Culture & Leisure Services
Red Doles Lane
Huddersfield, West Yorks HD2 1YF

D0726351

NONE OF THE ABOVE

Your vote is your voice
Don't stay silent

Rick Edwards

SIMON &
SCHUSTER

London · New York · Sydney · Toronto · New Delhi

A CBS COMPANY

First published in Great Britain by Simon & Schuster UK Ltd, 2015
A CBS COMPANY

1 3 5 7 9 10 8 6 4 2

Simon & Schuster UK Ltd
1st Floor
222 Gray's Inn Road
London WC1X 8HB

www.simonandschuster.co.uk

Simon & Schuster Australia, Sydney
Simon & Schuster India, New Delhi

A CIP catalogue record for this book is available from the British Library

Paperback original ISBN: 978-1-4711-4932-0
eBook ISBN: 978-1-4711-4933-7

Typeset in the UK by M Rules
Printed and bound by CPI Group (UK) Ltd, Croydon, CR0 4YY

For Emer and my mum and my dad

'Never use a long word where a short one will do'
George Orwell

'All the main parties are pretty similar'
Tinie Tempah

Contents

Intro   xi

1. Voting   1
2. Party Differences   8
3. The Rise of UKIP   17
4. Benefits   27
5. Broken Promises   38
6. Immigration   46
7. Coalition Government   56
8. The Housing Crisis   65
9. Devolution   75
10. The NHS   84
11. Leadership   96
12. Jobs and the Economy   104
13. Big Business   118
14. Climate Change   129
15. Representation   141
16. Public Finances   149
17. Drugs   159
18. Social Media   167
19. The EU   176

20. Inequality   189
21. Celebrity Involvement in Politics   200
22. Alternatives to Our Democracy   209

Glossary   221
References   229
Thanks   267
Outro   269

Intro

I have one very basic aim in writing this book. I'd really, really like to see a massive turnout at the polling stations on 7 May 2015. That's the date on which all of us* get to cast our vote in the general election, to make a collective decision about who will run the country for the next five years. Pop it in your diary or iCalendar or whatever. Another date to stick in is the 20th of April. That's when you have to apply to be registered to vote by. Seems annoying, doesn't it, that we have to register before we can vote? But for now, that's how it is. In fact, indulge me – if you haven't registered yet, or aren't sure if you are already registered, and you're over sixteen, why not register now? Even if you think you don't want to vote, at least you can give yourself the option come May. You never know, you might change your mind (I'm hoping this book might change it for you). It'll take less than five minutes, and then you can carry on reading. Grab your phone and go to this website:

https://www.gov.uk/register-to-vote

*Most of us – if you're reading this in jail, unlucky.

You will need your National Insurance number, but if you don't know it, just click on 'I can't provide a National Insurance number' and type in that you don't know it. The registration people will work it out. That's their job.

A very quick thought about voter registration: it could be automatic. No, it should be automatic. The government has all of the data it requires already – from your driving licence, or your NHS card, or school. Trust me, they know who you are and they know where you live. An automatic registration system would surely be cheaper than the existing one. As taxpayers, it is us who are footing that bill (and effectively, all bills). So our money is taxed and our time is taxed. Not only that, but some of us will inevitably forget to register and therefore be deprived of our right to vote, all because there is an extra hurdle in the way. That's another way of looking at the ambition of this book – to flatten hurdles. Or at least point them out, and stamp and shout about them.

So why do I want everyone to vote? I have been accused of being a 'government stooge' before, which I find bizarre. I'm 99 per cent certain that I'm not. If the government is appointing stooges then, firstly, they would tell you that you're a stooge so that you could do a good job for them; secondly, surely they could find better potential stooges than a 35-year-old TV presenter; and, thirdly, I remain to be convinced that the government does want everyone to vote.

My reasons for wanting people to vote are quite simple. I believe that the strength of our democracy is hugely improved when everyone has their say in choosing the government. It's clear to me that it would be better if the government had to consider the whole electorate when making policy decisions. And, conversely, I can see what

happens when certain sections of society don't vote: they
become invisible to politicians and decision-makers. For
example, austerity is a word that gets bandied about a lot.
All austerity means is that when the government doesn't
have enough money to run the country, it has to either get
more money (by raising our taxes), or spend less (on our
services), or borrow more money, or a combination of all
three.

We've been in a period of austerity and the government
has made cuts. Young people are voting far less than old
people, and so in many instances it's young people who
have felt the worst of these cuts. To me, that seems unjust
and unfair. It certainly doesn't seem like we're all in it
together. I'll talk more about that in the first chapter.

There are, unfortunately, some strong arguments to say
that I am writing this book a bit too late. Bruno Kaufman, a
Swedish election commissioner and journalist, has seen an
awful lot of elections around the world. He writes that the
places where he sees the highest turnout and the most participation are not always those where the media is
saturated with calls to vote, and party campaigns, and
books about politics by Z-list celebrities in the run-up to an
election. Rather, the process of engagement is much longer.
It requires normal people to 'connect with politics and
make collective decisions all the time, not just in election
season'. That seems obvious – if people are always
involved in their democracy, they will vote come election-
time, because it would be perverse not to. The challenging
part is – how? How can we achieve this ideal situation?
Bruno – I'm sure if I met him we'd get on well enough to go
with first names – has some ideas. And so do I.

In a way, I'm writing a book about politics that I would
want to read. I have no political background. I never sat at

the dinner table and chatted about the state of the nation with my mum and dad, we were too busy watching the telly. But in the course of hosting BBC3's *Free Speech*, a current affairs-based debate show for young people, I have been asked a lot of questions about politics. And I've asked a lot of questions myself. Some of them are straightforward to answer, some significantly less so. The one that threw me most was when I was chatting to a class of 17- and 18-year-olds about why they had no intention to vote. Several of them explained that they didn't feel that they knew enough about politics, or the parties, or the issues. And then one of them asked me where they could find the relevant information. I was stumped. Because there isn't anywhere. Not really.

The fundamental problem is a chronic lack of clear, accessible information. It's socially embarrassing to ask someone to explain a word or phrase or issue that you don't understand (like, what's 'austerity'? Every time I use a technical word or bit of jargon I will slap myself, put the jargon in bold type, and then attempt to explain its meaning at the back of the book, and then slap myself again). Picking through party **manifestos** (jargon klaxon!) is hard, thankless work. And who the hell does that anyway? Political conversations seem to be dominated by assumed knowledge – the people who know what they're talking about talk about it, and the people who don't (the rest of us), don't. That's not how it should be. Politics affects everyone and all it needs is for someone to bother to explain the basics. In the absence of anyone else doing it, I thought I might as well have a crack. I'm not an expert by any means, but I'm going to do my best.

So what I'm attempting to do is set out answers to some of the most common questions I get asked – the questions I hear again and again. And again. I'll try to write the answers in plain language and to give people at least a broad understanding of what is going on in our country. When I talk about the parties, I'll stick mainly to the nation-wide ones – the parties that have candidates standing for election in all or most of the four countries of the United Kingdom. So that's the Conservatives, Labour, Liberal Democrats, the Green Party and UKIP. If I had the time and space I'd cover every party but unfortunately, I don't.

I'll also be suggesting a few ways in which I think things could be improved – in fact, I've already made one sugges-tion: automatic voter registration.

By the way, I wish there was a better term for young people than 'young people'. I know it's hopelessly patron-ising, especially given that I am not one. I am open to alternative suggestions. For now, though, I'll persist with young people. Just know that I wince every time I write it.

Another thing I'd like to tackle before getting properly started is this poisonous myth that young people (wince) are apathetic, that they don't care. Let's look at what gets presented as evidence for that. We tend to measure people's engagement, or lack of engagement, by looking at whether they vote or not. So at the last general election, when 56 per cent of young people didn't vote, it was concluded by many that they were disengaged and apathetic. That they had no interest or concern about who got into power. Frankly, I think that's bollocks. Dave Meslin – a guy whose business card describes him as a 'community choreogra-pher', which I like – gave a brilliant TEDx talk a few years ago now, about redefining apathy. He suggests that this commonly voiced notion of 'they don't care' is totally false. That what is actually happening is that our systems are failing to allow potentially interested people to even access them. In this case, the system is politics. Politics puts up various barriers, intentionally or not, that exclude people. Perhaps it suits the system to do so. These are the hurdles I mentioned earlier.

So looking at that 56 per cent – how many of them truly 'don't care'? I would suggest, although I only have anecdotal evidence of this, that of those 18–24-year-olds who didn't vote, a great number of them may well have wanted to vote, but may not have felt that any of the parties represented their views or their needs. Again, that's not apathy – that's being let down. And that's why I firmly believe that there should be a *None of the Above* (hello, book title!) option on the ballot paper. A way of giving honest feedback and legitimately expressing dissatisfaction with the available options. That would carry a lot of power in itself because it would prove that people *are* engaged, they want to vote, but that none of the parties is representing them well enough.

Of course, if **democracy** and the political parties within it are working really well, you would hope that the vast majority of people would be able to find a party or an individual who will look after their interests, or most of them. At the very least, the political class need to accept some responsibility. They can't just write people off as apathetic, they need to work hard to make sure that people can engage, if they want to.

I've talked and written at length before about ways that we can get people voting. There are various practical solutions that will do it. But now I'd like to look at the less tangible solutions too. There are good arguments to suggest that somewhere like Australia, where voting is compulsory, you have an understandably high turnout of around 93 per cent, but not necessarily an engaged or informed electorate. Getting people to vote is in a sense only half the battle. A 100 per cent turnout would not guarantee that we had successfully engaged every member of our society. It may mean that, in the case of Australia, people just didn't want to pay a fine, and I believe that we can do better than that.

I'm not going to argue the case for voting, and wanting to vote, by talking about the lives that were lost in order to achieve universal suffrage. Suffrage, incidentally, just means the right to vote. I'm not belittling those lives or those efforts; I just think that there are such compelling reasons right now to vote that we don't need to lean on history. I'll also endeavour not to offer any strong advice on who or what to vote for – I don't care who everyone votes for, just that everyone votes.

One last thing before we get started – I am a freelancer, so although I sometimes work for various TV channels, I don't speak for them. In Twitter bio terms: these are my views, not the views of any broadcaster.

1. Voting

Why should we vote?

Your vote is your voice. Without a vote, you're silent, and you will be ignored. I'll expand on this some more because this is a book, not a slogan, but everything comes back to that simple point. Your vote is your voice.

Perhaps being ignored isn't so bad. It's not like it makes a difference to your lives anyway, right? Well, I'm afraid it does. For years now, there has been a steady and worrying decline in the number of young people voting. So young people have less of a voice. At the last general election in 2010, 76 per cent of over-65s voted, while only 44 per cent aged 18–24 did. This unequal turnout gives older voters a much greater influence on elections. Research has found that the UK has one of the largest differences in voter turnout between young and old people in the whole of Europe. That's an embarrassment. What's more, as young voter numbers dwindle, so too does the incentive for politicians to care about the issues most relevant to them. That's the thing that hurts. The government looks after the people that vote for it. So while pensioners get triple-locked pensions (basically, pensions that will go up with the **cost of living**, at least), young people get trebled tuition fees. And guess who is paying for all of those pensions for all those old people? Weirdly, it'll be young people. Because that's how our pension system works.

It's also young people who have been most affected by the evil combination of falling real wages (wages going up less quickly than living costs) and rising costs of essential goods. A study by the excellent Intergenerational Foundation has shown that the average weekly wages of workers aged 18–21 have fallen by nearly 20 per cent in real terms since 1997. Whereas workers in their fifties have seen their wages increase by 25 per cent over the same period. Public-spending cuts have hit young people the hardest too. A study has shown that, since 2010, in real, cash terms, over-55s are on average about £1,300 worse off because of the cuts, while 16–20-year-olds are £2,800 worse off. It really is that simple. On top of that, young people can't afford to buy homes because there aren't enough and the ones that are available are too damn expensive.

It feels as if an entire generation is choosing not to exert any influence over who gets to run our country, and therefore how they run it. The whole point of a **democracy** is that we get to collectively decide on the things that matter to us. We cannot do that if we don't vote. And for all our complaints about the system, we have to accept that if we don't participate in elections, we can't change anything. And we will get hit the hardest.

The number of young people volunteering in their local area and getting involved with campaigns and causes has never been greater. So as I said in the introduction, the low voter turnout is not down to apathy. Young people care about stuff. It's just that the link needs to be made between that stuff and politics. Because politics affects everything. What I hope to show you in these pages is not just what is happening in this country on a big scale, but also how the government's decisions and the policies of the parties affect our day-to-day lives; our jobs, our health and our families.

Obviously I would say this, but I think it's a really exciting time to be voting. It feels like the days of there only being two (or two-and-a-half) parties we can realistically vote for – Labour or Conservative (and maybe Liberal Democrats) – are over. Their dominance is slipping and the so-called minor parties are making up ground. Lots of people still maintain that voting for one of the minor parties is a wasted vote. I feel like even the term itself, 'wasted votes', is putting young people off voting. It just sounds so … pointless. These minor or 'fringe' parties, whether they're on the left or the right of the political spectrum, provide more choice. And choice is a good thing. The 'wasted vote' argument goes like this – if you vote for a minor party, you will be dividing the opposition. So let's say in a particular seat it is close between the Conservatives and Labour. The Conservatives would say that if you vote for UKIP, that will be taking votes from them, and you'll end up with a Labour victory. Labour would say that if you vote Green in that seat, you'll be taking votes from them, and you'll end up with a Conservative victory.

That may be true, but other people will say that this attitude is self-fulfilling and defeatist. By definition, if large numbers vote for a minor party, then they are no longer a minor party. That's exactly what has happened – the electorate have created a change. In 2010, the Lib Dems were the most prominent of those minor parties. This time who knows who it will be (polling suggests UKIP). This is, in the words of Green Party leader Natalie Bennett, 'really healthy for politics'.

I was genuinely thrilled when I saw a poll recently where people were asked 'Would you vote for this party if you thought they had a chance of winning in your constituency?' The results were fascinating. Labour and the Conservatives were tied at about 35 per cent, which is not far off where they poll generally. Then it was the Greens with 26 per cent, UKIP with 24 per cent and the Lib Dems with 16 per cent. The Greens on 26 per cent is extraordinary because in the standard polls (which ask 'Who are you actually going to vote for?') they had been scoring around 7 per cent. What is holding the Greens back is that people don't think they stand a chance of winning seats. Because 'they can't win'. Well, maybe they could. If all of that 26 per cent just put aside tactical voting, protest voting, not voting because there's 'no point' and voting out of habit – basically if those people put aside voting for any reason other than voting for who they think is the best candidate – then the Greens would win a lot more seats. And actually, the same thing applies to UKIP.

So what I am suggesting is – don't be put off voting by feeling that your vote will be 'wasted'. When you're working out who to vote for, and I hope that this book will help give some of you the information that you need to do that, don't pay any attention to the polls in your area. Or the national ones. Don't listen to the people who say 'it's only between Party X and Party Y around here'. When people listen to that, everything stays the same. Everyone needs to have an idea of what they want for our country and from our government, and equally they need an idea of what they want from their local MP. So take the time to work out which of the candidates and parties best match up with your vision, and vote for them. Don't worry about anything else. If everyone did that, we could see some momentous results. So if you want to vote Green – vote Green. If you want to vote UKIP – vote UKIP. And so on.

I realise that **safe seats** – you can read more about these in the Representation chapter – are frustrating. But they don't necessarily stay safe for ever. Nothing is fixed in that way. In 2008, Crewe and Nantwich, a safe seat that had only ever been held by Labour, was won by the Conservatives. Last year, there was a by-election in the constituency of Heywood and Middleton in Greater Manchester, which is Labour heartland. That seat has been considered safe for years, but Labour only won it from UKIP by the skin of its teeth. That's worrying for Labour, but great for our democracy. It shows that change can happen. It also means that the parties can't afford to neglect safe seats. They have to go after your vote, which is the way it should be. Nigel Farage has come out and said that he doesn't believe safe seats exist any more. Natalie Bennett agrees, saying, 'UKIP is a threat to both Labour and Tories, and its new-found popularity means that swathes of the country which were once considered safe seats are no longer secure.' Of course, it is in their interests to say that, but they are right. Everything is up for grabs.

What's more is that the youth vote has enormous power. There will be 6.8 million 18–24-year-olds eligible to vote in May 2015, that's nearly 14 per cent of the electorate. Studies suggest that around 190 seats could be decided by a 5 per cent shift in votes, and that means the youth vote could decide those outcomes. Another report by the Intergenerational Foundation concludes that, based on the 2010 election results, an increase of just 10 per cent in the number of 18–34-year-olds voting would change the result in 83 seats. So it is plain wrong to think that your vote doesn't count for anything. To put it in simple terms, at the last general election, if all of the eligible young people had voted for Labour, we'd now have a different party in government. That is a huge difference. The only thing that is guaranteed not to make a difference is if you don't vote.

This is all well and good but what if, after figuring out what you want from your MP and the government, you find that none of the parties and none of the candidates represent you well enough? That is perfectly possible. Then what should you do? Well, if you honestly don't feel that you can even identify a 'best of a bad bunch', don't vote for any of them. But you can still vote, and make your voice heard.

As the title of the book suggests, and as I said in the introduction, I hope that one day there will be a 'None of the Above' box on the ballot paper. They have just introduced one in India – the thirteenth country to give their people the option to reject all candidates. For now, though, there is a way around the problem: it's called 'spoiling your ballot'. What that means is that you have submitted your ballot paper but not made it clear who you've voted for. I find the name – 'spoiling' – annoying, because it makes it sound like a mistake, or an act of naughty rebellion. It doesn't have to be either. You could simply cross through all of the options and write *None of the Above*. You could even use a sticker from the cover of a book. That is a totally fair vote and, crucially, it will get counted. If you don't vote, that doesn't get counted and, trust me, you will get written off as apathetic. There is nothing apathetic about spoiling your ballot if you don't feel that you can vote for any of the parties.

There are other things you can do too. If you feel totally disenchanted with what you see on offer, why not join a political party and fight to change things from within? Or why not create your own political party? That sounds far-fetched, but in Spain a new party called Podemos (which means 'We Can') started in early 2014 and won five seats at the European Elections. It has the second largest membership of any party in Spain and it's barely a year old. That is incredibly inspiring. The simple fact is that the more people we have challenging those in power, the healthier our democracy becomes. And the primary way that we challenge and make our voices heard is by voting.

There are things that politicians could do to help increase the youth turnout. Voting should be online, and at some point it will be online. That is inevitable – there are several very well-funded companies developing the technology right now. Young people are digital natives, so it's obvious that we should be taking voting to where they are. It would also help anyone who has struggled to get to a polling station for whatever reason. Security concerns are exaggerated – if we're happy to bank online, surely we should be happy to vote online. I'm surprised that none of the parties has come out and said that they will introduce online voting by, say, 2020. Apart from anything else, just supporting online voting would itself be a vote winner with young people, simply because it would demonstrate an interest in getting them to vote. An interest that is sorely lacking at the moment.

I'll say it one more time. If you care about anything in this book – you have to VOTE.

2. Party Differences

Aren't all the parties the same?

In a word, no. What's striking is that this misconception actually suits politicians down to the ground. Because if you think like that, it means you're much less likely to vote. Which leaves politicians to focus on winning the support of the people who they know *will* vote (hello, old people), which is much more likely to get results than going after people who *might*. And as I explained in the previous chapter, the result of this is: young people getting screwed.

When Russell Brand talks about having no one to vote for, he is referencing this notion that the parties are 'all the same'. Actually, he would have to accept that that isn't true – what is holding him back from voting is that he doesn't feel that there is a party that represents his values, which is a different point. A colleague of mine once mentioned to Brand the idea of spoiling his ballot, and he responded by getting quite cross and saying that was childish, or words to that effect. I would argue that's what they

(I'm not quite sure who I mean by 'they' – the political class, maybe) want you to think.

Anyway, I maintain that the parties are fundamentally different, and that it is possible to tell them apart. The terms that get bandied about most when talking about political parties are 'left wing', 'right wing' and 'moderate' (or 'centrist'). What do they all mean? Well, depending on their politics, people answer this question in very different ways. Here's my best, simplified representation of how both the left and the right see things.

The world according to the left

'We on the left believe in equality. We seek to achieve this by sharing wealth around. One of the ways we do this is through taxation. We believe in fairness, and it is fair that the rich should give some of their money to the poor, so that ultimately, there is no rich and poor. When people are struggling, when people are ill, we believe the moral thing to do is to is to support them. The free health service is one of our ideas. So are welfare benefits.

'We are progressive. We have been at the forefront of pushing for the fair treatment of minorities. The left has always supported things like LGBT rights. People on the margins – be they the disabled, ethnic minorities, immigrants, or whoever – have friends on the left. We will always stick up for them. We won't give up on people who get in trouble either. We'll try to help you, not punish you.

'We have to regulate businesses, because otherwise they will run wild with their rampant **capitalism** and thirst for profit. The right are obsessed with the free market and it's "freedom to succeed", but it's not freedom to succeed – it's freedom to fail! It's not Survival of the Fittest, it's Death of the Weakest!

'We tend to be outward-looking and to work with other countries. In recent years we have tended to support being part of the EU, and other international institutions like the European Court of Human Rights. We believe foreign policy should be just, and believe it's not only morally right but in our own interests to help fund development overseas.

'When Ed Miliband went on political show *The Agenda*, he ended up having a disagreement with Mylene Klass over the mansion tax. They were never going to agree, because their worldviews are so different. It is fair that we tax the rich! She would never understand that.'

The world according to the right

'We on the right believe in equality and fairness too! But not like those Lefties. We want to live in a world where everyone has the opportunity to work hard and do well for themselves. We believe in a strong country that we can be proud of – and many of us say a strong defence is the first duty of government. We don't see anything wrong with putting our own people first.

'We are worried about the numbers of immigrants because of the pressure on public services, housing and wages. We also worry that they are not integrating and continue to live in separate communities. Although some of the business owners among us favour immigration, we all agree the test should be what's good for the country. If immigrants aren't good for Britain, then they can't keep coming here. We tend to be more sceptical of how effective international aid is.

'We believe there is nothing wrong with defending

traditional values and institutions – although we are willing to move with the times. Many of us supported gay marriage, for example. The left is obsessed with rehabilitation of criminals – all very noble, but victims should always be put first, and the deterrent by strong punishments will keep our citizens safe.

'Whenever governments interfere with the market, they tend to make things worse. The market has given us fantastic wealth and prosperity – what would you rather, the untold misery of a Communist regime?

'What Mylene Klass said to Ed Miliband was spot on – you can't just point at things and tax them! Of course you shouldn't tax people to high heaven who've worked hard to make money and then give it to someone who's done nothing! How is that possibly fair?'

The political spectrum, from left-wing, to moderate, to right-wing, doesn't totally describe the range of ideologies, and there are lots of issues – for example, civil liberties (things like freedom of speech and privacy) – which are hard to fit onto this left/right axis. In fact many people are sceptical of the definitions, and no doubt it's possible to pick holes in the accounts I've written above, but the truth is that these terms do still get used. They are clearly helpful for people trying to understand where the parties stand.

When you're choosing who to vote for, it's well worth having a think about these opposing positions. Work out which you agree with most. It's really important to figure these things out for yourself, don't just follow the lead of family or friends or whoever. Whatever you decide will be the right answer for you. Anyone who tells you otherwise is wrong. In this book, I'll try to get across the views of the left and the right so you can make up your own mind. And remember that when making your decision about who to support, you are unlikely to find a party that you think is correct about everything. There is a always bit of compromise. (Also, if you end up joining a party, you can work to change their policies to your taste.)

All of the parties have a range of policies, so it isn't quite as simple as saying 'Party X is left wing and Party Y is right wing'. However, in very broad terms, the UK has two left-leaning parties – Labour and the Green Party – and two right-leaning parties – the Conservatives and UKIP. The Lib Dems are somewhere in the middle. ComRes recently did a survey in which they asked the public where they thought the political parties sat on the basic left-to-right political spectrum, with 0 being very left wing, and 10 being very right wing. The Conservatives scored 6.91 (fairly right wing), Labour scored 4.13 (quite left wing), the Lib Dems scored 4.87 (very slightly to the left of centre), UKIP scored 6.61 (which places them as being less right wing than the Conservatives) and the Greens scored 4.06 (making them the most left wing of the major parties).

There is another version of the left-wing–right-wing political spectrum where there are two axes: one for social beliefs, and one for economic beliefs. The social beliefs axis goes from authoritarian (the government will tell everyone what to do) to libertarian (do whatever you like). The economic axis is basically left wing and right wing. The website politicalcompass.org shows the positions of the major UK parties within the two-axes model. According to this website, over the last forty years or so there has been a general drift by Labour and the Liberals towards the right, and towards being more authoritarian. That is more noticeable in Labour. Prior to the late 1980s, it was much more left wing, with a more libertarian social attitude. Over time, and especially with New Labour and Tony Blair in the mid-90s, the website shows them moving towards the centre, but also becoming increasingly authoritarian. Labour and the Lib Dems are now far closer to the Conservatives than in the past. The Conservatives themselves have also shifted towards the centre. The proximity of the parties is the main reason that people are finding it harder to distinguish between them.

However, is this convergence definitely a problem? There is an interesting economics model about selling ice-cream on a beach. If there is an ice-cream seller in the middle of the beach, where would you put your competing ice-cream hut? Intuitively I would guess at either end of the beach – as far away as possible from the original seller. But the answer that an economic theory (that I won't/can't go into – if you're interested, google 'Hotelling's Law') provides is that the best place is actually next to the original seller. The same seems to be true of political parties. If you want to sell lots of ice-cream/win lots of votes, set up near to your competition. The major parties have ended up occupying the same area of the political beach because that's where the majority of voters are – the British people are, on the whole, pretty moderate, and so the parties have become more moderate themselves. John Curtice, professor of politics at Strathclyde University, says that New Labour's shift to the centre had the effect of moving 'the electorate to the right'. Or perhaps, because Labour wasn't getting elected in the 1980s, the shift was a response to where the electorate had ended up.

The differences are still there though, at the heart of the parties. What I don't think the parties do enough of, in public, is give a really strong sense of that heart – what they stand for and how they believe our society should be run,

ideologically. An ideology is just a set of beliefs and values
that determines how we act and how we see the world. I
think that's what will get people excited about supporting,
or conversely being against, a party. Knowing exactly what
they stand for and why. There's something tribal about it.

Here is a very brief rundown of the parties, starting
with the Conservatives. Traditionally they are right of
centre, and believe in creating a strong economy through
free trade and a minimal amount of government interference in private business. At this election, they argue they
will be offering 'strong and stable leadership' and will
continue to rebuild the economy. David Cameron says that
'together, we are turning Britain around. Our long-term
economic plan is working'. The Conservatives are promising to cut income tax and corporation tax. They have
said that they will cap benefits payments 'so that it always
pays to work'. They claim that they will get control of
immigration (although they have failed to reduce it in the
past five years). They have pledged to protect the NHS
and schools budget. In order to try and reduce the amount
the government borrows each year (the **deficit**), the
Conservative Chancellor George Osborne has implemented austerity cuts – cuts to government spending on
things like local councils and the armed forces. All the
main parties want to reduce government spending in the
next few years but the Conservative's plans are the most
ambitious. Unsurprisingly, they claim that Labour cannot
be trusted to look after our economy.

Labour used to be the party of the working class (think
labour as in 'labourers'). It remains left wing but, as mentioned above, arguably not as left wing as it once was. Now
it describes itself as the 'party of the many'. It still believes in
redistributing wealth to reduce inequality. It says its values

are things like social justice and strong community. Labour, like the Conservatives, has said it will cut the deficit. In doing so, it will make sure that 'those with the broadest shoulders bear the greatest burden', meaning the rich – both individuals and companies – will pay more tax. Labour hopes its 'mansion tax' will contribute to a £2.5 billion increase in funding to the NHS. It has said that it will 'lead the fight to protect an NHS that puts people before profits'. Labour has pledged to freeze energy bills until 2017, cap benefits and also cut immigration. It is also committed to end what it describes as the 'cost of living crisis', by promising to increase the minimum wage.

The Liberal Democrats describe themselves as the 'radical centre' of UK politics. They believe in state help for the poorest (like Labour) but argue that they will be responsible with the economy and public finances (like the Conservatives). They believe in personal freedom and choice, hence the term 'liberal'. The leader of the Lib Dems, Nick Clegg, says that he would borrow less money than Labour, and cut less (from welfare spending and so on) than the Conservatives. They would increase the income tax allowance, but would also increase taxes on wealth (they'd introduce a new mansion tax for example). They also want to prioritise spending on education, making housing affordable and increasing power for local government. The Lib Dems have pledged that they will increase pensions. They say they will 'rewire the economy to cut carbon' and promise 200,000 new **green jobs**. They are pro-Europe and say that they are 'the only party that truly understands that Britain is stronger in the world'.

The Green Party is the most left wing of the major parties. It pursues environmentally friendly policies and wants nationalised services – the Greens would try to take the rail network back from private ownership, for example. They promise 'real change', and a move to 'public management of essential services not driven by corporate greed'. They say that they stand for 'a functioning National Health Service, free education and an affordable home'. They would put a cap on banker bonuses. They would not have a cap on welfare. The Greens would 'leave fossil fuels in the ground'.

I'll deal with UKIP in the next chapter.

If you agree or disagree with any of what these parties stand for – VOTE.

3. The Rise of UKIP

What does UKIP stand for?

As I mentioned at the start of this book, I don't want to influence the way that people vote. So describing the ascent of a particular party is tricky. In the case of UKIP, it's definitely worth doing – they have seen a surge in support in the last few years, and their rise in the opinion polls is one of the reasons this year's election is so uncertain. There are a lot of questions and controversy about the party and that's why I think it's worth giving the answer to this question a whole chapter. Whatever you think of them, the chances are you won't be able to move for coverage of them in the run-up to the election, so we might as well be clear on where they have come from and what they stand for. I'll try to just present the facts, although with UKIP things do tend to change pretty quickly.

The clue about UKIP is in the name – the United Kingdom Independence Party was formed in 1993, and wants us to be out of the European Union (EU). Badly. Their leader, Nigel Farage, has been banging the 'GET US

OUT' drum for nearly twenty years. The main reason being that the party thinks the EU has too much power over the UK, and it wants to take those powers back (including justice, home affairs and security policies). UKIP also wants to regain control of our borders and therefore restrict immigration. If we remain in the EU, then relaxed border controls mean that any EU citizen, pretty much, can move around the countries of the union as they please. So they can come to the UK and claim benefits and health care, are eligible to vote, and so on. Of course we can also do the same in their countries, but either way UKIP isn't keen.

If we leave the EU, we would stop making payments (as discussed in the EU chapter, there is some disagreement over how much we pay, although £11.3 billion in 2013 is often quoted – supporters of the EU estimate that membership is worth between £62 billion and £78 billion every year) and withdraw from all of our EU treaties. UKIP believes that we could then make 'bespoke' **free trade agreements** with European countries anyway, and be more open to trade with the rest of the world. The party claims that exiting the EU would save us £8 billion annually. (In case you're wondering, a free trade agreement basically makes trade easier and cheaper – often taxes are charged on imports, or countries say they'll only import a certain number of something, but an agreement like this means countries reduce the barriers on trade.)

Although UKIP has historically been a party with a single mission, they have in recent years started to come up with policies in all areas. Yet this process hasn't always gone smoothly. Farage himself famously described their 2010 election **manifesto** as 'drivel' and 'nonsense'. He also said that 'the idiot that wrote it has now left us and joined the Conservatives'. Farage wrote the foreword to that manifesto.

UKIP's anti-EU stance has always been very easy to get, though, and with its immigration implications, it is emotive. Over the years, that stance has seen UKIP gain more and more support in European elections, and in May 2014 they topped the vote. That was the first time a party other than Labour or the Conservatives has won a nationwide vote in over a century. It's always struck me as being quite funny that UKIP has the most success getting into a European Parliament that they don't want to be a part of.

For years, the political establishment dismissed UKIP as a single-issue party that would never be able to transfer its European election success to a general election. In 2006, David Cameron wrote them off as 'fruitcakes, loonies and closet racists, mostly'. It's worth noting that since 2008, UKIP has banned former BNP members from joining the party, and several candidates have been suspended for racist views. And although a lot has been made of far-right nationalists like Nick Griffin (former leader of the British Nationalist Party) and Tommy Robinson (former leader of the English Defence League) coming out in support of UKIP, it's fair to say that no party will turn down votes from anywhere.

To understand why UKIP is able to win the European election but has never won a single seat in a general election (the party currently has two MPs, but these were Conservative politicians who switched party and were then re-elected in by-elections), you have to look at the voting systems for each, which are totally different. In the Europeans, they use something called the Closed Party List – essentially, you add up all the votes in each area for each party, and seats are awarded in proportion to each party's area total. Across the UK, UKIP got 27.5 per cent of the votes, which translated to 23 out of the total 73 seats.

For comparison, the Conservatives and Labour won 18 seats each. The general election, however, is done with a system called **First Past the Post** (FPTP), which I'll talk more about in the Alternatives to Our Democracy chapter. Farage has bemoaned FPTP as 'brutal to a party like us'. It's fair to say that it throws up some counter-intuitive results. For example, in 2010 UKIP got three times as many votes in the general election as the Green Party, but won no seats. The Greens took one in Brighton. The system really doesn't favour parties that get a lot of votes in a lot of places, coming second and third in many, but coming first in few (or none). UKIP hopes that will be different at this election and it'll get some seats. Its by-election successes suggest that its campaign will be in better shape than in 2010. The Liberal Democrats have managed to build support over the years by concentrating on certain parts of the country like the South-West, and by focusing on local issues they've built up a decent number of seats over the years. Their abilities as local campaigners are one reason why, despite low polling, many believe the Lib Dems will hold onto a fair number of MPs in this general election.

Farage himself is a fascinating leader. I don't believe a person's background completely defines them, not by any stretch of the imagination. However, it is worth saying that, for all of his 'man of the people', pint-and-fag protestations that he is not like the rest of 'em, Nigel Farage's background is quite a lot like the rest of 'ems. He's a privately educated former City trader and former member of the Conservatives, although he argues his background in business, and the fact that he didn't go to university, makes him unique. Many argue that even if he seems anti-establishment now, he does nevertheless come from the Establishment. Whether that makes him less electable is anyone's guess.

The way he presents himself is intriguing. I don't know if he's pulling a very successful confidence trick, or if he's genuine. Also, it's interesting that Farage has said that Ed Miliband is 'a product of his upbringing and his life ... disconnected from ordinary people'. Presumably he doesn't think the same is true of himself.

As recently as 2013, Farage said that he is 'a conviction politician, I'm not doing this for a career ... I'm here as a campaigner'. In a time when people are pretty fed up with 'professional politicians', it's clever how he tries to distance himself. Doesn't seem too different to the kind of clever move you might expect of, say, a professional politician. Farage's biggest success is that he has created a party that, even if you have no idea what it stands for beyond being anti-Europe, you know is not like the others, which all seem to merge into one. At the last general election, Nick Clegg presented himself in the leaders' debates as an outsider – different to the two main parties that had played 'pass the parcel with your government for ages'. Five years of being in government means that it's now harder for Clegg and his party to make that claim. Today Farage says the main three parties are all just **social democrat** parties squabbling over minor details, and he claims to offer the alternative.

Over the years, Farage and his party have acquired a reputation for being libertarian, favouring minimal government interference in either people's personal or economic lives. The description on their website used to read, 'UKIP is a libertarian, non-racist party seeking withdrawal from the European Union'. However, recently some commentators have noticed a shift away from their **Thatcherite** roots – especially in the party's insistence that it strongly supports the NHS (more on this later) – as it tries to attract voters in traditionally Labour-voting areas. Farage has even spoken recently about the 'big, big problem' of the rich getting richer. As they target more seats outside of their traditional heartland in the South-East, these shifts may continue. Sometimes Farage's libertarianism puts him at odds with the rest of UKIP. For example, while Farage himself would favour decriminalising some drugs, he says, 'This is one [subject] where I differ strongly from my party'.

Who is voting for them?

There can be little doubt that support for UKIP in the polls has risen since the last election, and while all the other major parties' membership has been falling for years, UKIP's has been rising steadily (as has the Green Party's and the SNP's). And that's true of their youth membership too, which is up by a third since February 2014.

In the past, UKIP was only really attracting unhappy Tories. Unhappy because, under David Cameron, the Tories have moved towards the centre, leaving the right-wingers feeling betrayed. Let's call them 'old' UKIP. But now UKIP is gaining support from across the board – taking Labour and Lib Dem voters. The proportion of UKIP voters who were previously Labour voters has risen from 7 per cent to 23 per cent. These are 'new' UKIP (or NewKIP, as some are calling them). The academic Matthew Goodwin has studied the rise of UKIP and he's identified three key factors driving this surge in support: anger with Europe, anger with immigration and anger with politics (and what UKIP cutely refers to as the **LibLabCon**) in general. A fifth of all voters are angry about all three. Around a third are angry about two of the three (which ain't bad).

Not just that, though – the fall in living standards and the impact of government spending cuts over the last few years has driven some working-class voters to UKIP. When people are struggling, they are more likely to look outside of the perceived 'mainstream'. Forty-three per cent of voters as a whole are termed 'working class'; 51 per cent of old UKIP support was 'working class' and 63 per cent of new supporters are too. So UKIP now have an unlikely span of votes from the right, the left and the centre. Their supporters are much more likely to be male than the general electorate (which Farage puts down to women being 'a bit more sceptical than men') and they're also more likely not to have gone into higher education. But while being largely male and working class, arguably the only thing unifying those ideologically opposed voters is anger, whether it's anger over the economy, immigration the EU or politics itself.

One of the problems that Farage will have to solve is that it's unlikely that anger will be enough to glue his people together in the long term. His party is filled with voters and activists with entirely different ideas on how the economy should be run, and that must be a serious obstacle to any kind of political cohesion. Farage claims to be untroubled by this, though, believing that you 'get different shades of opinion with any political party', and that he is ready and willing for the people within UKIP to argue for different approaches. He also denies that the by-election successes were simply protest votes – believing that people who vote UKIP intend to stay UKIP (for the general election).

Last year Farage had to contend with a seemingly endless barrage of scandals – from UKIP candidates and associates making homophobic and racist remarks, to sexual harassment claims, to a party donor making unsavoury remarks about rape. And yet, none of it seems to have affected the party's popularity in the polls. Matthew Goodwin guesses that either their voters haven't seen the negative coverage (which is mainly in the broadsheet papers) or they just don't care. Goodwin also observes that 'now, the same tabloid newspapers that have spent more than twenty years telling these voters that they are right to feel anxious about immigration, the EU and politicians in Westminster, are telling them that they are wrong to support a party that is campaigning on the same message'. UKIP's supporters, he argues, aren't buying that.

The question is does UKIP's rise represent a public desire to create an alternative party of government? Or are the public just tiring of the old guard? Either way, there is no doubt that UKIP have the momentum. Previously, European success has never led to success at the general election. This time could well be different.

What are their policies?

So what exactly will UKIP voters be voting for? It's fair to say that UKIP policies have been prone to some movement, which doesn't fit perfectly with Farage's straight-talking image. The party's position on the NHS is particularly hard to read. In 2012, Farage said that he 'would feel more comfortable that my money would return value if I was able to do that through the marketplace of an insurance company' – in other words, an insurance-based health-care system, like they have in America. Then in January 2014, he said it would be 'ridiculous' to protect the NHS from spending cuts. Most recently, UKIP has been campaigning as the only party that will protect the NHS from **privatisation**.

When UKIP's economic spokesman, Patrick O'Flynn, suggested the party would introduce a 'luxury goods tax' on designer handbags and the like, it took less than two days for Farage to state that that definitely wouldn't happen. The UKIP chairman, Steve Crowther, then explained that the 'shambolic' nature of UKIP is actually a positive, because the party is 'liked by its electorate because it is not always as slick and as polished as the other political parties'. I'll talk more about that 'everyman' appeal in the Leadership chapter. Perhaps UKIP's U-turn on gay marriage – the party was against it, and now it's OK with it – is similarly appealing.

Embarrassingly, Farage recently told an audience of young people that he had never advocated banning sex education in primary schools. Yet UKIP's website explicitly states that it would do exactly that. Farage's explanation? He missed the start of his deputy leader's speech at the UKIP conference.

Mark Reckless, the newly elected UKIP MP and former Tory, said that some immigrants might be sent home after a 'fixed period'. This sounded quite a lot like **repatriation** and caused an outcry. UKIP then clarified its position, which is not to backdate any future border controls. Hard to know what happened in this case – perhaps Reckless was so new to the party he simply wasn't sure of the correct policy, or perhaps he was just tired, as Farage said at the time – but it supplied ammunition to the party's opponents.

One interpretation of all this would be that UKIP is developing its policy as time goes by – a less kind one would be that the party is making it up as it goes along. What has never been in doubt is that UKIP would leave the EU and end the UK's 'open door' borders – current net annual immigration into the UK is around 260,000 (in spite of David Cameron's promises to reduce this to 100,000). UKIP says it would limit it to between 30,000 and 50,000, using the same kind of points-based system found in Australia to assess immigrants' suitability for the UK.

UKIP would get rid of inheritance tax (tax paid on money or assets left to you by relatives) and increase the personal tax allowance (which is the amount that you can earn before paying tax) so that anyone earning the minimum wage would be free of income tax. They would also try to introduce a tax on turnover (the amount of money going into a company) to try and stop some big businesses from paying next to no corporation tax. UKIP says it wants a 'simplified, streamlined welfare system', which would include a benefits cap. They want welfare to be a 'safety net for the needy, not a bed for the lazy'. They would abolish the **bedroom tax**.

Other key policies are: the re-introduction of grammar schools, which they believe will provide better opportunities for all children, regardless of background; a massive reduction in foreign aid; scrapping all green taxes and subsidies; the repeal of the Climate Change Act 2008; and the somewhat controversial development of shale gas, with financial incentives to communities in which the **fracking** is being done. Give them some money – they'll keep quiet about the earth tremors!

It is also UKIP policy to legalise handguns in the UK, although if that appears in their manifesto, I for one will be amazed. Then again, UKIP is full of surprises.

If you agree or disagree with UKIP's vision for the UK – VOTE.

4. Benefits

Are we spending too much on welfare in the UK?

First things first. The 'welfare state' is a system through which the government gives assistance to those citizens who need it, from cradle to grave. So the state provides an education when you're young, health care when you're sick, and tries to help you into work when you're unemployed. However, questions like the one above are typical in that, these days, when we say 'welfare' we are usually referring to the money that is getting paid to people who aren't working. Those payments go to the retired (pensions), the unwell (Employment And Support Allowance), the unemployed (Jobseeker's Allowance) and so on. There are also payments to help with the extra costs of disability or bad health (Personal Independence Payments, for example), having children (Child Benefit) and tax credits, which are there to top up low pay – in effect, trying to deal with poverty. The reason we need payments to help with poverty is that the UK – despite being one of the richest countries in the world – has around 13 million people living in poverty. A statistic made all the more staggering when you consider that half of those people are living in working families, where one or more members of the family is in employment.

Now, there is a subtlety here. The word 'poverty' tends to conjure up images of people starving in the developing world. For the purposes of measuring their numbers, there is a definition of an 'absolutely poor person' as someone trying to survive on an income of less than the equivalent of $1.25 (less than a pound) a day. You'd be hard pushed to find many people living in those conditions in the developed world. What is usually meant by poverty in the UK is actually 'relative poverty' – worked out by comparing a household's income to the average (median) income. Anyone whose income is 60 per cent or less of that average income is defined as living in relative poverty. That works out at just under £14,000 per year.

Recently, the welfare system and the people claiming benefits have been given a bit of a kicking by certain sections of the British media, and by some politicians. From multiple opinion pieces about the most extravagantly fraudulent claimants, to the 'poverty porn' of Channel 4's *Benefits Street*, to Chancellor George Osborne's reference to the people behind 'the closed blinds ... sleeping off a life on benefits', some commentators have argued we're being led towards a 'strivers *vs* skivers' narrative. Where hard-working folk (the 'strivers') have to foot the bill for the indolence or mistakes of these lazy workshys (the 'skivers'). On the whole, we seem to be buying into that. We believe it's true. In 2012, a YouGov poll showed that an astonishing 74 per cent of us thought that the government was spending too much on benefits. Sixty-nine per cent believed that the welfare system has created a 'culture of dependency', and that people need to take more responsibility for themselves. In other words: it's their fault. What's more, it seems benefit 'scroungers' – people who lie about their circumstances to get more welfare money – are bloody everywhere. The Trades Union Congress (TUC) did a poll in 2012 and found that, on average, people thought 27 per cent of the welfare budget was claimed fraudulently. The official figures for that year state that fraud accounted for a mere 0.7 per cent of the total welfare budget. In fairness, for obvious reasons, this is only an estimate. Presumably a lot of fraud goes undetected (if the fraudsters are any good at it). But it still seems likely that we think fraud is a bigger problem than it really is. The Department for Work and Pensions (DWP) has the largest budget of any government department – it was around £166 billion in 2011/12. Nearly half of that goes on pensions, and yet we're not angry with pensioners for taking our money. I don't think we are, anyway.

Perhaps it is to be expected that in tough economic times we look for scapegoats. We all feel poorer and we want someone to blame and, luckily for us, the media has provided us with benefit fraudsters, and in fact anyone claiming out-of-work benefits. Since the 1980s, there has been a decline in the number of people who agree that the government should spend more money on benefits. In 1987, 55 per cent supported higher spending on welfare. By 2013, that percentage had fallen to 36 per cent (although that had risen from 28 per cent in 2011). It seems that over the past three decades, opinions have changed.

So is the welfare system doing what it's supposed to? Well no, not if 13 million people are living in relative poverty, and nearly a million people are using **food banks** – although, according to Employment Minister Esther McVey, there is 'no robust evidence linking food

bank usage to welfare reform'. In fact, the coalition government argues that the number of those hungry in Britain
has come down, and the number of delays in paying benefits – one of the biggest reasons people use food banks –
has been reduced. They also criticise Labour for stopping
job centres making referrals to food banks while in power,
something which the current government reversed in
2010. Either way, if people can't afford food, something is
going wrong. And 83 per cent of Trussell Trust food banks
surveyed said that welfare sanctions – the withdrawal of
benefits – were the reason for people coming to them.

What the welfare system is trying to do is provide the
needy – the most unfortunate people in our society – with
enough money to live on, but not so much that there's no
point in working. That feels like a reasonable ambition. We
don't want to encourage a culture of worklessness – that
can't be healthy for either the individuals themselves or for
society as a whole. But that is exactly what's happening in
some cases. People are getting stuck in a **benefits trap**.
You've probably heard that term before. Essentially, going
out to work ends up giving you so little extra money, compared to what you were getting on benefits (many of which
are taken away as soon as you find employment), that there
is virtually no incentive to go to work. At least in financial
terms.

That's where **Universal Credit** (UC) comes in. One of
the coalition government's biggest projects, UC is a single
monthly payment, like a salary, that will replace six of the
main working-age benefits (i.e. not pensions): Jobseeker's
Allowance, Working Tax Credit, Income Support, Housing
Benefit and so on. Universal Credit will be available to
people out of work and in work on a low income. It aims
to avoid the benefits trap, by letting people keep some

benefits as they do more hours of work. It should also be easier for people to move in and out of employment with ongoing financial support, meaning any amount of work will be worthwhile. Also, because the payment is a monthly lump sum, people will need to budget for themselves, which it is hoped will provide an important lesson in responsibility.

Universal Credit also hopes to make the system simpler. In the current system, there are over fifty different types of benefits that an individual can apply for. Unsurprisingly, that requires a huge amount of administration and filling out of forms, which is both time-consuming and really expensive. That's a problem, but the much bigger problem is that it's a total nightmare to navigate for someone making a claim – it's too bloody complicated. That's why you end up with millions of households who are eligible for benefits missing out – because they either don't know about the benefits they're entitled to, or are confused and overwhelmed by the complexity of the system. That complexity also means that it's extremely hard for an individual to work out whether he or she will be better off in employment, and that in itself is another deterrent from work.

Ultimately, the system of Universal Credit aims to be cheaper to administer too, although the costs of bringing it in are high and it is proving difficult to implement. Consequently, the government is rolling it out very, very slowly. Originally, the plan was for it to be fully operational by 2017, with a million people supposed to be using it by April 2014. The National Audit Office found a mere 17,850 people on UC in October 2014. The latest target is to have 500,000 people claiming UC by 2016. Iain Duncan Smith, the Work and Pensions Secretary, is now aiming for 7 million claimants by 2019. That's a long way off. The

whole process has been plagued by technological problems. A minister who has dealt with Duncan Smith on the
reform said of UC, 'I do think it'll work, but whether I'll be
alive to see it finished is another matter.' I don't know how
old or well he/she was when they said that.

In its aim to make work pay, Universal Credit combines
stick with carrot. If you work, you and your family will be
better off, but until then this will keep you afloat (that's the
'carrot'). If you aren't looking for work when you could
and should be, you will have your benefits taken away
(there's the 'stick'). Those on Jobseeker's Allowance sign a
'Claimant Commitment' which outlines what job seeking
actions you must carry out to keep receiving the money. If
you don't do what you promised, your benefits are suspended. The stick is in good working order. A total of
789,000 sanctions were imposed in the year to September
2013, punishing people for not looking for work, or missing
appointments, or not getting involved with back-to-work
programmes.

It's worth mentioning – while we're on the topic of the
stick – that by and large there is a political consensus that
sanctions are a necessary part of the welfare system. They
are part of the deal: the state will look after you, so long as
you are trying to look after yourself. The idea is that as
well as being a punishment, sanctions also act as a spur –
to encourage people to find work. But does it work like
that? Not everyone thinks so. An Oxfam report found that
between October 2012 and June 2014, the increased use of
sanctions did not reduce unemployment.

Another concern is that under-25s are much more likely
to experience sanctions than older people. Again, the reasons aren't really known, but it is probably a combination
of factors. It may be that they are more able to rely on help

from family; that their lifestyles are a bit more chaotic, which makes meeting the benefit conditions harder; or it may be that they just have less experience of the benefit system and find it more difficult to navigate.

A government-commissioned review found that communications with claimants needs improving – too often people aren't aware that their benefits have been stopped, or why they've been stopped, or don't know that they can appeal against sanctions. There are horror stories about people's benefits being taken away unfairly, though you might argue this is more to do with the administration of the sanctions than the principle itself. The Liberal Democrats think too many people are being unfairly punished, and have proposed a 'yellow card' system – so that any claimant will get an official warning for a first offence.

There is actually a good amount of cross-party support for Universal Credit, with the Labour Party supporting the system in principle. Labour is worried about the delays and the costs, though, and would pause the project if elected until the National Audit Office has done a report on it.

The question is, while the stick is in place, is there enough carrot? Some argue that even when people get work, what's available is often badly paid and comes with no job security. Sanctions, or the threat of them, make people take those lower-quality jobs and hardly give employers an incentive to offer better pay and conditions. These low-quality unsecure jobs can be positive if they lead to a better job. But if they don't, and they result in people falling back on benefits, there will be no long-term improvement. In fact, we know half of the families living in relative poverty have a family member working. The danger is that without those better-paid jobs, the best-case scenario is that you shift people from out-of-work poverty to in-work poverty. And that is a terrible best-case scenario.

But what is the solution? One idea is for the government to dictate the creation of secure, well-paid jobs. Labour has promised taxpayer-funded jobs for young people who have been unemployed for more than a year. The Conservatives and other parties question the government's ability to 'magic up' jobs, and generally those on the right feel the best way to create jobs is to reduce taxes and '**red tape**'. Those on the right are often also sceptical of things like the minimum wage (though the Conservatives support it and, like Labour, promise to increase it), arguing that if the government forces businesses to pay wages they can't afford, that will just result in fewer jobs and more struggling businesses going bust. I'll talk more about the minimum wage, the living wage and **zero-hour contracts** in the Jobs and the Economy chapter.

Maybe Universal Credit will be a success if and when it finally replaces the current system. Another possible solution – a form of which is supported by the Green Party – is a thing called Basic Income (BI). It goes further than UC, in that it would replace all anti-poverty welfare payments with a single payment to every citizen. The means-testing would be very straightforward – the same amount would be given to everyone until they entered employment, and then it would be tapered off. This challenges our whole notion of welfare. Currently, we will only get help from the government if we can prove that we need it. This idea questions whether it has to be that way. This is an 'all carrot, no stick' solution. One objection is that you have to retain a bit of stick, or you'll just end up with a growing number of people sitting around doing nothing, living off the state. Setting the rate wouldn't be easy either – you'd

want the payment to just cover the basic costs of living, so
that no one had to live in poverty. That way, at least the
incentive to work is still there, because if you want anything above and beyond that very simple life, you will need
to earn money on top of the BI. But regional variations in
living costs make a one-size-fits-all lump sum difficult to
imagine. In its favour, it is very easy to grasp, not like the
current welfare system. One way of structuring it is that the
more you earn, the less of your BI you get (much like with
UC), but you will always have more money than if you
weren't working. So say the BI is £10,000. If you don't
work, you just get £10,000. If you earn £5,000, your BI will
now be less than £10,000 – £7,500, say – but you still have
more in total (£12,500) than you would have done without
working. If you earn £10,000, your BI drops to £5,000, but
again you have more (£15,000) than you would have done
without working. There would be a cut-off, after which you
would receive no BI, but your wage is now decent (£20,000
say).

There is another way of doing it, which is even simpler
and even bolder. It's an idea that's been knocking about for
a while – Martin Luther King Jnr spoke about it. You get the
same amount of Basic Income no matter what you earn on
top of it. There is no means-testing at all, and there is no
requirement to demonstrate that you are actively seeking
work.

Both forms of Basic Income are open to criticism.
Politicians from the left and the right have talked about
ending a 'something for nothing' culture. But this is exactly
that. If voters think that the current welfare system is creating a 'culture of dependency', they're unlikely to go for
this. Another worry is that although BI sounds very neat
and simple, it may not be able to cope with all of the

inevitable exemptions and special cases – people with severe disabilities, immigrants, people having to pay London rents and so on.

There is not any agreement on the overall cost of a Basic Income system. As with so many areas of politics, it's hard to get a consensus. These things aren't black and white. Supporters say that while it may be expensive, the extensive means-testing of the current system is also expensive, and those costs would be removed entirely under BI. A lower cost of administration, so the argument goes, means that more of the welfare budget can end up with the people who need it (the same will also hopefully be true of Universal Credit). We wouldn't need to have government employees hunting for benefit frauds, because by definition, benefit fraud couldn't exist. Also, the stigma of claiming benefits would be eradicated entirely. People could not over-claim (and I'm sure television people can find something else to make programmes about).

Another potential problem with the system of Basic Income is that it could mean people getting less welfare money than they do currently. That might be a difficult shift. Also, if the policy ended up costing a lot more, then of course we would need to find that money from some-where, presumably via taxation. Again, the notion of paying more tax to fund the welfare system doesn't sit well with many people, and nor does the principle of the state paying people to (potentially) do nothing.

The Green Party is alone in favouring the Basic Income, supporting an unconditional form of the system. The Conservatives argue that their reforms – capping benefits so 'no out-of-work household can claim more in benefits than the average family earns in work', and reducing the rate at which benefits increase in value to beneath inflation – have been effective at providing a safety net for people, while maintaining the incentive to work. Labour has talked about offering up extra training to help people get back into work, with sanctions if training is refused. Labour has also trumpeted (as mentioned above) its 'jobs guarantee', which it says would mean that 18–24-year-olds out of work for a year would be offered a taxpayer-funded job for six months – with those who refuse losing benefits. Nick Clegg claims that the Lib Dems have protected welfare from more cuts by the Conservatives, and boosted income for the poor. But he has also stated that the government won't provide benefits with 'no strings attached and with no questions asked'.

UKIP argue that welfare should be a 'safety net for the needy, not a bed for the lazy'. They also say they will enrol unemployed welfare claimants onto community schemes or retraining workfare programmes (where you have to work in order to claim your benefits), and restrict benefits to those who have lived in this country for at least five years.

Whatever party's approach you favour, if you care about how welfare should work, then make sure you help to choose the next government – VOTE.

5. Broken Promises

Why do politicians lie?

You've probably heard someone, at some point, tell you that all politicians lie. Ironically, that might be a lie, but it's fair to say that almost every successful, and unsuccessful, leader you can think of has broken promises. It feels like we are constantly being reminded by the press and the opposition parties that the government lies. That makes it hard for us to trust the government, and trust has to be earned.

I absolutely believe that most politicians enter politics for the 'right reasons'. I think they want to make their country better. What gets in the way is that the campaign period is the time for the parties to try and win our votes. That's the most important thing. That's what is happening right now. The promises that are being broken are often the promises made in the run-up to an election – when all of the parties are enthusiastically laying out what they will do if and when they get into power. You could argue that, once a party is in power, the best time for it to break its promises is straight after the election – as far from the next election as possible, by which time the electorate might have forgotten ...

It's no surprise that the parties who don't win the election spend so much time highlighting the broken commitments of the party in power – because they want to undermine confidence in the government, and it's quite easy to be judgemental when not in power. They can say with total assurance, 'We would do this, we would do that, we would never have behaved like this shameful government', because there's no way of testing that claim. The Opposition can't really break promises because they have no power. And you can be sure that if the Opposition do eventually get into power at the next election, roles will be reversed, and they will be the ones getting criticised for breaking promises made in their campaign. That's just how it goes.

A survey published in 2009 showed that, on average, across Europe and America, parties keep 67 per cent of their campaign promises. Actually, I don't think that sounds so bad. Perhaps if we, the public, just accept that one in three promises will be broken, we'll be much less disappointed. The trick is working out which are the ones that will get the axe. And also exactly how they will get the axe.

There are a few different types of lies, in political terms. There is the *outright lie*: we promised that we would do this, and now we are doing the opposite. There is the *delay-until-the-people-forget lie*: yes, we know we promised to do this, and we will do it, just not yet. There is the *total-ignorance lie*: we have no idea what promise you're talking about. And there is the slippery *technically-we-haven't-lied lie*, which is my personal favourite. Picture the scene:

you're having dinner with a politician (weirdly). You need
to go to the loo, and you say, 'Mrs Politician, please promise not to eat my chicken wings.' The politician replies,
'OK, I have no plans to eat your chicken wings.' Happy
with her answer, you go to the loo, and are furious when
you return to the table to find your plate littered with bones
and the politician licking her lips. 'You said you weren't
going to eat my chicken wings!' 'No, I said I had no plans to.
At the time, that was true. But while you were in the loo, I
gave it some thought, formulated a new plan, and ate them.'

That sounds far-fetched, doesn't it? And yet, if you
replace 'eat my chicken wings' with 'introduce top-up fees',
and 'Mrs Politician' with 'Tony Blair', you have a fair
description of what happened when Labour introduced
top-up fees in 2004. In 2000, Tony Blair said, 'We have no
plans to introduce top-up fees.' That was also in Labour's
2001 election **manifesto**.

So I think there are several questions that need to be
asked. Why do politicians lie? Why do we allow them to
get away with it? And how can we stop them?

The truth (ha!) is that election promises are not really
promises in the way that we normally see promises. They
are signals of intent and priority, as opposed to genuine
commitments. They should qualify each statement with,
'This is not what we *will* do, it is what we would *like* to do.'
Effectively, they are statements that describe what the party
would do in an ideal world, but of course we don't live in
an ideal world. We live in a world where there are many
limits and constraints – money being the main one. It's
actually not difficult to come up with solutions and policies if you think of them as all operating on their own, and
with no budget limitations. Unfortunately, policies do
affect one another, and the budget is limited.

Elections require the parties to try and build the widest range of support and therefore the largest number of votes, so they strive to make a wide range of 'promises'. Often, politicians have a choice to make: stick resolutely to their guns and their principles, or try to maximise their votes. Very rarely will those two aims be compatible. Once in power, politicians simply won't have the means to keep all of their promises. Another thing is that circumstances change. What may have been the best thing to do when the promise was made may not be the best thing to do when it's time to act on it. Politicians then have to figure out whether the benefit of breaking that promise outweighs the cost of betraying those people who may have voted for it. Given that parties keep 67 per cent of their promises on average, I guess 33 per cent of the time they do think the benefit outweighs the cost.

The most intriguing reason that politicians make promises that they don't deliver on is that they are, in their minds at least, doing it in our interests. For our own good. That seems perverse, but what happens is parties make commitments that they know will be popular, and that will win them the votes they need, and then they do stuff when they're in power that is unpopular but the right thing to do. The idea being, the electorate don't know what is good for them: popular doesn't mean right. If they did what the voters wanted the outcome would be bad, and the party would lose popular support anyway. So basically, making the 'promises' before the election attracts popular support, and breaking them afterwards will, in the slightly longer term, maintain the popular support. At least that's the theory.

As voters, do we need to take some of the blame for this situation? Are we letting politicians get away with lying to us? To some extent, yes. Sometimes, we simply don't realise that we've been lied to – politicians are good at covering their tracks and confusing us with jargon. That's quite deliberate. They can use a combination of any of the different types of lies I mentioned earlier. Sometimes, we do realise that we've been lied to though and our response to this is more interesting.

You might think that if a politician breaks a promise in clear view, all of the people who voted for that politician or party based on that promise would vow never to vote for them again. Likewise with the people who weren't fussed about that particular promise, but do dislike dishonesty. However, it seems that we are much more forgiving than that. We seem to fundamentally put up with lying. We've seen it before; we'll see it again. Perhaps our expectation is that everyone will lie in roughly equal amounts, and therefore there is no overall effect. If collectively we said, 'If you lie, not one of us will ever vote for you again', I don't think politicians would lie. Or they'd at least do it less. Unfortunately, it's hard to visualise how we could organise or implement that collective decision. I'll come back to that ...

If you've voted for a party, the chances are that you will agree with many of the rest of their policies, some of which are being implemented. That will make you prepared to downplay and forgive the odd fib. And then there are people who will have disagreed with the policy in the first place. So let's say, taking the example of tuition fees, that you don't think higher education should be paid for by the taxpayer, then you would have been delighted when Labour, twice, and then the Liberal Democrats failed to do what they said they would (that is, to cap tuition fees, or to scrap them altogether). I think a lot of us also understand the constraints of being in government – we get that it's not possible to do everything. We also get that things don't always go to plan.

You could argue that the way our political system works encourages broken promises. We now have five-year fixed-term governments. So even if we wanted to punish our politicians for U-turns, broken promises and lies, we have to wait until the next election, and do it with our vote (by not voting for them). That's the problem. Five years is a long time to wait and many voters will forget, or be wooed back on side with other policy decisions, or both. As discussed in the Leadership chapter, some voters will vote the same way at every election anyway, but their voting intentions may be reinforced if a government they haven't voted for does something especially 'wrong'. While some voters will absolutely hold a grudge ('I will never forget the time you did that!'), you could argue that it doesn't even really make sense to vote on the basis of frustration over a promise broken years ago. Of course trust is important, but I would have thought that people are probably better off voting on the basis of what is being promised this time round.

Many people think we need a way to punish MPs who lie to us or are guilty of serious wrongdoing. Currently, we have no ability to do that. Which is where **recall** comes in – it doesn't exist in the UK, but it may well do soon, in some form. Let's say our local MP has done something awful, or totally gone back on what they said. That's fairly easy to imagine. If 10 per cent of voters in a constituency then signed a petition the MP would have to stand down and face a by-election, where he or she could be replaced, depending on the result of that election. Recall gives us, the voters, the power to make our MP stand down.

Given that MPs are our representatives, some people think it is absurd that we have no way of expressing dissatisfaction with them. Recall would allow us to have our say on an MP's actions where their behaviour has 'fallen below the standards expected of an MP'. There's an easy joke in there about the standards that we expect of MPs, which I'll leave you to make yourselves. As I write, a bill is being discussed by MPs to introduce recall, but there is a serious effort being made by some MPs to water the proposal down. The recall I've described is 'pure recall' (or if you prefer, Total Recall) – the people make the decision to get their MP removed from his or her position. With the watered down version, a parliamentary committee would have to decide that the MP in question had been 'engaged in serious wrongdoing' before a petition could be made. Campaigners for pure recall say that means that the only time the public would be allowed to use recall is when their MP is on the brink of resigning anyway. Which seems to make the public's role almost redundant.

It's a bit of a 'turkeys voting for Christmas' situation – highly unlikely to happen. MPs in **marginal seats** might be in favour of pure recall because they already know that they have to fight to win their constituents' approval, but MPs in so-called **safe seats** would be put at risk by recall in its original form (I talk more about this in the Representation chapter). As it stands now, the constituents of MPs in safe seats are almost entirely unable to get them out. I guess that's quite comforting for them, but not for us. The Tory MP Zac Goldsmith is championing pure recall, trying to convince his fellow MPs to see the positive impact that he believes this could have on our **democracy**. Goldsmith thinks that giving us the authority to punish MPs would help to convince us that they care what we – the people they are supposed to represent – think. That they care about our view. Some of the arguments against recall are that by-elections are expensive (the average cost is £240,000), and they might get unduly influenced or triggered by special interest groups. There is also the concern that if you end up having loads of by-elections, it might destabilise the government and stop anything getting done. Zac Goldsmith points out that the American people have recall powers, and have only used them forty times in a hundred years.

My final thought about how we might be able to reduce the amount of promise-breaking comes from the economist Robin Hanson, who says, 'Politicians who really wanted to show they would keep their campaign promises would post bonds, judged by neutral third parties, and forfeit if they broke their promises.' Essentially, get politicians to put their money where their mouths are. If they make a promise, and then break it as judged by an independent board, they lose their money. That's probably never going to happen, but it could have a huge effect. Although, you might end up with an awful situation where only the richest politicians can afford to lie!

If you care about punishing politicians for breaking promises – VOTE.

6. Immigration

Do we have an immigration problem in the UK?

This question breaks down into two bits: do we *actually* have an immigration problem, in terms of numbers and money and so on, and do the public *think* we have an immigration problem?

Before we start, it's worth noting that we, as a country, are talking about immigration again. That is a good thing, because ten years ago we weren't. If you so much as mentioned immigration, or questioned its levels, you were denounced as a racist. Labour in particular was guilty of this. In 2005, when then Conservative leader Michael Howard made a speech about immigration, saying, 'It's not racist to want to limit the numbers. It's just plain common sense', he was attacked by Labour minister Peter Hain, who accused him of 'scurrilous, right-wing, ugly tactics'. Shutting a debate down in that way is rarely helpful. Now, although there is still a bit of that – the standard left-wing put-down of UKIP is that they are a 'racist party' – the newer problem is that the conversation about immigration doesn't seem to be rooted in what is actually happening. That's partly because for every 'fact', there is another 'fact' that will show the exact opposite.

For example, a UCL report found that immigrants from the EU, between 2000 and 2011, made a net contribution (which is their actual contribution after all relevant deductions have been made from their gross contribution) to the UK finances of £20 billion. The same report found that immigrants who arrived since 2000 were 43 per cent less likely than British people to receive state benefits or tax credits. The report is very clear – immigrants are net contributors to our economy. But then Migration Watch, a group that is in favour of tougher immigration laws, has strongly disputed the findings of that UCL report, saying that some of the assumptions were flawed. Migration Watch claims that immigrants might actually have cost around £140 billion in the last seventeen years. So who are we to believe?

Some figures that we do know, and that aren't contested, are for net migration. Net migration is the difference between the number of people coming (immigrating), and the number of people leaving (emigrating). Before David Cameron became prime minister in 2010, he said that he wanted to return net migration to 1990s levels and to see 'immigration in the tens of thousands rather than the hundreds of thousands'. When Cameron said this, he was effectively setting himself a target to reduce net migration to under 100,000. In 2010, net migration was 244,000. And although it dropped a bit over the following years, it is now back up to 260,000. Higher than when he set the target, and nowhere near the target. So more people are definitely coming into the UK.

The truth is that it's impossible, at the moment, for us to

control two of the three factors that affect net migration. We can't influence how many people leave the country, and we can't influence the number of people who come in from the EU (39 per cent of the total influx in the year to June 2014). That's because our EU membership means that EU citizens can come and go as they please. This is what UKIP would like to see stopped. What we can control is the number of people coming in from outside the EU (47 per cent of the total influx in the year to June 2014). Apart from anything else, these statistics highlight that 'immigrants' are not one uniform group of people; some come from the EU and some come from outside the EU; some come looking for work, while others may have simply married a UK citizen or decided to retire here. And then, crucially, some are unskilled while others are highly skilled. We must try not to lazily lump them all into one category.

We know that immigration increases our population size. That means that there will be a greater demand for our public services and that, inevitably, we need to build more of everything – houses, roads, airports. That will cost money, and generally speaking people don't want those things getting built near them. However, more people also means, theoretically at least, more tax revenue to build all those things. The government would argue that the high immigration numbers are due to the economy doing really well – the UK is an enticing prospect.

An obvious question to ask is – are the native British people who are unemployed being kept out of work by migrant workers? Again, this is difficult. Sorry. On the one hand, it seems kind of obvious that if an immigrant comes to the UK and gets a job, then by definition a British worker can't have that job. On the other hand, others say some industries wouldn't thrive without the skills and hard work of immigrants. In other words, some of those jobs wouldn't exist at all. It's not simple. Theresa May talked about a Migration Advisory Council report at the end of 2012, saying that 'for every additional 100 immigrants, they estimated that twenty-three British workers would not be employed'. There were lots of caveats to this statement though: this study is only about non-EU immigrants; the immigrants have to have been in the UK for less than five years; and this only applies to periods of economic hardship (in other words, when unemployment is higher there are fewer jobs, so the impact on British workers is higher).

The Migration Advisory Council's report was questioned by Jonathan Portes of the National Institute of Economic and Social Research, who said that the majority of the data showed that overall, there was 'no statistically significant impact of migration on employment'. There is, however, some agreement among politicians and academics that migration has an effect on wages. According to Fullfact.org, which reviewed the evidence from both sides of the argument, migration tends to increase wages at the top (high-paid jobs), and lower wages at the bottom (low-paid jobs). So some would argue that, when things are tough, immigration is both reducing British workers' chances of getting a job, and squeezing the pay of the same jobs.

The main parties all agree that immigration is an issue, but they have different ideas on how to tackle it. According to the Office for National Statistics (ONS), 236,000 people in the UK are paid less than the minimum wage. Immigrant workers get exploited more because they are less likely to know what they're entitled to. And in turn, native British workers don't get those jobs because the employers know they can get the labour cheaper by under-paying immigrants.

The parties all recognise that the 954,000 so-called NEETS (young people who are Not in Employment, Education or Training) need assistance. Most of them didn't do well at school. One thought is that schools should be trying to identify those kids early, and then focusing on giving them the basic skills that will make them more employable. Those aren't just academic skills; they are things like teamwork, confidence and flexibility ('soft skills').

As things stand, we rely on migrant workers. UKIP would argue that this is a bad thing and we need to be less reliant. They are confident that if we reduced the number of migrant workers, native British workers would fill the gap, and with no extra pressure being put on public services. That may be true in some cases, but in others it may not be. There is a measure of how easily employers can find the skills they need in the workforce. According to the recruitment firm Hays Group, in areas like engineering, construction and IT – 'skilled jobs' – the UK has a 'talent mismatch' of 9.6 out of 10. A higher number means greater difficulty. The UK's score is 9.6 out of 10! We are struggling to fill high-level positions. Ideally, in the long run, we need to drastically improve and encourage the training of our own workers, but in the short-term we need people to come in from outside of the UK. Those skilled people are in demand – other countries want them too – so we need to compete.

In the short-term, until we can train British people to take the jobs, we need to attract these skilled immigrants, or the worry is that our economy will be damaged. The NHS is a prime example of a sector that relies upon migrant workers – an estimated 11 per cent of the NHS workforce are immigrants. Without them, you'd assume that the NHS would struggle. Some people also say that our

ageing population will need more, not less, migrant workers to support it – because immigration provides a supply
of young people. A report in 2013 estimated that we will
need an extra 7 million migrants over the next fifty years.
They will not only be in employment, but also paying all-
important taxes to support our elderly.

It's curious that facts and figures are almost always over-
shadowed by anecdotal evidence. Partly because every
argument seems to be able to find facts and figures to support it! Both sides can claim that the numbers are on their
side. That means that if someone has a friend or family
member who has lost a job, directly or indirectly, to an
immigrant, then that is what sticks. Nigel Farage, when
asked about the evidence that immigrants contribute to the
economy, which he disputes anyway, said that 'there are
some things that matter more than money'. It's an interesting, and smart, answer. Farage recognises that this debate is
about more than numbers – it's about how people feel.

It is also all too easy to dismiss anti-immigration feeling
as just a fear of the unknown. And, of course, during times
of economic difficulty we will tend to look for someone to
blame. One thing that probably hasn't helped is David
Cameron's 2010 pledge to reduce net migration to below
100,000. The point here is that it doesn't matter whether
immigration is a good thing or a bad thing, what matters is
that the government has failed, quite spectacularly, to do
what it said it would. And whatever the reason, the impres-
sion it gives is that the government can't control the
number of people coming in. The danger then is that
people feel like our borders are open to anyone and sure
enough anyone is flooding in, in spite of whatever the government is (or isn't) doing to stop them. It's hardly
surprising that the public find that worrying.

The relationship between public opinion and the media is tricky to figure out – it's chicken and egg. Are the public wary of immigration because of the media's coverage of it, or is media coverage being led by the public mood? A study was done recently by The Migration Observatory at Oxford University on the type of language used when the media covers immigration and migrants in general. Across all newspapers, left and right wing, the most commonly used terms to describe immigrants and **asylum seekers** are 'illegal' and 'bogus'. Of the headlines about asylum, 31 per cent are negative. Of the text about asylum, 53 per cent is negative. Yet asylum seekers make up a tiny proportion of inward migration. In 2010, of 17,790 who applied for asylum in the UK, only 3,480 were successful. Hardly enough to warrant this negative attention. Although, you could perhaps justify describing the high proportion that are denied asylum as 'bogus'.

Those concerned about immigration often reject the argument that their concerns are born of fear and a need to blame someone. For many, integration is also an issue. After spending a couple of days with a Muslim family in Birmingham in 2007, David Cameron said, 'the challenges of cohesion and integration are among the greatest we face'. In my ideal version of the UK, we have people of all different religions and races all mixed up and living together. Everyone bringing bits of their own culture and identity to the table and forming our society – the people of our country united.

Many worry that that is not what's happening. There's not enough integration. Instead, we have isolated pockets of people here, and isolated pockets of people there. In 2012, Ed Miliband said that 'separation means isolation and you can't succeed in Britain if you are isolated.

Isolation also breeds ignorance and ignorance breeds suspicion and prejudice.' In a country that has a welfare state, which supports its people with money, health care, education and housing, we need to feel that every member is part of the wider community. It doesn't work if we are just a collection of individuals, we need to feel solidarity with everyone else. Otherwise, as Miliband suggests, we may well start to resent those who feel to us like they are not part of our society. And that's not to do with their financial contribution. That's – and I realise this is vague and a bit hippy-ish – to do with their emotional contribution. How can we help new migrants to integrate into British society? Some will say that reducing their numbers will make this easier.

In a recent Ipsos MORI poll, British people on average thought that just over 24 per cent of the UK population is made up of immigrants. The actual figure is around 13 per cent. What I find interesting about that is this: in Germany, the immigrant population is around 13 per cent too but the German people believe it's higher, around 23 per cent. Very similar to the British public, but there is one *huge* difference. In Germany, 62 per cent of the people think that immigration is an opportunity. In other words, they welcome it, believing it will strengthen their country. In the UK, 64 per cent think that immigration is a problem. Whether it's right or wrong, Germany has a more positive perception of immigration. Why is that? There's a lot we might be able to learn from their experience. For example, since 2005 they have run compulsory 'integration course' for new immigrants. Boris Johnson, the Mayor of London, has said that he thinks everyone is a little bit xenophobic, that it is a part of human nature. He believes that we have to keep telling people about the 'benefits of having talented people, and having a welcoming policy to people that will work hard'. If we are still to have immigration – and only the BNP opposes all immigration – what Johnson says is true.

Immigration is one of the key issues at this general election. The British people are definitely worried about it and UKIP is getting support from many of those people. Where UKIP stands on this is very clear. It wants to end freedom of movement within the EU so that we can 'take back control of our borders'. UKIP says it wouldn't allow any new migrants access to schools, housing or health care for their first five years in the UK. It would introduce a tougher system (like Australia uses) for prospective migrants, and reduce net migration to 50,000 or less a year. Interestingly, though, Migration Watch has done an analysis of the Australian system and believes that it would be entirely unsuitable for the UK. Nevertheless, UKIP says it is the only party that anyone categorically trusts to be 'tough on immigration'.

You may well have heard the phrase 'You can't out-UKIP UKIP'. Still, that seems to be what the other parties are trying to do. That's essentially because all except the Greens agree that immigration needs to come down.

The Conservatives, perhaps somewhat embarrassed by their failure to meet their own immigration target, say that they have clamped down on benefits and health 'tourism' (where people are said to be coming only to claim benefits). David Cameron has once again promised to cut net immigration by focusing on non-EU migration (the only thing he can focus on, remember). The Conservatives have said that they are going to reduce non-EU immigration to 'levels not seen since the late 1990s'. He also plans to bring in a 'new citizen test with British values at heart'. Presumably that's a way of tackling the integration problem I mentioned earlier.

Labour is planning to stop employment agencies from recruiting exclusively from abroad. Those immigrant agency workers can be legally paid less than the UK minimum wage at the moment, which seems ridiculous. Bringing an end to that should help both migrants and British workers from being excluded from jobs or being underpaid. Miliband has said he will close the legal loophole that is currently allowing that to happen. He also wants to double the amount of time that an immigrant would need to live in the UK before they can claim any benefits. This would, he hopes, serve as a deterrent to would-be 'benefit tourists'. Any big changes to the benefits migrants from the EU receive may well need agreement with the EU, and would presumably lead to fewer benefits for the British citizens living in Europe. Labour would also re-introduce exit checks at UK borders to identify people who have stayed longer than their visa allowed. I'm not sure what the punishment would be, but the Lib Dems would also do this.

The Lib Dems say they would implement a 'firm but fair system'. They think that highly skilled immigrants can contribute to building a stronger economy, but people 'need to trust the system to work properly'. The Lib Dems will shut down 'bogus colleges' that bring 'students' over who then work instead of study.

The Green Party is the only party that would reduce UK immigration controls, and not set caps on numbers. The Greens are far more pro-migration than any of the other parties.

If you care about the people who live and work in our country – VOTE.

7. Coalition Government

Will we have another coalition government after the general election in May?

I'd like to quickly clear up the difference between Parliament and government, if only because it confused me for ages. Government is led by the prime minister, and is made up of a team of MPs from his or her party (plus others if there is a coalition). The government sets the agenda, deciding how to spend our taxes and so on. Parliament is the MPs in government, plus all the rest of the MPs in the House of Commons and all of the members in the **House of Lords**. Parliament is responsible for changing and approving the country's laws. It also keeps an eye on how the government is doing. Those MPs in Parliament are representing us, the people, and trying to ensure that our best interests are being looked after. Also, if someone says 'during this Parliament' they mean 'in the time since the last general election when all of these MPs were elected'.

In answer to this chapter's question, it's very possible that another coalition government will be formed. There are 650 constituencies in the UK, and therefore 650 seats up for grabs. To get an overall majority and form a single-party government, a party needs to win a minimum of 326 seats (just over half of what's available). In 2010, no party did that, and we were left with what's called a Hung Parliament. A recent publication by the website Election Forecast UK suggested that the probability of another Hung Parliament after this general election – with no overall majority for any party – is 91 per cent. Of course, everything could still change . . .

This is what happens in the event of a Hung Parliament. First, the sitting prime minister, in this case David Cameron, will get the opportunity to form a coalition with another party or parties, who will bring enough seats with them to give the coalition a majority. In 2010, the Conservatives won 307 seats, Labour won 258 seats, the Lib Dems won 57, and the remainder were won by smaller parties. So when the Conservatives (307) joined forces with the Lib Dems (57), they had a total of 364 seats, enough for a majority. That allowed them to form the coalition government. Coalition governments have been extremely uncommon in the past. Because coalitions require a degree of compromise from all the parties involved, if the parties' ideals and policies are too far apart, they can be impossible. For example, in 2010 Labour had an opportunity to do a deal with the Lib Dems but they were unable to agree on enough to form a 'stable' coalition and negotiations broke down (Labour had been in government for a long time and Gordon Brown was unpopular, and that might have put the Lib Dems off too). The Conservatives and Lib Dems, however, were able to come to an agreement, and outlined various common aims. David Cameron said he wanted to 'put aside party differences and work hard for the national interest'. Nick Clegg hoped the arrangement was 'the start of the new politics I have always believed in'. I'll talk about how that panned out later.

To figure out why having a majority, or not, is so important, you have to look at the way that laws are passed. Any MP can propose a bill, which is essentially either a suggested law change or a new law. Now, if the bill is proposed by an MP who is a member of the government, it will probably get voted on. If the bill is a Private Members' Bill (a bill proposed by an MP who is not in the government), it is much less likely to get voted on, or even debated. Basically, it's not easy getting a bill passed if you're not in government. If a bill gets to the voting stage, it will be voted on by MPs in the House of Commons. If the bill gets the majority of votes, it will stand a very good chance of becoming law (although the House of Lords can reject it).

Where not having a majority can be especially dangerous is if an Opposition MP proposes a 'vote of no confidence'. In 1979, after a few Labour MPs had defected to other parties, the Labour government found itself in a minority (having previously held a very small majority). The Leader of the Opposition, Conservative Margaret Thatcher, proposed that 'this House has no confidence in Her Majesty's Government'. The Labour government lost by one vote and a general election was called. That is a danger that looms over any government with a minority – it can fall at any moment. A **minority government** will always need to make deals with other parties if they are to win any votes in Parliament, whereas a majority government should be able to pass all of its bills without help from other parties. That is useful when trying to run a country, and that is why Cameron and Clegg were keen to try and make their coalition work.

There are two different types of vote in the House of Commons: a 'free vote' and a 'whipped vote'. In a free vote, the parties don't tell their MPs how to vote – they are free to choose their own positions. In a 'whipped vote', the party's Chief Whip makes it very clear how the party is expecting everyone to vote. If an MP goes against that, the party will not be pleased. An interesting vote to look at is the one on gay marriage in 2013. That was passed, overwhelmingly, by 400 votes to 175 (with a fair few **abstentions**). David Cameron declared the vote a free one, but also that he was in favour of gay marriage. He would have hoped that his party would follow him of their own accord, but that didn't happen – 139 Tories voted against, with just 132 voting for. That kind of division within a party is both embarrassing and, if the vote had been tighter, worrying.

At this election, if David Cameron and the Conservatives are unable or unwilling to form a coalition with one or more of the smaller parties, then they will have the option to form a minority government. Minority government is when a party forms a different, weaker alliance with a party or parties – much weaker than a coalition. The parties don't agree on enough to form a coalition but will have loose agreements on certain issues. So the party forming the minority government can count on support on those issues only. The strength and formality of these agreements vary. There is something called a 'jumping majority', which is extremely fragile, where the government will try to persuade parties to support it in votes on a case-by-case basis. These governments don't long! Then there are more secure 'confidence and supply' deals, where parties formally agree to support certain key legislation, like the budget. This allows the government to function, but outside of those agreements the other parties will stick to their own policies and views. If the Conservatives fail to form a coalition or a minority government, then the biggest opposition party, likely to be Labour, will have a go.

In the past, coalition and minority governments have come in for criticism. Many argue that majority governments are strong and can pass laws swiftly. That means they can react to situations quickly. The government will almost certainly serve its full five-year term. But the opposition parties have very little power beyond holding the government to account – so the government basically gets to do whatever it wants. Compare that to a minority government, which has to rely much more on the support of the opposition parties when trying to pass laws. This takes longer, but at least all of the parties get a say. All of the parties have to work together. That's no bad thing. Some would argue that this will never lead to radical change – because lots of parties have to agree – but others would say that in fact bolder decisions might end up being made, because of the shared responsibility.

Scandinavian countries have a long and fairly successful history of coalition and minority governments, but in December 2014 Sweden's left-wing minority government fell after only three months in power. The far-right, anti-immigration Sweden Democrats (to some extent, the equivalent of UKIP here – in the European Parliament, MEPs sit in groups determined by political leaning, and UKIP sits with the Sweden Democrats) was the third biggest party, with 13 per cent of the public vote. Neither the centre-left (like our Labour Party) nor the centre-right (like our Conservative Party) would team up with the Sweden Democrats formally, meaning that the Sweden Democrats ended up holding the 'balance of power'. Balance of power basically means whichever bigger party the smaller party decides to side with, on any issue raised in parliament, will win. So effectively, the smaller party dictates what happens. In this case they, the far-right, voted against the government's first budget and defeated it, triggering another election. It is precisely that sort of balance of power that UKIP, the Green Party, the Lib Dems and the SNP will hope to hold.

Being the smaller party in a coalition can be difficult, as Nick Clegg and the Lib Dems have found out. The public perception is that if you're in government, you should be delivering on the promises you made in the run up to the election. That isn't always, or even often, possible in a coalition because of the compromise involved – you have to pick and choose your battles with your coalition partner. The Conservatives have more power within the coalition. Many young people are furious at Nick Clegg over the issue of tuition fees because he said that he would scrap them, but under this government they were trebled. Clegg is at pains to point out that he is not prime minister – he is not in charge of the government. But the Lib Dems did make some of their policies deal-breakers – they made firm agreements with the Conservatives on some issues. Unfortunately, getting rid of tuition fees wasn't one of them. They didn't prioritise it.

One of the things that the Lib Dems did demand was a referendum – a nationwide vote – on Alternative Vote (AV), a voting system that the Lib Dems favour over the current system used in our general elections, called **First Past the Post** (FPTP). (You can read more about this in the Alternatives to Our Democracy chapter.) The Conservatives agreed to the referendum, but then attacked the Lib Dems and Nick Clegg personally to ensure that AV was voted against. In May 2011, 68 per cent of the public voted 'no' to

AV. So less than a year into the coalition, all the talk of 'putting aside party differences' seemed to have been forgotten. The two parties are currently feuding over plans for the economy, with Cameron describing the Lib Dems as 'all over the place' and Clegg saying that the Conservatives are 'kidding themselves and seeking to kid the British voters' if they think they can balance their budget plans. The cracks that appeared so early on in the coalition are now chasms. Interestingly, recent polling suggested that the Lib Dems will do better in this election under FPTP than they would have done under AV. So the Conservatives might have inadvertently done them a favour!

Clegg will argue that their time in the coalition has been worthwhile, because the Lib Dems have achieved many of their aims. To name a few, they've raised the income tax allowance, created more apprenticeships and protected pensions. To the public though, that doesn't seem to matter. His reputation has been severely damaged. The party's popularity has plummeted, with it now regularly polling below UKIP and the Greens. After the TV debates in 2010, Clegg was rated the most popular party leader since Winston Churchill. Now he is really struggling. That is the danger of a coalition government for the weaker partner.

The fortnight after May's election may well be as dramatic as the campaign itself. That's because the chances of a single party winning a majority are so low. The bigger parties – the Conservatives and Labour – could be scrambling around trying to form a coalition or minority government with one or more of the smaller parties. Those smaller parties will be able to ask for certain things in exchange for their support. How much they can ask for depends on how many seats (and votes) they can offer, and how extensive the support they promise will be.

Let's look at each of the smaller parties in turn, and what they might want from an alliance. UKIP has said it will 'do a deal with the devil' in order to get a referendum on EU membership – so it will get into bed with anyone. It's unlikely that the Tories or Labour would go into a full coalition with UKIP, but they may entertain a less formal arrangement. So, UKIP could support either one of the bigger parties in a minority government. The Greens have said that they will not go into coalition with the Tories. They only have one MP at the moment and it remains to be seen if they can pick up any more at this election – with only one, they would offer very little to a coalition. Much like UKIP, the FPTP electoral system doesn't currently favour them winning seats, so they would probably push for electoral reform in any alliance negotiations. If the polls are to be believed, the Lib Dems are likely to lose a fair few seats at this election, so will probably not be able to form a coalition like last time, even if they wanted to. About half of their members say they would ally in some way with Labour, given the chance, but unsurprisingly very few would want a repeat of the Conservative alliance.

The regional parties – the SNP in Scotland, the DUP and Sinn Féin in Northern Ireland and Plaid Cymru in Wales – would all want more devolved powers to their regions in return for any support they offered. The SNP has said it would not go into coalition with the Tories, and a coalition with Labour would be difficult because the SNP would have just fought against Labour and possibly wiped it out in Scotland. The former leader Alex Salmond believes that the SNP will win enough seats to hold the balance of power after the election. Latest polling suggests that the SNP might take 45 out of 59 seats. Labour would fall from 41 seats to 10. In Wales, Plaid Cymru currently has 3 seats.

David Cameron has apparently been courting the DUP, which may offer him support in exchange for some funding for pet projects.

Given that it is so likely that there will be a coalition or a minority government, the significance of the smaller parties is that much greater. They can play the role of 'kingmaker'. They may find themselves in a position to make demands relevant to you. Every party could have a say in the next government and this is why every vote counts.

If you want to have your say too – VOTE.

8. The Housing Crisis

When will I be able to afford to buy a house or flat?

That depends, because house prices are going up, and up, and up. If the price of food had risen at the same rate since 1971 then a chicken would now cost £51. Last year a report showed that four out of five homes for sale in England are unaffordable to the average working family looking to buy their first home. Renting in England and Wales has never been more expensive either, and the cost is still rising, so it's no wonder that a quarter of under-35s are still living in their childhood bedrooms. Most of them are working, but can't afford to move out of their parents' home. So what's going on? Why can't average people afford to buy any more? Or even rent? And whose fault is it?

There are a few reasons for the current situation, but the main one is very basic: our population is increasing, and over the last forty years or so we just haven't built enough homes. So there simply aren't enough properties – the shortfall is 1 million, and that number is steadily increasing because we are thought to be building 100,000 fewer homes, every year, than we need in order to meet demand. In 2013, fewer than 110,000 new homes were completed in England – one of the lowest levels since World War II. There are various estimates for the number of homes that we need in order to keep pace with demand, but most agree that it is around 250,000. Could we build that many homes in a year? Well, in the 1960s and 1970s we regularly churned out in excess of 300,000 a year – the record number was 425,000 in 1968. There was a lot of demolition happening then, so the total number of additional houses wasn't quite at that level, but that's missing the point – we have the ability to build a lot of houses. We just aren't.

Many would argue that the bare minimum we should expect from a civilised society is that it provides decent, affordable homes for its people. And many voters see the government as responsible. I guess they shouldn't be surprised if some voters get angry and disillusioned, when it seems clear that successive governments – of various parties – have failed. What we need is: lots of houses being built, at a low price. What we have is almost the exact opposite of that: very few houses being built, at a high price. Not only are there too few houses, but the houses that are being built are too small – smaller on average than almost all other European countries. Some people suggest that we should have minimum space standards for all new homes. If nothing is done then Shelter, the housing and homelessness charity, believes that we will fall further into 'a spiral of increasing house prices and rents – making the current housing crisis worse'. Property website Rightmove thinks prices will rise another 30 per cent over the next five years.

That's one problem area. The other is renting, and social housing. The whole idea of social housing is that it provides accommodation for people on low incomes, with rents that are limited by law. And unlike the growing private rental market, social housing is allocated on the basis of need, rather than whoever can pay the most. Margaret Thatcher thought home ownership, not renting, was the key to a happy family life. So in the 1980s her Right to Buy scheme allowed council tenants to buy their homes with generous discounts. Unfortunately the majority of those homes, which were social housing, were not replaced.

We now have so little social housing available, and so many families unable to buy homes, that more and more are being forced to move into privately rented properties. These often have short-term contracts, rents that could rise at the drop of a hat and a lack of security – not what these families need. The Joseph Rowntree Foundation has forecasted that, if no action is taken, the average private rent will rise from £132 a week to £250 a week in 2040 – that's double as fast as incomes will rise. That in turn will put another 2.6 million people into relative poverty, and add another £20 billion onto the housing benefits bill. Central government already spends twenty times as much on housing benefit as it does on grants for the building of affordable housing.

There has been a big change since the house-building heyday of the 1960s and 1970s. Back then, houses were being built by a combination of private building firms and local councils. These local authorities, funded by the government, were building about 90,000 homes every year. Not any more though – council-building has been replaced, in theory at least, by housing-association-building. This is also not for profit, but they build far fewer. From 1978 to 2013 those associations have built an average of only

18,800 new homes a year, and those numbers are even lower now after their budget was cut by over 50 per cent in 2010. What this means is that we have become extremely reliant on private firms to build housing stock. That wouldn't be a problem if these private firms were putting up enough new, affordable houses. But they aren't!

If you want to build a house, the two things you need are land to build on and money to pay for the construction. Actually if you're a private building firm, you need a third thing. You need to believe that the build is 'viable'. What viable means, in plain English, is profitable. That makes sense – why would a private company build houses or flats for social tenants who pay affordable rents ('affordable rents' are set at 80 per cent of market rents, the rate that private landlords charge normally) when they could sell or rent them to those who can afford to pay more?

One way of persuading developers to supply good quality social housing would be to offer tax breaks (build these for us, you'll pay less tax) in return. They do this sort of thing in the US and France, and it seems to work. You could, for example, say that in return for renting out properties as social housing at a fixed rate for twenty years, the developer would then be able to sell the property on without paying any capital gains tax (that's a tax that you pay when you sell something that has increased in value).

Given that it's currently hard to find incentives for private firms to build social housing, almost all of the affordable housing that is going up is being built by housing associations. One idea is that we need to allow them and local councils to borrow more money so that they can build more. The government has been wary of doing this in the past because it fears what happens if a local council recklessly borrows too much, leaving the government to pick up the bill when things go wrong. However, if it meant people moving out of more expensive private rented accommodation, this could reduce the rising housing benefit bill. That might help the sums work. The independent research company Capital Economics concluded that 'an increased budget for central government capital grant is the most straightforward, practical and efficient method for stimulating building'.

While some argue finding the money is relatively simple, finding the land itself is tricky. Where can we build these homes? Our planning laws mean that getting permission to build is not straightforward. The **green belt** areas around towns and cities are protected from development. And local residents tend to strongly object to any new building – a phenomenon known as NIMBYism (Not In My Back Yard). This is typified by pressure groups like the Campaign to Protect Rural England (CPRE). Even they admit that only 24 per cent of the green belt within the M25 is deemed of outstanding natural beauty – much of it is golf courses and pony paddocks. The government needs to find ways to settle these planning disputes, essentially by emphasising that our need for new homes must take priority over 'the countryside' and by giving councils more control. Currently, there is no strategic planning above the most local level. Councils need to be able to work together to win popular support for new developments. Kristian Niemietz of the free market Institute of Economic Affairs (IEA) is adamant that planning regulations have to be relaxed – he would abolish greenbelt protection and even abolish height restrictions (build 'em high!).

Another issue is land speculation. Near Oxford, a plot of land the size of one-and-a-half football pitches would be sold for about £20,000. If planning permission is granted there, it can suddenly be worth £4 million. So the building firms with the most money to invest compete to buy up the little available land, in the hope that they may get permission to build. If a firm ends up paying over the odds for land, it will usually then spend less money on the houses, which means the quality of the build will suffer.

Even when permission is granted, developers often sit on the land and don't build. That's because, with house prices rising so fast, they know that the longer they wait to build, the more they will be able to sell the houses for. As I said before, these building firms are driven by profit, not a desire to get people housed. Labour leader Ed Miliband has previously suggested that a way of dealing with this would be: use it or lose it. So planning permission would be withdrawn after a certain period. Another option would be to start charging council tax on that undeveloped land. Both measures would provide incentives to build, though opponents say they could also scare smaller building firms from the market place.

So far I've been talking about development on 'greenfield' sites. These are basically bits of countryside that haven't been built on, like in the green belt areas around cities. There is another type of site called 'brownfield'. These are sites that have been built on previously but are now derelict or abandoned. They aren't always in areas where housing demand is the highest, unlike greenfield areas. Sometimes existing buildings on brownfield can be refurbished and turned into housing, otherwise the land will need to be cleared. This means they are sometimes more expensive to build on. If the sites were used industrially then occasionally they may need to be decontaminated, which isn't cheap. The benefits of building on brownfield sites are that, unlike greenfield, they don't increase so-called 'urban sprawl' – the spread of cities into the countryside. However, although 80 per cent of us live in towns and cities, less than 7 per cent of UK land is classified as urban, so perhaps there is room for some 'sprawl'.

The construction consultancy WSP Group, who worked on The Shard in London (which is built on top of London Bridge train station), have a novel idea for building new homes in the capital, where house prices and demand are highest. They propose that we pay private firms to rebuild and refurbish our public buildings – hospitals, libraries, prisons, fire stations, schools etc. – and add a few floors of affordable housing on top of them. These firms can then sell or rent out the accommodation. The problem with that is that most of us don't want to live above a hospital or a school. However, what about offering these homes to the people who work there? So with hospitals, for example, we provide nurses with somewhere affordable to live that is (very) close to their work. These are workers who are currently being priced out of London. It would even reduce the pressure on our transport system. We could house old people there too, so they are close to treatment. This kind of development is already happening in New York and there are plans for flats to be built above a primary school in King's Cross.

Given that people want to live in cities, schemes like the one above are potentially useful because they increase the density of homes in desirable places (the number of homes in any given area). On the subject of desirable places, another thing we could be looking at is council housing in wealthy areas of cities – it would be possible to sell at least some of those off, for a high price, to fund the building of many more social homes in a cheaper area. That would be contentious, because obviously it would mean kicking the existing residents out of their homes, and finding them new ones.

One aspect of social housing that has become controversial is occupancy by those with high incomes. In 2013, Chancellor George Osborne said, 'There are people on incomes of £60,000 or £70,000 living in council homes. I would look at that issue.' There are an estimated 11,000 to 21,000 council tenants with an income of £60,000 or more, although that amounts to a small minority. As it is, once you are allocated social housing you are not subjected to any more means-testing. That might need addressing. One suggestion is that people in social housing who start earning over a certain amount of money would have to declare it, and the council could increase their rent to a market level. That way these high earners would not have their housing subsidised by the taxpayer any more, because they'd either be paying 'full price', or could choose to move out and allow people on council waiting lists to move in.

It's interesting to think about who benefits from the forced movement of families from social housing to private rentals. Clearly, it's private landlords – people who own more than one property and rent out the ones they don't live in. At the last count, one third of MPs are private landlords. Some would say that constitutes a conflict of interest when dealing with housing.

All of the parties recognise that housing is a big issue and their policies around it will probably play a significant part in their election campaigns. David Cameron has pledged 100,000 new homes will be built on brownfield sites for first-time buyers under the age of forty, who will be able to buy the homes at a 20 per cent discount. The Conservatives also champion their Help to Buy scheme, which gives first-time buyers a loan of up to 20 per cent of the home's price. Opponents argue that these initiatives don't help with rented social housing and that removing the need for the new houses to comply with the zero-carbon homes standard (which will be the case with the 100,000 houses built on brownfield sites) will mean they're not as energy efficient as they could be.

Labour has promised to get the UK building 200,000 homes a year by 2020 – still not enough, it must be noted, to meet demand. Labour also has plans to increase the tax on vacant properties. Ed Miliband has promised to introduce rent controls, specifically a cap on the amount that private landlords can put rents up, and making them offer three-year tenancies. Opponents say evidence from other countries shows rent controls lead to fewer homes being rented and ultimately higher rents as a result.

The Lib Dems say they will aim to build 300,000 new homes every year and have plans to create new 'garden cities'. Garden cities would be high-quality new towns with spacious homes and good **infrastructure** – both of which are necessary in order for people to want to live in them. They argue this is vital, because you have to try and spread the housing demand out – our existing cities can't cope. Nick Clegg says that he would ensure that at least ten were established. In March last year, George Osborne announced a new garden city with an initial 15,000 homes would be built at Ebbsfleet in Kent, the first for many years, as development is often opposed by local communities. The Lib Dems would fund some of this new building by creating a new not-for-profit Housing Investment Bank. Savers could deposit money and the government would guarantee steady returns. The bank would provide low-cost loans for private firms and housing associations that are building social housing.

The Green Party is concerned about the environmental impact of new housing developments, which they want to minimise. They would try to empower local councils to use the 1.1 million empty homes (at the last count in 2011) in the UK. They want to 'ensure everyone is provided with housing appropriate to their needs'. They want to use money from 'carbon taxes' to pay for housing insulation, which will reduce consumer's energy bills. Like Labour, the Greens would introduce a form of rent control, focused on providing tenants with more long-term security.

UKIP has no up-to-date details on its housing policy at the time of writing, but in 2013 its then housing spokesman, Andrew Charalambous, said that the party favours building on brownfield sites and protecting green spaces. He also said that UKIP would eliminate all **stamp duty** from brownfield properties and speed up the planning process in non-contentious cases. UKIP also believes that the housing situation would be improved if net immigration is reduced, which is obviously true. They have said they would prioritise social housing for people whose parents and grandparents were born locally.

If you want somewhere to live – VOTE.

9. Devolution

What is devolution and why does it matter?

Devolution is a form of decentralisation – the transferral of some powers from one central place (Westminster, in the UK's case) to more local institutions (the individual countries). The United Kingdom is made up of four countries – England, Wales, Scotland and Northern Ireland. The relationship between those countries has changed over time, but let's just look at the recent history. For a long period, until the late 1990s, the Parliament in London ran the whole of the UK – controlling everything in all four countries. The UK Parliament is made up of MPs in 650 seats, which breaks down like this: 533 English seats, 40 Welsh seats, 59 Scottish Seats and 18 Northern Irish seats. That is broadly reflective of the populations of each country. The simplest argument for devolution is that the regions all have their own unique cultures and problems, so it makes sense for at least some decisions to be made more locally to the people those decisions affect. Laws and decisions made in Westminster might not apply so well outside of England, or even London.

There is a principle called 'subsidiarity' that is used in the EU, and it's related to decentralisation. The idea is that you try to make any decision or perform any task at the most local level. If that doesn't work, try it at the national or regional level. If that still doesn't work, then you go to the highest level – the EU. This is kind of like school. If a kid misbehaves in class, the teacher will deal with it. If the teacher can't deal with it, he might then get the Head of Year involved. And if there's still a problem, maybe the head teacher deals with it. But crucially, the head teacher is not who you go to first. You always try to deal with the issue at the most local level. That is another argument for decentralising the power of the UK Parliament. However, some critics say that more and more devolution will eventually lead to the break-up of the UK.

In the mid-70s the Labour government – which was an unstable **minority government** – made plans for devolution in return for the support of the Welsh and Scottish nationalist parties. The plans weren't realised back then, but when Labour got back into government under Tony Blair in 1997, they finished the job. The Scots, the Welsh and the Northern Irish all voted for, and got, devolution. The National Assembly for Wales, the Northern Ireland Assembly and the Scottish Parliament were formed – along with the Greater London Authority, which has control over London's transport and policing among other things.

'Devolved powers' are decisions that, before 1999, were made by the UK Parliament, but are now made by the devolved institutions. The degree of devolution varies between the three countries – the distribution is uneven. So for example, Scotland has more powers over itself than Wales does. Scotland controls its own education system, its climate change policy, its NHS and can also move income tax 3p either way of the UK rate (although it has never used this power). Wales has power over education and its NHS. All of the regional parties (SNP in Scotland, Plaid Cymru in Wales and DUP and Sinn Féin in Northern Ireland) want more devolved powers. The decisions that are still taken by Westminster on behalf of the whole UK are called 'reserved powers' – things like foreign policy, energy, defence and some economic powers.

Each of the regions gets given a lump sum of money by the UK government. The amount that they get is worked out by something called the Barnett Formula, which takes into account the level of devolution (how many areas they will control their own spending in) and the population of the region. This has been controversial because the total public spending per person in Scotland is significantly higher than the spend per person in England. In 2012/13, it was £10,152 in Scotland and £8,259 in England. In Wales it is between the two, at £9,709. Northern Ireland gets more spent per person than the other regions (although much less in absolute terms, because there aren't many Northern Irish people).

Of course, what these figures miss is how much each of these areas contribute in terms of tax. London is an obvious example. The amount spent on average on each Londoner in terms of services is higher than the average, but then the amount London brings in in taxes is much, much higher. Scotland also contributes more in taxes – though this may change with the fall in oil price – than it spends. Think of it like when you order lots of food in a restaurant, all to be shared. One of your friends starts wolfing down more than anyone else, which might lead you to think she's being unfair, but if she then pays more when the bill arrives, all is well. Whatever the fairness or unfairness of these arrangements, not everyone is convinced. According to a British Social Attitudes survey, 36 per cent of the English population thinks that the Barnett Formula is too generous to Scotland.

If Scotland had voted 'yes' to independence, it would be getting no money from the UK. But they voted 'no'. The Conservatives, Labour and Lib Dems wanted that result and promised to devolve more powers to Scotland, and soon. This is called 'devo-max' (as in, maximum devolution), and should result in more powers for the Scottish government. The Smith Commission report was prepared after the referendum and gives the details of this deal. Scotland will have much more autonomous power over its economy, taxation and welfare, although the SNP argues it doesn't go far enough, estimating that the deal on offer will only give Scotland control of less than 30 per cent of their taxes and less than 20 per cent of welfare spending.

Having promised this deal to a Scotland that remained within the UK, on the morning that Scotland rejected independence David Cameron turned his attention back to the English, saying, 'Now the millions of voices of England must be heard.' He said that he wanted a definitive answer to the West Lothian Question. The West Lothian Question, so-called because it was posed by the MP for West Lothian back in 1977, asks: should MPs from Scotland, Wales and Northern Ireland be allowed to vote on matters that only affect England? Because with devolved powers, the reverse isn't true – English MPs don't get votes on issues only affecting Wales, and Scotland, and so on. Nearly forty years after the question was first asked, it's more relevant than ever, but the answer is still not clear.

In 2004, a vote on the introduction of top-up fees for university students in England acted as a good example as to why this question is so important. Education is devolved to Scotland, so English MPs could not vote on an equivalent bill up there. The bill was passed by 316 votes to 311. Forty-six Scottish Labour MPs voted in favour – meaning that, without the support of these Scottish MPs, the bill would not have been passed. As it was, students at English universities would have to pay higher fees. Meanwhile, students at Scottish universities pay nothing. The Tory shadow education secretary at the time, Tim Yeo, was furious, saying, 'It is completely wrong that a bill which imposes higher charges on students attending the English universities should only be carried ... using the votes of Scottish MPs when the students attending universities in the constituencies of those Scottish MPs do not have to pay those higher charges.'

However, it's possible that the problem of MPs from outside of England voting on English issues is being overstated. The Houses of Parliament produced a report to show what effect removing Scottish MPs votes from all of the votes since 2001 would have had. There have been about 3,600 votes and a mere 22 (0.6 per cent) would have had different results. One of those was the vote on student top-up fees. Then when you look at this Parliament (so, since 2010) and how English MPs have voted compared to how all UK MPs have voted, you see that they voted with the majority, 99 per cent of the time. Compare that to Scottish MPs, who agreed with the majority 24 per cent of the time, and Welsh MPs who agreed 26 per cent of the time. In other words, while English MPs tend to agree with the way that votes go in the UK Parliament (partly because there are so many English MPs in Parliament, obviously, and partly because many of those English MPs are in governing parties – the Conservatives and Lib Dems), Scottish

MPs and Welsh MPs only agree on about one in four. For many that is a compelling reason for them to have devolved powers, but not England.

What David Cameron is pushing for is English Votes for English Laws – which has the pleasing acronym EVEL. Many criticised the timing of his speech. After months of campaigning to maintain the union, to convince the Scottish people to stay in the UK, the first thing Cameron did was talk about devolving powers to England. Which some have argued is not a very union-minded move, and has created another surge in support for the SNP in Scotland. Polls suggest that they might win 45 seats at the election, which might well make them the third largest party in the UK Parliament. They would be in a strong position to negotiate more devolution for Scotland and maybe even another referendum on independence.

Cameron got William Hague, leader of the House of Commons, to go away and draw up some proposals for how EVEL might work. The first of the three options he gave was the most radical – non-English MPs being excluded from all English-only votes. That is the purest form of EVEL. This would favour a party that has predominantly English MPs – for example, the Conservatives. In Scotland they won just one seat out of 59 in the 2010 general election, which led to the observation that there are more giant pandas in Scotland than there are Tory MPs (there are two pandas in Edinburgh Zoo, Tian Tian and Yang Guang, if you're interested). Labour agrees that English MPs should have more say over English matters, but not with this form of EVEL. Partly because they think it would create two classes of MP and partly because they have in recent times had a lot of Scottish MPs, so they'd like them to be involved in votes, thank you very much. Without the

support of those Scottish MPs, a Labour government might
not even be able to vote through its own budget. Up until
now, SNP members have chosen not to vote on English-
only issues, but their former leader Alex Salmond has said
they might rethink that if their support was required to
prop up a minority Labour administration after the May
general election.

Hague's second option would be to give English MPs
control over the early stages of a bill (that is, a draft law).
This is quite boring, but bills don't just get passed on a
single vote. They go through several stages, getting rewrit-
ten and tweaked until the final vote. So this would allow
English MPs to determine the exact nature of the bill that
gets to that final vote stage, at which all MPs, from across
the UK, would be involved. The third option is to give
English MPs the power to overrule (veto) a vote on some
English-only laws. One of the big difficulties with any form
of EVEL is that it won't always be easy to decide whether
something only affects England. There may be subtle
knock-on effects to the regions.

Both Labour and the Lib Dems want to create a committee of English MPs that looks at bills before they go to the
vote. The make-up of their committees would differ slightly
but they are basically the same idea. Crucially, neither
Labour nor the Lib Dems will support the Conservatives'
plans for EVEL. Without that support, the Conservatives
will find it extremely difficult to push any form of those
plans through. Some people think it is still useful to them
though, because it lays down a marker that says: we care
about the English. David Cameron may make this a key
part of the Conservative Party's election campaign, in the
hope that it will attract some would-be UKIP supporters. It
used to be that more English people identified themselves

as British than English – now it's about half and half. Michael Kenny, an authority on 'Englishness', thinks that this rise in English identity has been a factor in UKIP's increasing popularity. The former deputy PM John Prescott has accused the Conservatives of trying to rush what would be a big constitutional change, just to win favour at the election. He is making the argument that as a country we shouldn't want something of this magnitude decided by party political manoeuvring. Gordon Brown, the former Labour prime minister, said, 'When one part of the union is 84 per cent and the others are 8 per cent, 5 per cent and 3 per cent ... the rules needed to protect the minority are bound to be different from the rules to protect the majority, who can always outvote the minority.' In effect, Brown is arguing that England is big enough to look after itself without the introduction of something like EVEL.

Labour also argues that EVEL would in effect be centralising English power in Westminster, when what we should be doing is decentralising within England. They tried to devolve power to regional assemblies in 2004, but a vote for a North-East assembly was defeated, and plans were scrapped. Labour are keen to have another go at creating these regional assemblies though, each about the size of Scotland – so taking power from Westminster and giving it to cities and city areas (much like the Greater London Authority). The Chancellor, George Osborne, would also like to see 'serious devolution of powers and budgets' to cities that are interested. Manchester and West Yorkshire may be the first to get these powers. A report last year suggested that devolution to the fifteen biggest city areas in England would give a £79 billion a year boost by 2030, and perhaps reduce the UK economy's reliance on London.

UKIP also agrees that it's unfair for MPs from devolved

nations to vote on English-only issues, but hasn't yet said how it would overcome this. The party would introduce national referenda on 'issues of major public interest'. It would also reduce the amount of money given to Scotland, Wales and Northern Ireland by the Barnett Formula, but give them each more power over their own taxes to sweeten the deal. The Greens are totally in favour of devolved powers because they want to see decisions taken as locally as possible – they believe in subsidiarity. The Greens would give all of the devolved nations total control of their own tax affairs, and would allow another raft of votes on independence for each nation.

Plaid Cymru wants Wales to get the same amount of money per person as Scotland, as calculated by the Barnett Formula. The DUP and Sinn Féin in Northern Ireland may have some influence in the next Parliament because the chances of a Hung Parliament are so high. They will also ask for more devolved powers.

If you care about what happens to the United Kingdom – VOTE.

10. The NHS

What's going to happen to the NHS?

To work out what's going to happen to the NHS, it's worth looking first at where it came from. Immediately after the Second World War, a man called Aneurin 'Nye' Bevan became the new Labour health minister, and pushed the principle of a free health service for all, paid for with tax money. Prior to that, many people didn't have access to a doctor, and hospitals were run by charities and local councils. The war had, for obvious reasons, put the existing health service under enormous strain, and it was close to going bankrupt. The NHS came into being in July 1948 and marked the first time anywhere in the world that completely free health care was made available to everyone, rather than on the basis of fees or insurance premiums.

Bevan's plans were met with significant opposition. Some leaders of the British Medical Association viewed the move as a step towards National Socialism and a letter in the *British Medical Journal* described Bevan as 'a complete and uncontrolled medical dictator'. It was even suggested that an NHS system was like something from Nazi Germany, overseen by a 'medical Führer'. Nevertheless by the time the Conservatives came back into power in 1951, it seemed that the battle for free health care had been won. That same year the government set up a committee to look at the effectiveness of the NHS. The committee concluded that the service was both efficient and worthy of funding.

Many countries use an insurance model for their health care – it's often compulsory to have insurance, but you get to choose your provider. You or your employer pay a monthly amount to your insurance company, and when you get ill, they cover the costs. That's fine unless you end up getting taken to the wrong hospital – one not covered by your plan, say. Insurance can work but the danger is the poorest, who can't afford to pay monthly premiums, are likely to suffer. In the US, where more is spent on health care than anywhere else in the world, 41 million people are still uninsured. Not so in the UK, where everyone gets cared for. No one gets turned down for care by the NHS because they have a 'pre-existing condition', i.e. are actually ill and need care! This often happens in countries that rely on insurance.

Throughout its history, the NHS has undergone reforms – changes of structure and ways of operating (pun intended, thank you). These reforms have been driven by the same two factors: how good the service is, and how much it costs. In 2014, the NHS came top of a Commonwealth Fund study of ten countries' health-care systems – most of whom spend more per head than the NHS. It's not perfect and there have been some notable scandals in recent years, but we still seem to think it's fundamentally a good thing. Many people regard free health

care as their national birthright, and worth maintaining
and protecting.

What the creators of the NHS didn't anticipate was how
the expense would spiral up and up. The simple fact is
that it costs a lot of money, and the costs are going up
quicker than inflation. There are several reasons for that,
the biggest of which is our ageing population. Advances in
medicine, which are making medicine itself more expensive, mean that we can keep people alive for much longer.
When the NHS was founded in 1948, the life expectancy
for men was 66, and for women, 71. Today those figures are
78.7 and 82.6. I don't want to be down on the fact that lots
of people are living longer (oh no, we're all going to live!),
but the truth is that as old people tend to require more
medical care, and medical care costs more than it used to,
the fact that we are living longer means that the cost of the
NHS is rising very quickly. Back in 1948, the annual cost of
the NHS per head, per lifetime, was £200 (in today's terms).
In 2012/2013, it was nearly £2,000 per head. And there's a
lot more of us now. With no intervention, the NHS in
England will face a £30 billion shortfall in its budget by
2020. That's partly why the NHS will be another of the
main battlegrounds for this coming election.

Politicians know that there aren't that many ways to deal
with this huge shortfall. Either you make cuts elsewhere, or
you cut the NHS budget, making it harder to keep the same
level of services. Or you make the service more efficient
(that's unlikely to be enough on its own). Or you get more
money for the running of the NHS by raising taxes somewhere (a poll showed that two-thirds of us are unwilling to
pay more tax to fund the NHS, preferring reforms). Or you
try to save money by farming out services to private sector
firms. Or you try a combination of all of the above.

The UK government only runs the NHS in England. The NHS in Wales, Scotland and Northern Ireland is devolved – they run their own health services. In Wales, Plaid Cymru wants to integrate social care and health care, while the Scottish National Party is planning to cut the number of managers by 25 per cent to make savings. In England, various proposals are being made by the various parties. And while they only directly apply to the NHS in England, the problems that need solving are in many instances the same for the devolved institutions too.

Undoubtedly the NHS will continue to exist, and to the casual observer/sick person, it will probably exist in pretty much the same form as before. You'll get ill, you'll go to your local GP or hospital, you'll wait for a while, and at some point get free treatment (as paid for by your taxes). All of the main parties have committed to keeping NHS services 'free at the point of delivery'. You will probably be charged for any prescription you get. So far, so good. But changes will be occurring. They are occurring right now. The name will remain the same but the question many people are asking is, with all the changes behind the scenes, will it still be the same NHS?

Well, a lot of the conversation about the NHS is centred around whether it is being privatised or not and, if so, to what extent. Privatisation has traditionally meant selling things that are publically owned to private firms. That's what happened with the railways, British Gas, British Telecom and the water companies in England. For the most part, this is different. It's not that ownership is changing hands as it did with the railways and with BT, rather it's that bits are being run by the private sector (although many would say the result is the same – a bigger role and more money for the private sector – it is nonetheless different to

what happened with those other public institutions).
Getting the private sector to run parts of public services has
been happening for a while. Basically Clinical
Commissioning Groups (CCGs), representing different areas
and run mainly by doctors, have the option to award private firms contracts to provide medical services. This was
the change in the organisation of the NHS that has been so
controversial while the coalition has been in power – the
'top-down reorganisation' that the Conservatives promised
wouldn't happen. In 2009, David Cameron said that there
would be 'no more of the tiresome, meddlesome, top-down
re-structures' of the NHS. However, it's worth pointing out
that if Labour are now against 'privatisation', it was New
Labour under Tony Blair that started the process of transition, bringing in the private sector in an attempt to bring
down waiting lists and increase 'patient choice'.

The Health and Social Care Act (which introduced the
system of doctors' groups – CCGs – buying services) was
passed in 2012 and Labour argues that it has paved the way
for further privatisation. Over 200 MPs and Lords who
voted on that bill have financial or vested interests in private health care (you can find the list on the Social
Investigation Blog online – have a read). Those interests
will all have been declared, but you have to wonder
whether huge decisions on the future of the NHS should be
taken by people who could have something to gain from private sector involvement. Stephen Dorrell, a Conservative
MP and the former Chairman of the House of Commons
Health Select Committee, has just taken a job as an advisor
with a private firm that is reportedly intending to bid on a
£1 billion NHS contract. He himself has said that the two
roles are 'incompatible' and so will be standing down as an
MP at the election, but the way politicians move into

private sector jobs so easily causes many to worry. Will current MPs and ministers treat private companies favourably because they hope one day to get well paid jobs from them?

Even if you believe those parliamentarians should not have been able to hold those financial interests, that's still not to say that privatisation is necessarily bad, or the wrong choice. Assuming that we still receive our health care for free, and keep the cost to the taxpayer steady, then many will ask, does it matter who is providing those services? So long as we have a cost-effective system working well, then the level of private involvement is almost immaterial, isn't it? Competition, so the argument goes, improves the quality and range of choice for patients, just like competition between supermarkets makes for a better customer experience when they're buying groceries and so on. Elizabeth Wade, the deputy director of policy at the NHS Confederation (which aims to represent all the different parts of the NHS, from hospitals to CCGs), says that it's 'vital' that the NHS is free to buy from private firms when they offer better value and better service.

So why does Andy Burnham, Labour's Shadow Health Secretary, say this: 'I believe we [Labour] let the market in too far [when they were last in government], and it's my view that if you carry on with this experimentation with the market in the National Health Service, you will in the end destroy everything that is precious about it'? Well for him and other opponents of the NHS changes, private health-care providers and public health-care providers are *not* the same. Their goals are totally different. In the public sector, doctors will try to make sure they have enough money to treat people. Treatment is their priority. But with private firms, they are trying to turn a profit. Money is the priority. Again, you could look at that as being a positive – private firms can't afford inefficiencies, so the services might be more streamlined and cost the taxpayer less. The chance to make a profit may also encourage new service providers to innovate in a way that is good for patients. The concern, though, is that corners might be cut and treatment will be lower quality. Cost reduction and efficiency might take precedence over the serious business of giving care.

In fact, defenders of the NHS reforms argue that there have always been private providers (drug companies and manufacturers of medical equipment like stethoscopes and plasters, for example) and managers have had to shop around to get value for money. All that's changed, they say, is that these managers now work with GP groups. They also point out that voluntary organisations and other non-profit groups are free to try and win contracts. Whoever ends up doing the work, they say, it's right and sensible that doctors' groups, spending the money on behalf of patients, make the decisions about which provider is best.

At the moment, we have a mix of public and private service provision – the total budget of the NHS is around £100 billion, and in 2012, private firms were taking £8.7 billion of that. Due to the way the system has been structured, that proportion is changing, though – the private sector will almost certainly grow as the public sector shrinks. The private sector will inevitably try to take all of the potentially profitable bits of the NHS. Maybe we won't notice. Maybe people won't care that their health care, which is still free, is being provided by private firms. Possibly not, unless the care gets really bad. But if that does happen it might be difficult to reverse the process.

There is another potential problem. If medical facilities can only make money from selling, then they might not think like advisors to the public. They might think like salesmen, interested only in their profits. In fact, there's some evidence this culture is already in place. When the NHS was worried about doctors missing cases of dementia they started to pay GPs £55 for every diagnosis. The boss of NHS England, Simon Stevens, defended the payments. He said the NHS was trying to get treatment to as many patients with dementia as possible – currently only half are believed to be diagnosed. But offering a financial incentive to doctors for the diagnosis of a specific condition is a first, and should make us think about what we want from our NHS.

So can privately run NHS hospitals be a success? The Circle Partnership is a large private health-care group, co-owned by the doctors and nurses that run their hospitals. Hinchingbrooke Health Care NHS Trust was the first privately run hospital in the UK and soon after Circle took charge, its patient ratings were some of the highest in the UK. That gave encouragement to those who support private involvement in the NHS. At the time of writing, though, Circle has said it is planning to pull out of its contract, blaming 'unprecedented A&E attendances' (too many sick people! How dare they!) and funding cuts. The hospital had just been rated 'inadequate' by a health watchdog. The watchdog's chief inspector of hospitals did point out that their findings were 'not a judgment on the role of the private sector in the NHS or on franchise arrangements. Where hospitals are failing to promote good care, we will say so regardless of who owns and runs them.' It's very hard to draw firm conclusions from one case, but opponents of private sector involvement will use this to say that it shows that a private firm will run at the first sign that their profits are at risk. For those in favour of private involvement and the benefits they say it brings – efficiency, expertise and innovation – Hinchingbrooke is a setback.

Another huge area of controversy when it comes to the NHS is the **Transatlantic Trade and Investment Partnership** (TTIP) deal that is currently being negotiated by the EU and the US, mainly behind closed doors. It's a trade deal that aims to reduce tariffs and regulations between Europe and the US and so make trading easier; some fear it will open up the NHS to US health care and pharmaceutical companies, meaning that they might be able to bid to supply services and products to the NHS. Increased competition may benefit services but the deal is believed by its critics to pose a further threat to the NHS. They think it will allow US firms to sue the UK government over NHS decisions. The fear is that a private company will sue if a contract is cancelled, or a drug banned due to side-effect or safety concerns. In November, the Labour MP Clive Efford laid out a bill to explain how Labour would make the NHS exempt from TTIP. They also promised to get rid of the Health and Social Care Act, thus halting – they say – the advance of privatisation (specifically it would cancel the requirement to put all NHS contracts out to tender, remove the freedom that allows NHS hospitals to earn up to 49 per cent of their income from treating private patients, and make the secretary of state responsible for the NHS again). Labour has said the Conservatives are destroying the NHS through 'a toxic mix of cuts and privatisation'. Defenders of the TTIP trade deal say that, with more trade, the economic benefits will be great and that the NHS will be exempt. In November 2014, David Cameron said: 'It's our National Health Service. It's in the public sector, it will stay in the public sector. That's not going to change ... There's no threat, I believe, from TTIP to the National

Health Service and we should just knock that on the head as an empty threat.'

One area where the NHS has been much criticised is in its treatment of mental health issues. Reliable statistics are hard to come by but it's often quoted that one in four of us will have mental health issues at some point in our lives. Provisions to deal with mental health are poor, though. The wait for treatment is far longer than it is for physical complaints; and a report showed that in 2013 fewer than half of the patients who sought help from the NHS for depression and anxiety got treatment. From what I've heard talking to young people affected by mental health issues, there is often a general lack of compassion too. Not enough is being done to get people the help they need – in fact, mental health services have had their funding cut in recent years. Leading mental health organisations estimate that two-thirds of people suffering with depression will receive no treatment. There's an argument to say that we should be doing more to help for economic reasons too: mental illness costs the country around £70 billion every year, through lost working days and higher benefit payments and so on. Nick Clegg's announcement that from April 2015 there will be waiting time standards introduced to mental health treatment is, ironically, long overdue. It is a step in the right direction, though, and should ultimately see mental health given the same level of attention and care as physical health. The Lib Dems have pledged to increase funding to the NHS as a whole, giving an extra £1 billion per year. They have also promised to get more money and focus on mental health services.

Labour has also said that it will increase NHS funding and staffing – investing £2.5 billion extra a year to pay for 20,000 more nurses – but without any more large reforms, although they also plan to integrate health and social care. Which is itself, you'd think, a big reform. The hope is that integration will ultimately save money, but that's not been proven as yet. Labour says that waiting times in A&E are unacceptably long. It also claims that under the coalition government it has got harder to see your GP within 48 hours. Labour says it would guarantee a GP appointment within 48 hours.

The Conservatives have said that they will give 'everyone access to a GP seven days a week by 2020'. They've also pledged to ring-fence the NHS budget – ring-fencing means guaranteeing that the allocated money won't get spent on anything else. They've also pledged to increase real-term NHS spending every year (in other words, the money will be higher every year, even when you take into account inflation). The Conservatives are also promising to reduce bureaucracy and **red tape** to free up money to pay more doctors and nurses, and make services more efficient for patients. They also maintain that the only way to safeguard the NHS is by ensuring that the economy is strong – something that they say Labour will not provide.

The Green Party says that it is the only party committed to keeping the NHS publically owned. It would also try to take back those bits of the NHS that are already being run by private companies. It's not clear how it would do that. The Greens would get rid of prescription charges and reintroduce free eye tests and dental treatment for everyone. They plan to increase taxes on alcohol and tobacco to fund real-term growth in the NHS budget.

UKIP's NHS policy has been subject to some controversy (see the UKIP chapter for more on UKIP's policies), but for the election it says it will ensure that the NHS remains free at the point of delivery, and oppose charging for GP appointments. It has also said that it will make visitors and migrants have NHS-approved private health insurance when they come into the country – UKIP believes that will save the NHS £2 billion a year. UKIP's two MPs supported the Labour anti-privatisation bill.

If you care about the future of our free health care – VOTE.

11. Leadership

How do we choose our leaders?

In the UK, we don't directly choose our prime minister; we vote for the party that we want to form the government, and the leader of that party becomes prime minister. If the party in power changes leader for some reason, then the new leader will take on the role of prime minister. We have no control over that. This happened when Tony Blair stepped down as Labour leader in 2007, and Gordon Brown took over as leader of the party and country. So, although we don't technically vote for our prime minister, we absolutely know that a vote for, say, Labour, is in effect a vote for Ed Miliband to become PM. And that means that we give a lot of consideration to those party leaders and their suitability for running the country.

Before looking at what we're after in a leader, let's look at the different types of voters. There are voters who vote for the same party at every election, irrespective of who the leader is, because that's just what they do. These voters are, with respect, not very exciting to think about because they are extremely predictable. Then you have the disenchanted voter, who has grown tired of his party's failings and is starting to look elsewhere. But the most interesting voters are ones like me, even if I do say so myself. We are swing voters, or 'swingers' (yes, hahahaha), who vote according to which party, at that moment in time, seems to be offering the best deal for the country, or for us personally. Swing voters can also be broken down further. Some swing voters are well informed but have a range of views that just don't fit neatly into any of the stated positions of the parties. And then there are the many voters who – through no fault of their own – feel that they simply don't have the information required to make a judgement, and who therefore rarely, if ever, vote. The whole point of this book is to give those people information.

None of the following applies to voters whose voting habits are fixed. This is about those of us who, in the run-up to an election, are still trying to make our decision. There are two ways in which we size up our potential leaders. The first is assessing whether they have the qualities that we deem desirable in a leader. The second is, in a way, much more intriguing: in the words of psychology writer Michael Bond, we are led by 'instinctive biases' – subtle influences that we are blissfully unaware of. Until now!

So what are the qualities we know we want to see in a prime minister? Well, I think some of them are very clear. We want someone who is engaging and a charismatic speaker. The power of charisma should not be underestimated. It can inspire devotion and confidence. I think people want to feel confident in their leader, and an accomplished orator offers that. This has become increasingly important with the recent move towards American-style televised leaders' debates, which showcase precisely these qualities. Or lack of them.

Boris Johnson's clown-like version of charisma certainly doesn't seem to have hurt him in his career.

If we're looking for 'experience', that's a much harder thing to pin down, because experience can come in a variety of forms. Some would say that the best kind of experience comes from time spent working within the political system, because politics is so complex and difficult that you need to learn how it works before you can take on the big job. Of our current party leaders, only one – Ed Miliband – held a ministerial position in government before becoming the leader. As I mention in the Representation chapter, other people believe that career politicians, who have never worked a day 'in the real world', can't possibly understand what normal people need or want. Cameron, Clegg, Farage and Bennett have all worked 'in the real world'. It's often well-regarded if the leader has come from a 'normal background' too. On top of that, if a candidate is especially young – irrespective of their career path – they may be deemed not to have enough experience of, well, anything.

The academic Alex Haslam believes that the best leaders feel like members of their 'group' – a leader who is obviously one of the people and in touch with their concerns. Haslam cites George W. Bush as a good example of this. He thrived after 9/11 because he clearly shared the electorate's fears; he may have been mocked for his famed verbal stumbles, but they made him seem like a normal person. Nigel Farage is doing something similar; he's managing to tap into how many people feel, and his regular apologies on behalf his party seem to make him more human and relatable. He's also not afraid to personally attack his rivals, saying, 'These men are utterly hopeless, dull as bloody ditchwater.' Of course, Farage knows that he's not going to become prime minister (that would certainly be an unexpected election result!), which allows him to play this 'everyman' role with freedom – he is clearly enjoying being a thorn in the side of the other leaders. Miliband and Cameron, as the two most likely contenders, do not have that freedom and have to behave in a more considered way. Ironically, this probably makes them feel more out of touch with the electorate.

What I think must be the next vital component seems almost too obvious to mention: popularity. The leader has to make his policies appeal to as many of us as possible, while also remaining faithful to the fundamental principles of his party. It's no use for a leader to be popular only with his core supporters – those boring voters from earlier – because they won't usually win an election on their own. The leader has to be able to broaden the appeal. It's a tricky balancing act that has confounded many leaders in the past. And, as discussed in the chapter on broken promises, it can create problems for the government later down the line.

When occupying a position of power, you will be subjected to criticism, often from every direction. I think the capacity to deal with that is another key leadership skill: someone who remains calm and unflustered when attacked by the media or a pitbull interviewer. Not just in public, either – I really want someone who is able to deal with it privately too. Someone who has a thick skin.

I haven't mentioned ability or intelligence specifically; whether the public think the person is bright enough and talented enough to actually be our leader and run our country. That's not because my criteria are all 'style over substance', but because all of the things I've discussed contribute to overall ability. Also I think it's reasonable to assume that anyone who rises to a high-up position in a political party isn't going to be stupid, even if we don't agree with them about anything.

So, taking all of these factors into consideration, in summary what I reckon we want is an engaging and charismatic orator, not too old and not too young, who started with nothing, but who built up their own small business before entering politics and successfully running a government department, making policies that have wide appeal, and all the while laughing off any criticism they might receive. Surely that's not too much to ask? And yet, even if that super-candidate emerged, would they definitely win?

Not necessarily, no. There are many more factors that we aren't consciously or rationally considering. For example, in the vast majority of US presidential elections in the last 100 years, the taller candidate has won. Isn't that insane? Perhaps I should stand as an MP (I am 6'5"). Psychologists such as Professor Gad Saad believe factors like that, which they call 'peripheral cues', are often more important than policy issues. Some other cues that make a good leader in our eyes are a strong jawline, a 'bright smile' and a deep, authoritative voice. In America, people want someone who just seems 'presidential'. Increasingly, it seems the same is true in the UK.

Research published in 2009 also suggests that the faces of candidates strongly influences voters. Students at the University of Lausanne were shown pictures of the faces of two French political candidates for one second. Seventy-two per cent of the students correctly guessed the eventual winner. Children aged 5–13 were able to predict Obama's win in 2008 when shown pictures of the presidential candidates and asked 'Who would you rather be captain of your ship?' (which would be a fun way to liven up the ballot papers, by the way). We make fleeting judgements about someone's competence to lead based on their face. And what we're looking for varies too. Research in the Netherlands has shown that during times of war we want an older, masculine face; in times of internal conflict, a feminine face; and when things are stable, a youthful face. We are quite fickle, it turns out.

The media's presence nowadays is pervasive; we are exposed to more and more pictures and videos of our politicians, and not just the carefully orchestrated photo-calls with sick children, or the approved press shots. That means it's much harder for people in politics to manage and manipulate an image. We know how they move, how they smile, how they scowl, how they flinch, how they struggle to eat a bacon sandwich. We see everything – and sometimes we won't even realise that we are making judgements. So whose face will fit at the next election?

A lot has been made of Ed Miliband's skills as a speaker. He missed out a large chunk of stuff about the economy – a massive election issue – during his speech to the Labour party conference. He's not the most photogenic either but, as he says himself, 'there is more to politics than the photo op'. Perhaps he's right and these things shouldn't matter, but then again, what does that mean? Who gets to decide what should and shouldn't matter? Recent polling suggests that only 13 per cent of the British public believe that he is ready to be prime minister. His approval ratings six months before the election were the worst for any main party leader in the last forty years. However, when you look at the 'likeability' of Miliband, Cameron and Clegg, averaged over the last four years, there isn't much of a difference. On a scale of 0 to 10, Cameron's average is 4.2, Miliband's is 3.9 and Clegg's is 3.3. All pretty low, but perhaps heartening for Miliband that he is only trailing

Cameron by such a small margin. Especially since like-ability tends to be a good indicator of how people will vote. Gideon Skinner of Ipsos MORI, a leading market-research company, summarises the situation like this: 'Labour is the most liked party, but Ed Miliband still hasn't convinced the public on his prime-ministerial qualities – where David Cameron has the edge, but is hampered by being seen as out of touch and leading a more disliked party.' Cameron has the distinct advantage of seeming more prime-ministerial because he *is* Prime Minister. Seems silly to say it, but I think it makes a difference. Clegg has suffered from being unable to deliver on election promises in the coalition government, in particular tuition fees. There seems to be little danger of a repeat of the 'Cleggmania' that accompanied the 2010 election campaign, when he performed so well in the TV debates.

Natalie Bennett, of the Green Party, is certainly the least well known of the leaders. She is strong and competent but probably lacks the charisma of someone like Farage. She wasn't invited to take part in the upcoming TV debates, but that has galvanised her supporters – thousands of people signed an online petition saying that she should be in the debates, and her party membership is rising. Bennett and the Greens have had more media exposure than ever before. The sense that the Establishment (who-ever they are) is trying to exclude the Greens is working in their favour – the public love an underdog. Some voters might be put off because she is Australian, but she has a good line on this, saying that she chose to be British – it wasn't just 'an accident at birth'.

There are some other extraordinary factors that affect how we vote, that have nothing to do with the candidates themselves. The 'Primacy Effect', in voting terms, means that a candidate is more likely to get voted for if they are listed first on the ballot paper. A study that looked at state elections in California found that 82 per cent of candidates performed better when listed first than when listed later. In California, they rotate the names on the ballot paper to avoid this having an influence on the result. However, in Florida, they don't. In the 2000 American election, George W. Bush was listed first on every ballot paper across the state and won by less than 1 per cent. One of the authors of the study says, 'If Florida had done what California or Ohio do, by rotating name order, we have very strong evidence to suggest, that most likely, Al Gore would have been elected president.' So – the Primacy Effect may have determined who was the President of the USA. That blows my mind. There is also some evidence that people favour names listed on the left-hand side of the paper. For right-handed people, that's because they are the first name they read (because we read left to right) – the Primacy Effect again. But for left-handed people, as well as the Primacy Effect, there is an additional bias because apparently they have positive associations with things on the left.

Whatever happens, it's important to acknowledge that some or all of these factors play a surprising part in our decision-making, not only because it's fascinating but also because anything that makes us think more about our choices and why we're making them is worthwhile. Incidentally, David Cameron and Nick Clegg are the tallest of the major party leaders, so presumably they'll do just fine.

If you want to have a say in who runs our government – VOTE.

12. Jobs and the Economy

How does the economy affect me?

'The economy, stupid' was a slogan stuck on the wall of Bill Clinton's campaign office when he was running for President in 1992. It's come to mean that during an election, one of the biggest issues will always be the economy. Forget everything else, it's the economy, stupid.

And sure enough, during this campaign we are hearing a lot about the economy. About how well businesses are doing, how many jobs there are, how well paid those jobs are, whether we, the public, are spending money ...

But what exactly are the politicians talking about? One of the most common measures of whether the economy is in a good state or not is **Gross Domestic Product** (GDP), which is the main way of assessing the size of the economy, and therefore how well it is doing. If GDP goes up – the economy is growing, and the government is delighted. If it goes down, or is only going up slowly – the government is not so happy. The Office for National Statistics (ONS) is responsible for coming up with this GDP figure every three months (once a 'quarter' – as in, a quarter of a year), and it is a mammoth task. They do a survey of tens of thousands of businesses across the UK. They want to know how much they are selling, how much they are buying, how much they are paying their employees, whether they've made any investments ... There are three different ways of working out GDP, all of which, in theory at least, give the same result.

The Conservatives are keen to make this election about the economy because at the moment GDP is growing. In the July to September quarter in 2014, it grew 0.7 per cent. This was 2.6 per cent higher than in the same period in 2013. At that time, the UK had a faster growth rate than Italy, Canada, France, Germany, Japan and the US, although the US is now growing much more strongly. That's pretty good news. The awkward thing about the economy is that it's extremely hard to figure out when it's going to grow quickly, or grow slowly, or shrink. I don't just mean hard for the likes of you or me – I mean hard for economists who spend their lives examining and trying to explain and predict these trends. There is an excellent line by Harry S. Truman (the 33rd US President), about economists: 'Give me a one-handed economist! All my economists say, "On the one hand ... On the other."' What politicians want is for things to be black and white, so they can say, 'We're going to do this, and then that will happen.' But in economics, things are usually grey. What this often means is that the government claims credit when GDP is growing, and washes its hands of it when it isn't. Our GDP is also affected by things that are happening elsewhere in the world, which we have little control over. Of course, there are things that the government can do that it hopes will increase growth, but there is never any guarantee.

The other thing about GDP is that it doesn't really mean much to the majority of people. It's just a bit too abstract – people don't tend to care whether the GDP and economy are strong if they don't feel it in their pockets. The questions that we are more likely to use to judge how things are going are: do I have a job? How much money do I have? Do I feel better or worse off than before? It was ex-president of the US (and ex-Hollywood star) Ronald Reagan who asked, 'Are you better off than you were four years ago?' This is such a crucial issue. On the whole, if people feel better off, they will reckon the government to have done a good job with the economy – and perhaps trust it to carry on. If they feel worse off, they will reckon that the government has done a bad job – time to give someone else a go.

Let's start by trying to answer the jobs question. Current employment statistics are very encouraging. Unemployment peaked at 2.7 million people in late 2011. Since then it has been dropping and the figures are now below 2 million (which is about 6 per cent of the working age population) for the first time in six years. The latest figures show that 30.8 million people (73 per cent of working age) are in work, which is a record high. The Conservatives point to this as evidence that their long-term economic plan is working. David Cameron said that the drop below 2 million unemployed and rising real wages (more about that shortly) marked 'an important moment for our country'. Paul Johnson, director of the Institute for Fiscal Studies, says that 'given economic performance, employment is amazingly high'.

Those on the right, advocates of the free market, continue to argue that the best way to achieve jobs growth is by allowing businesses to flourish. They think that the way to do this is by deregulating – getting rid of time-consuming and expensive rules and regulations that might hold businesses back – and lowering taxes on business, so that they can save money and afford to grow and employ more people. This is what the Conservatives say is working, and will continue to work.

Youth unemployment is also falling. The number of 16–24-year-olds seeking work peaked at over a million in late 2011, but that was down to 767,000 by June 2014. However, that is 16.6 per cent of all 16–24-year-olds, which as David Kern, chief economist at the British Chambers of Commerce, said is 'still nearly three times the rate of unemployment as a whole'. Young people's job prospects have clearly been hit harder by the **financial crash** than those of any other age group. The Institute for Public Policy Research (IPPR) says that around 700,000 young people have never had a job. They also claim that there is a mismatch between what young people are training to do, and what jobs are actually available. For example, in 2011/12, 94,000 people trained in hair and beauty for 18,000 jobs, while only 123,000 people trained in engineering and construction when there were 275,000 jobs advertised in the sector. That's ridiculous. It's not necessarily the government's responsibility to address this – can people not figure it out for themselves? – but something obviously needs to be done. Many also argue that the non-academic path ('vocational route') into employment needs strengthening. That is where apprenticeships come in. Since 2010, over 2 million people have started one, with 86 per cent of people getting a job (with the same company or elsewhere) after completion. The coalition government is proud of this. Having said that, the IPPR claim that there aren't enough

high-skill apprenticeships. Internships are a good route
into many professional careers, but 31 per cent are
unpaid. That means that only those from wealthy backgrounds can afford to do them, which will clearly have a
negative effect on **social mobility**. Of course some would
say that an unpaid internship is better than no internship.

Nevertheless, the overall employment growth in the UK
is welcome. The government is right to say that 'more
people are in work than ever' and will point to the fact that
95 per cent of the rise in employment last year was due to
'full-time' jobs. That sounds good – full-time jobs should
allow people to work enough hours to take home enough
money to live on. However, some have questioned the type
of job that is being taken. The Resolution Foundation did
some research that shows that the employment growth is
being driven mainly by the London jobs market (which is
healthy) and a huge rise in self-employment. In fact,
between 2008 and 2013, in nine out of twelve regions in the
UK the number of employed jobs fell.

So these 'full-time' jobs are largely coming from
London, where in that same period 285,000 employed
jobs were created, and the spike in self-employment.
There are 4.5 million people working for themselves,
which is 15 per cent of the total workforce, the highest it's
been since records began. In 1975, it was only 8.7 per
cent. You could look at self-employment as being an
encouraging sign of entrepreneurialism, but since 2007
the average self-employed wage has fallen by a massive 20
per cent. The average self-employed person now earns 40
per cent less than the average employee. The Office for
National Statistics thinks that the rise is partly due to limited opportunities to leave self-employment. So where

people would once have been self-employed for a bit and then found a job, now they are having to stay self-employed. And it doesn't stop at low-pay – the self-employed get no sick or holiday pay, or contributions from an employer to their pensions, and they work longer hours on average too. However, the government would argue that the majority of people in self-employment are happier than they were in regular employment. A Royal Society for the Arts report found 84 per cent of the self-employed claimed they were more satisfied in their working lives than they would have been in a conventional job. The report also says that many self-employed people enjoy the greater freedom, and 'value different things at work, the softer benefits over the harder ones'. And besides, there are some 'hard benefits' – reduced childcare and commuting costs, for example.

Many on the left argue that self-employment is bad for the economy as a whole. People on low pay need more in-work benefits (which costs the government money, clearly) and don't pay very much tax (which makes the government less money).

Self-employment is not the only indicator of job insecurity in the UK. The Trades Union Congress (TUC) has produced a report that says that one in twelve workers is now in 'precarious employment' – including **zero-hour contracts**, agency work and part-time contracts with variable hours. The ONS estimated that at the start of 2014 there were 1.4 million zero-hour contracts, offering no security at all – no minimum hours or pay. Those contracts do offer flexibility, which can be useful for some people (students, for example), but many say having no fixed income and being at the mercy of your employer for working hours is a bad thing. A study by Scottish Friendly found that on average the unemployed have £174 left every month after paying for essentials, while people on zero-hour contracts have £130. That is the definition of a benefits trap – it says that, on average, it's better not to work than do zero-hour contract work. Ed Miliband is promising to deal with this, having focused on Sports Direct, the high street retailer, as a 'bad place to work'. Sports Direct has thousands of workers on zero-hour contracts but has said they are 'reviewing' their employment practices.

Obviously, having a job is really important but it's not the end of the story. In a purely financial sense, feeling 'better off' or not will be determined by how much you're getting paid. Since it's been in opposition, Labour has been using the phrase 'cost of living crisis'. Of course it's to be expected that the Opposition will talk about how badly everything is going, because they want to undermine the government. After the financial crash, wages increased more slowly than inflation (which determines how much things cost). That meant that even if people were getting paid a bit more, because stuff was more expensive, they in effect had less money. That's one way of working out whether people are richer or poorer – calculating 'inflation-adjusted wages' or 'real-term wages'. When inflation is greater than wage growth, real-term wages fall, and so people are poorer. This has been described by the TUC as 'the most severe squeeze on real earnings since Victorian times'. That sounds like a joke but it appears to be absolutely true – things hadn't been that bad since the 1860s and 1870s. The financial crash was global, and yet in the period 2010–13 it was British workers that suffered the biggest fall in real wages of all the **G20** countries (twenty of the world's major economies). Real-term pay was increasing in the US, France, Germany and Canada.

Wages in Italy and Japan were also falling, but not as quickly as in the UK. In 2013, real UK pay fell by 0.3 per cent compared with a 2 per cent increase globally.

In terms of how much people are earning in the UK now, there's good news and there's bad news. The good news is that, as of late 2014, average real earnings are rising, after six consecutive years of decline. That's because earnings are finally rising more quickly than inflation. And inflation is falling, so that will help real-term wage growth, too. James Knightley, an economist at Dutch bank ING, said: 'With inflation running at just 1 per cent and set to fall further, we are soon going to be seeing quite a pickup in real take-home pay'. One of the reasons for that is that global oil prices are collapsing, so people will be spending less on heating their homes and running their cars, leaving some extra cash for other stuff. That's the good news.

Wages are rising, but less quickly than they did before the crash (it used to be around 4 per cent, but according to the ONS it's been averaging 1.4 per cent between 2009 and 2014). The bad news is that because wages have been lagging behind prices for so long, according to Shadow Chancellor Ed Balls, working people are now £1,600 worse off (in real terms) than they were in 2010. Fullfact.org points out that this £1,600 figure is calculated with a measure of inflation (RPI) that isn't used that much any more – with the current measure of inflation (CPI), the figure would be more like £1,150. Either way, Chancellor George Osborne blames the previous Labour government, saying, 'Britain is poorer because of what happened to it in the Great Recession [in 2008]. People in the country are poorer because of what happened in the Great Recession.' Analysis of official figures shows that real wages have indeed fallen since the start of this Parliament five years

ago. So on that basis, the answer to Reagan's question is –
no, people are not better off now than at the start of this
Parliament. Although, as the Conservatives point out,
while things have been tough, they are starting to pick
up.

It's important to realise that average earning figures
don't necessarily tell the whole story, too. They can be
dragged up by big pay rises for people on high incomes –
bankers' pay, you'll be unsurprised to hear, is going up
much more quickly than the average pay. So an increase in
average earnings doesn't always mean that people on low
incomes are getting paid more. However, the opposite is
also true. If lots of new jobs are created (the government
says it has helped create 1.7 million new jobs) at the lower
end of the pay scale, that will bring the average down. The
ONS looked at the wages of people who have been in their
job for a year or more, and found that those show 'consistently higher growth rates, and in April 2014 earnings for
this group grew by 4.1 per cent compared with April
2013'.

The government has ultimate control over the wages of
most of those who work in the public sector. At the end of
2014, NHS workers went on strike twice to protest their
pay – the first time nurses have gone on strike for over
thirty years. And more strikes are planned. An independent
board recommended a 1 per cent pay rise for all NHS
employees, which the government rejected. It has now
compromised and will give the 1 per cent rise to around
half of the employees. Bear in mind that what we're talking
about is a 'pay rise' (1 per cent) that is only half a per cent
higher than current inflation (0.5 per cent). Christina
McAnea of the trade union Unison, said: 'Our members'
pay has been frozen or held down for the past five years

and there is no end in sight.' Of course the NHS has serious funding problems, as mentioned in the NHS chapter, and the government argues that if they were to award the 1 per cent increase across the board then they would have to cut 10,000 **frontline jobs**.

An independent board also looked into MPs' pay and recommended that they get a 10 per cent increase from about £67,000 to £74,000 a year. The House of Commons may reject that rise – Cameron, Miliband and Clegg have all said it would be unacceptable, given the hardship being faced by many in the UK. It's difficult not to make a comparison between the NHS workers and MPs. The total cost of the 10 per cent increase for MPs would be around £4.5 million, a tiny fraction of the £450 million that the 1 per cent increase for the NHS would require. But it's not really about the figures themselves – it's about what they seem to represent. Even though it's not MPs who are suggesting this big salary hike, the perception is inevitably, 'Oh, so they think they deserve a 10 per cent pay rise while the rest of us struggle to make ends meet'. That doesn't feel like the right way to win favour with the electorate.

The National Minimum Wage (NMW) is set by the government and is designed, fairly obviously, to increase the income of those on the lowest wages. The level that it is set at is obviously the subject of debate. Currently, for people aged twenty-one and over it is £6.50 an hour. That is significantly less than the UK 'living wage' of £7.85 an hour, which is published by the Living Wage Foundation. This amount is calculated according to the basic **cost of living** in the UK. Quite a lot of companies pay a living wage, but it is not compulsory. Those people who earn the minimum wage are not earning enough to live on, and are therefore eligible for working tax credits – basically, where the government tops up their low pay. Many on the left argue that the taxpayer should not have to do this. If the NMW were raised to a living wage, then working tax credits would not be necessary, saving the taxpayer money. The cost of such a raise would be borne by employers. It would eat into their profits.

Initially, that seems fine. Why should the taxpayer effectively have to subsidise the profits of employers? The problem is that economists on the right believe it will have a negative impact on the employment prospects of the very people it's trying to help – predominantly the young and the unskilled. If the government enforces a higher minimum wage, some employers may not be able to afford to have so many employees. Or they'll just choose not to, to try and protect their profits. Big companies may simply leave the UK if the cost of labour went up in this way. Smaller companies may go bust. We had this debate on *Free Speech*, and Leanne Wood (leader of Plaid Cymru) pointed out that when the minimum wage was first introduced in the mid-1990s, many businesses and the Confederation of British Industry were expressing the same worries (businesses won't be able to afford it), but those issues never materialised.

There is another subtlety here too: a lot of workers in the UK who earn less than the living wage (so, who are on minimum wage or just above) are young and from families that are, income-wise, in the top half of the country. In other words, many of the people who would benefit from an increase in the NMW are from relatively well-off families. At least working tax credits are targeted specifically at the people who need help.

Clearly, wage increases will make people feel better off.

Another way of achieving that would be by attempting to reduce the price of essentials, like housing, energy, childcare and food. People on low incomes suffer higher inflation than wealthier people – this is because people on low incomes have to spend a greater proportion of their wages on things that suffer inflation, like food and energy. The bottom 10 per cent of the UK, in spending terms, have experienced an average annual price hike of 3.7 per cent since 2003, while the top 10 per cent have experienced a 2.3 per cent annual rise.

I've talked about ways of making housing cheaper in the Housing chapter – essentially, the government needs to grant more planning permission and keep pushing to build more houses. Energy prices have been rising and it's not really through greedy energy companies making huge profits – they make around 5 per cent, which they say is not unreasonable. Renewable subsidies have driven the prices of energy up. Those subsidies are important in terms of climate change measures (more about this in the Climate Change chapter), but I totally get why some people would recommend scrapping them entirely in order to reduce the cost of living.

So what are the parties going to do for the working population? The Conservatives want to 'abolish youth unemployment' with their Earning or Learning policy. What that means is that young people have to either be working, looking for work, or in training or education. This will be 'encouraged' by taking away benefits. Furthermore, 18–21-year-olds will not get any housing benefit (unless they have a child) and will lose their Jobseeker's Allowance after six months of not finding a job. The Conservatives are pleased with the number of apprenticeships they've brought in during this Parliament. On the economy as a whole, David Cameron says it's a choice between 'competence' under the Tories and 'chaos' under Labour. They argue that their economic plan is working and to abandon it would be a huge risk. In January 2014, George Osborne spoke about how economic growth and job creation under the coalition government means that 'Britain can afford a higher minimum wage'.

Labour is looking towards apprenticeships too. It wants to ensure that the 50 per cent of young people who don't go to university get training, through apprenticeships and new technical qualifications. Labour is also planning to offer any 18–24-year-old who has been out of work for a year a guaranteed six-month job, paid for by the taxpayer. Refusal to accept the job would mean losing benefits. Rachel Reeves, the Shadow Work and Pensions Secretary, says that Labour would raise the minimum wage, incentivise employers to pay the living wage and make sure benefits were adequately supporting the self-employed. Ed Miliband has been clear that he wants to stop the abuse of employees under the zero-hour contracts, saying he will ban them for people who work regular hours.

The Tories' coalition partners, the Lib Dems, are proud of the apprenticeships that have been taken up but they recognise that more needs to be done to tackle youth unemployment. They say they will keep pushing firms to invest money in training young people and equipping them with the skills they need to work. The Lib Dems will also increase the income tax allowance – so people can earn more before getting taxed on their pay. UKIP would also raise the income tax limit, to the level of the full-time minimum wage. This would mean that no one would pay income tax until they were earning above the minimum

wage (around £13,500 a year). The current threshold is
£10,000. UKIP would allow businesses to 'discriminate in
favour of young British workers' and introduce an appren-
ticeship qualification to schools to replace four non-core
GCSEs. The Green Party would raise the minimum wage to
the same level as the living wage, make sure all interns are
paid the minimum wage, and scrap all university tuition
fees.

If you want to have enough money to live on – VOTE.

13. Big Business

Are big businesses paying their way?

Supporters of **capitalism** say that it allows individuals and companies the freedom to make money better than any other system out there. Capitalism is all about promoting economic growth, and providing opportunities. Some companies have grown and grown and grown, until they are bigger in economic terms than many countries – in fact, eight of the fifty largest economic entities in the world in 2011 were corporations. Many would argue these big businesses are pure, capitalist beasts and they exist solely to make money for their shareholders. I think we all understand that. The problem is that we need taxes to pay for public services, and publice services are hard to afford without contributions from business.

The famous economist Milton Friedman said, 'The social responsibility of business is to increase its profits.' So we shouldn't be surprised when we hear stories about low wages for workers, tax avoidance, customers getting a raw deal etc. In fact, there is plenty of support for the idea that so long as big businesses follow the law and pay all of their taxes, they should be allowed to make as much money as possible. So what role should the government have?

In a totally 'free market', there is no government intervention whatsoever. No one keeping watch over the activity of business. If they provide low quality services or goods to their customers, people won't buy from them anymore, and they'll go bust. You let the private businesses run the economy and then see what happens. The prices for goods and services are set by a sort of mutual consent between the supply (the businesses) and demand (us, the consumers). There's a price the businesses won't sell for less than; there's a price the consumer won't pay more than; they meet somewhere in the middle. The businesses also control wages and the payment of bonuses and so on. The government does not interfere. Many people argue that this is the best, and fairest, means of wealth creation. And that ultimately everyone will benefit.

A 'controlled market' or 'regulated market' is one where the government does interfere – there are a variety of ways in which they can do that, including setting the prices of things, controlling who or what can produce and sell certain things, setting taxation levels, imposing wage restrictions etc. Most major global economies are mixed, so that there is a bit of both. The economy is mainly run by the private sector, but the state still plays a role, in some cases even owning companies and businesses.

In the UK we have a mixed economy, where the government exerts a certain amount of regulation over big business and also provides some public services that could otherwise be private businesses (like the NHS, and schools). The size of the UK's public sector has declined from its peak in the 1970s. Since then, various governments have sold off various public industries to private companies. Most recently the Royal Mail was sold, apparently for less than it was worth (although admittedly these things are hard to judge).

So let's have a look at the tax situation first. The UK government sets the taxation rates and taxation laws, and is also responsible for enforcing and collecting. Is it working? Many would say no, because there is a 'tax gap'. This is the gap between the amount of tax the government should be receiving, and what it actually receives. The tax gap is made up of three bits: tax avoidance, tax evasion and tax debt. Tax avoidance is, as the name suggests, a way of avoiding paying tax through legal means – exploiting loopholes in our tax system. Sticking your profits where the government can't touch them. Tax evasion is the illegal equivalent – avoiding tax through deceit and careful manipulation of your accounts. And tax debt is the amount that companies and individuals know that they owe, but have managed to delay payment of. The size of the tax gap in the UK depends on whose figures you believe. There is an organisation called Tax Research UK that estimates the tax gap in 2013/14 to have been around £120 billion (more than the annual budget of the NHS). The Inland Revenue (HMRC) says that is a wild overestimate and that in 2012/13 it was more like £34 billion. What occurs to me is – even if you accept the lower figure – how are we letting corporations and the rich get away with not paying £34 billion in tax? As a nation, we are having at least £34 billion effectively stolen from us. That is insane. Especially when you compare that to something like the Department for Work and Pension's estimated cost of benefit fraud, which in 2013/14 was (only!) £1.2 billion.

Of that £34 billion, HMRC estimates £22.3 billion is lost through tax evasion – illegal tax avoidance. Tax Research UK says that it's much higher (£73.4 billion), and that it's been rising quickly over recent years and showing no signs of abating. It seems obvious that we have to stop this (or 'clamp down', as we always seem to say). A recent report written by a committee of MPs has found that HMRC is 'unacceptably slow' in recovering lost revenues. It also said that it 'does not do enough to tackle companies which exploit international tax structures to minimise UK tax liabilities'. Tax expert Chas Roy-Chowdhury, of the Association of Chartered Certified Accountants, offers some defence, saying that tax collection is very complicated and that HMRC is under-staffed to do the job properly. Chancellor George Osborne said in March 2014 that he would increase HMRC's budget in order to 'tackle non-compliance'. But then a memo was leaked that showed that HMRC would lose 300 members of staff by 2015. Mark Serwotka, the general secretary of the Public and Commercial Services union (PCS), whose members work for HMRC, said that the government is actually 'making it harder to chase down these wealthy individuals and organisations'. HMRC has said that these size reductions are part of a long-term plan to become more highly skilled and operate out of fewer locations. The Financial Secretary to the Treasury, David Gauke, said that 'since 2010/11 the percentage tax gap [as a proportion of **GDP**] has stayed lower than at any point under the previous government ... avoidance overall is down'.

Richard Murphy, a global tax expert, believes that the rich have managed to control both the writing of tax laws, and the enforcement of them. HMRC enlists the help of big accountancy firms to design our tax policy. These same big accountancy firms then advise their clients –

huge corporations and rich individuals – on how to get
round the policies that *they have helped design*. In the
meantime, small businesses and individuals who can't
afford expensive accountants get hounded for payments.
So while for the big players taxes seem to be negotiable,
you can be certain that the little guy is paying his in full.
That hardly seems fair.

Given the financial pressures we're under, it seems
important to start making sure that companies pay the
right amount of tax, so why has the government, and previous governments, not done so? There are a couple of
possible explanations. One is that as soon as the government manages to shut down a loophole, the companies,
with their crack team of tax lawyers, have found the next.
The companies are always one step ahead. Another
reason may be that the government is worried that if it
cracks down on these huge multinational corporations,
threatening to reduce their profits, the corporations will
relocate to somewhere that has less strict tax laws. And if
a corporation relocates, it takes with it its jobs, its investment and its tax revenue (whatever little amount they
may have been paying). These companies are global and
mobile. So when David Cameron comes out fighting and
says firms will be pushed 'to damn well pay', many like
Richard Murphy think these words – like the words of
previous governments – are empty. In fact, Murphy
believes that the UK economic climate actually makes
tax avoidance easier. The recent report by the committee
of MPs backs this claim up, saying that HMRC is using
tax breaks to lure companies to set up in the UK, and
these same tax breaks might lead to tax avoidance.
Moreover, standards are slacker in the UK than the rest
of Europe. Murphy also insists that David Cameron's

government actually created a new tax loophole – an incentive called the 'Patent Box' – which enabled aggressive tax avoidance. Germany and other countries objected, and the government has since reached a compromise on it, which George Osborne describes as 'a great deal for Britain'.

In 2012, Starbucks, Amazon and Google were asked to explain why they were paying little or no tax in the UK. Starbucks claimed that it was making no profit from its 700 stores in the UK (so why, you might ask, not shut them down?). However, its thirty coffee traders in Switzerland (where conveniently the tax rate is half that of the UK) made a healthy 20 per cent profit. Starbucks in the UK would be profitable but it pays large fees for 'product development'. These fees are paid to another part of Starbucks based in Holland, where they had a private tax arrangement, which is now being investigated. Amazon wouldn't disclose in which countries they made their profits – but they make very little profit here. To many it seems hard to justify how a UK order, coming from a UK warehouse, could end up on their Luxembourg accounts. Google argued that their European profits were being made possible by their work in America and so should be taxed in America. That makes some sense, except their European profits ended up in Bermuda where they had to pay – yup, zero tax. All of this behaviour is designed to maximise profits. Why would we expect anything else?

After being called out on their dubious tax arrangements, Starbucks agreed to pay some tax – £20 million over two years, which is a figure that they seem to have plucked out of thin air, but better than nothing. Although it's very hard to imagine an individual business person who had sold £3 billion worth of goods over fourteen years and who had only paid £8.6 million in tax, being allowed to choose their own, rather low, liability. Starbucks' chief executive, Mark Fox, said that he wants governments to draw up more coherent tax systems, and that 'it needs to be the policy-makers that change things'. It feels like he's got a point there. The government has to take charge if it wants corpo-rations to behave differently.

One seemingly straightforward way of dealing with multinational companies that have divisions spread out across various countries, some of which are 'tax-friendly', was devised by the District Economics Group. It involves taxing companies on where sales are made, not where they report their profits. So let's say Starbucks makes 10 per cent of its global sales in the UK. Then it would pay tax in the UK on 10 per cent of its overall, global profits. If Starbucks doesn't want to pay our tax rate, then it will have to stop selling in our country. That might be fair, but no doubt incredibly hard to actually implement, given the cooperation between countries that would be required. That said, the UK government, along with fifty-one other countries, has recently signed a pledge to share tax infor-mation openly with one another to try and reduce tax evasion. Unfortunately the US, home to some of the largest multinational corporations, has not signed the pledge.

UKIP has a similar policy idea. It would make corpo-rations pay a 'turnover tax' on their UK revenue (turnover being the amount of money going into a company). That sounds sensible, but you have to worry that firms with clever tax accountants will be able to make sure that their turnover appears overseas. In November last year, Labour announced it would introduce penalties for tax avoid-ance and evasion. Currently if, by some miracle, HMRC actually catches a corporation avoiding tax, they just have to pay what they owe, but no fines. The Liberal Democrats and Conservatives argue they have done lots to crack down on what, in 2013, George Osborne called 'morally repugnant' tax avoidance. They point to their introduction of a general anti-abuse rule (GAAR) in July 2013, which aims to avoid the task of having to introduce new legislation to tackle individual loopholes. The Liberal Democrats argue their idea of a mansion tax would be very difficult for the rich to avoid. The Green Party says it would close any existing loopholes so that company profits earned in the UK were taxed here, even where this would mean that profits of transnational corporations may be taxed twice – once in the UK and once again in a foreign country.

The next thing to look at is how these companies are sharing out their wealth among their employees. The FTSE 100 is a list of the top 100 companies listed on the London Stock Exchange – it's one way of identifying the most valuable companies operating in the UK (although lots are international firms). The High Pay Centre, an independent non-party **think tank**, has looked at how much the bosses of those companies are paid (referred to as 'executive pay'), relative to their average employee. In 1998, the average FTSE 100 chief executive officer (the boss) was paid forty-seven times as much as their average employee. They are now paid 130 times as much. Executive pay is increasing rapidly, while for the last six years real-term average wages have been falling. Are executives getting paid more because they are doing a much better job than they were in 1998? Are average workers not doing a better job?

The coalition government has tried to act on this. In 2013, they gave shareholders the power to vote against executive pay if they thought that it was too much. So far, every vote at a FTSE 100 company has supported the levels of executive pay. The average FTSE 100 boss earned £4.7 million in 2013, up from £4.1 million the year before. So if the shareholders are happy, and they have a clear vested interest, shouldn't we be too? Apparently not – 78 per cent of the public would be in favour of a maximum limit on the amount that the highest paid employee can be paid in relation to the lowest paid. The majority of the public isn't happy with the level of inequality.

The government could bring in a maximum pay ratio. It could have different ratios for different sectors of business. Some firms have already chosen to adopt pay ratios – TSB and John Lewis have a 75:1 high to low pay limit, meaning that the boss can only be paid 75 times more than the lowest-paid employee. The problem with pay ratios is that they may be easy to get around. For example, if a company sacked a load of its lowest paid workers, its pay ratio would be seen to 'improve'. Companies could also compensate for lower salaries to their top executives by paying them bigger bonuses (although new EU legislation has put limits on this) and giving them shares. One idea for combating that would be the introduction of compulsory profit-sharing. So if the company does well, everyone who works there will benefit. The New Economics Foundation thinks that simply making companies disclose their pay ratios in public might shame them into 'more equitable arrangements'. Labour says it would raise the top rate of tax for individuals so people would hand over 50 per cent of everything they earn over £150,000 to the government, which wouldn't affect the pay ratio, but would hit the pockets of the top executives. They would also raise the minimum wage, which may have some effect on pay ratios.

There is an interesting argument about wages put forward by fans of capitalism and the free market. They would say that the same 'corporate greed' that makes companies push for profit will actually, in certain circumstances, make them pay their workers more. If that seems counter-intuitive, here's how the logic goes: this greed makes the companies want to get bigger, sell new products in new locations and beat their competition. To get bigger, a company needs more workers. It needs to attract those workers away from competing companies by paying a bit more. In other words, the greed creates a push and pull – a push to pay as little as possible and a pull to pay a bit more to attract workers to enable growth, so you reach a fair equilibrium. The problem with this model is unemployment. When you have unemployment, there is a large number of people who are, in lots of cases, desperate to work, and who companies can therefore offer minimum-wage employment to. Also, it assumes that big companies don't take advantage of **globalisation** and source their workers from somewhere they can pay them even less.

The more general argument against introducing pay ratios or enforcing higher minimum wages or increasing top rates of tax for individuals or corporations is that any form of government regulation will make the situation worse. This is the free-market position. Anything that restricts the growth of a company, or dissuades someone from trying to start a business, will limit the economic growth of the country. That will have a knock-on effect on the number of jobs being created, which won't help anyone.

Even without additional government regulation, there are some companies that choose to run themselves in a different way. I mentioned John Lewis earlier – they operate as a kind of 'economic democracy'. Each employee has part-ownership of the company so they get a share of the profits and decide how the business is run. The idea is that this means the employees will be more inclined to work hard, because they benefit directly if the company does well and there are no outside shareholders influencing the business. The Green Party supports this kind of business, which fits its aim of 'equitable distribution of resources, wealth, opportunity and power'. I suppose the truth is that not every company is going to adopt this method.

Tax avoidance is something that the government can tackle if they really commit to it. The problems of pay inequality, though, may or may not be solved by government action.

If you think big business needs reining in, or should be left to get on with things – VOTE.

14. Climate Change

What should we be doing about climate change in the UK?

Disclaimer: many, many years ago I did a degree in Human Impact on the Environment, and this stuff gets me angry.

That said, it's important to note that the question doesn't imply that climate change may or may not be happening. Because climate change is happening. Honestly, anyone with half a brain (me) has known that for years, but now there is a global scientific consensus. The latest Intergovernmental Panel on Climate Change (IPCC) report stated that the effects of climate change, if unchecked, will 'bring high risks of severe, widespread, and irreversible impacts'. More than that, it says that humans are extremely likely to be the dominant cause of the rise in global temperatures since the 1950s. This is the most conclusive and comprehensive report yet,

collated from five years of worldwide research by people
wearing lab coats. At the release of the report, the UN
Secretary-General Ban Ki-moon was plain when he said:
'Science has spoken. There is no ambiguity in the message. Leaders must act. Time is not on our side.' It's not a
coincidence that that sounds like the tagline for a big
budget action film (*The Day After Tomorrow*, anyone?),
because if we can do anything about climate change,
whether that is stopping the warming, or getting ready for
its effects, it is going to need a big budget and require a
lot of action.

As a quick aside, if you're ever unlucky enough to meet
a climate-change doubter (they don't like being called
'deniers') – there are a few knocking about – just shout
'extreme-weather-conditions-global-poverty-flooding' and
then walk away.

However, where there is debate is on the scale of the
problem, what action we should take, how quickly we
should take it and how much it will cost, both in the UK
and globally. There are three basic options: accept that
changes will occur due to climate change, that we can't
alter that, and so look for ways to adapt to these changes
(symptomatic treatment); try to combat the climate change
itself (preventive treatment); close our eyes and hope it
will all be fine (fingers-crossed treatment). Or, we can try a
combination of the above. The really tricky bit is that
having a global scientific consensus on the problem is not
the same as having a global political consensus on the solution or solutions. Which, as Ban Ki-moon suggests, is what
we need.

So, if we ignore climate change, and carry on blindly,
will it all be fine? Not really, no. But before we get to the
details, it is important to acknowledge that there is a large

degree of uncertainty in climate change projections —
because they are trying to model something incredibly
complex (the earth and its atmosphere and the sun, and so
on). Climate-change doubters point to this as evidence that
scientists don't really know what's happening or what is
going to happen. Actually, scientists are increasingly confident that the projections provide very good indicators of
climate trends.

What those trends tell us is that in the UK we will experience more erratic rainfall and wetter winters. The
government thinks that by 2080, flooding damage could
cost the country up to £27 billion annually. It costs
around £1.1 billion now. Nearly four times as many properties might be at risk of flooding in the next twenty years.
In spite of all the rain, its increasingly unpredictable
nature will mean that water storage will become more of a
challenge. By the 2050s, anywhere between 27 million
and 59 million people — there's that uncertainty — could
be living in areas with water supply problems. A country
with rampant floods and a patchy water supply sounds
absurd, but that could be our reality. Average temperatures, which have risen by one degree Celsius since the
1970s, will continue to rise. We will have drier, warmer
summers — that might be good for tourism, but it'll see our
ageing population struggle to cope with the heat and put
even more pressure on the NHS. And these are just some
of the things that are predicted to happen in the UK.

The global effects of climate change will have a big
impact on us too. Our **cost of living** is likely to go up as
raw materials and crops get scarcer. People will be forced
to migrate from the searingly hot equator to cooler areas
like the UK, which will put even more of a strain on our
infrastructure.

But can we seriously hope to halt the advance of climate change? If we are serious about trying, then what we have to do is reduce our carbon emissions – I'm sure everyone remembers from school that carbon dioxide is a greenhouse gas that warms up the planet. Currently, global emissions are very high. In the UK in 2008, we passed the Climate Change Act, which set the aim to reduce our emissions by 80 per cent (from the 1990 level, which is the benchmark) by 2050. It established the world's first legally binding climate targets. In order to meet those targets, we will have to take measures to conserve energy, and try to switch from fossil fuels to renewable or clean sources of energy. Something that may have increasing significance in future attempts to lower CO_2 levels is **carbon capture and storage** (CCS). This is a relatively new (and expensive) process that effectively grabs CO_2 from the fumes of power stations and similar industrial plants, and stores it in the ground. The first coal-fired power station using large scale CCS in the EU is awaiting final approval. The site is in Yorkshire. Parliament's Energy and Climate Change Committee has called for more of these CCS plants to be fast-tracked because they are 'vital to limit climate change'.

The switch to renewable energies like wind, solar or hydroelectric is contentious though. These renewable technologies are up and running but they aren't cheap. Their costs will come down, as with any technology, but for now they are expensive. The government is putting money ('green subsidies') into solar farms, wind farms and other renewables projects. It also has measures in place (a 'carbon tax') to discourage carbon emissions, and that increases the cost of power from coal, oil and gas. A report by the Climate Change Committee estimates that these subsidies and measures increased the cost of the average gas/electricity bill by £45 in 2013. The same committee found that these costs will add £175 to the average household bill by 2030. The cost of energy to business and industry is set to double by then, which will probably increase the price of goods and services. This is why some people object to renewables. Why should the public have to pay to subsidise these projects?

The government has changed tack a bit with their funding of green energy. Previously, they were making power companies supply a certain proportion of renewables; now they are trying to strengthen renewables producers, to make them competitive in their own right. This is key – the aim is to make renewables competitive. The justification for green subsidies has always been that while fossil fuels will get more and more expensive (as they run out), renewable technology will get cheaper and the subsidies will eventually fall away to nothing.

Unfortunately for this plan, oil prices have been falling dramatically, and are expected to fall further. That wasn't predicted, but it's great news for consumers and motorists, and bad news for the renewable energy industry. Anne Robinson of the uSwitch price comparison website said, 'More subsidies are likely to be needed [for renewable power] as the gap between the cost of fossil fuel power and renewable power gets bigger.' Those subsidies would have to increase consumer energy bills. Which is unlikely to go down well. Renewable energies may be seen as offering very bad value. Which is especially problematic because renewable power plants are expensive to build and need massive investment. That investment is less likely to be offered if the economic case for building them is weakened.

In 2010, David Cameron made assurances about running

the 'greenest government ever', but in the latest environmental check-up (called the 'environmental audit'), it was
found that no satisfactory progress has been made in any of
the ten environmental areas it looked at. Three – including
flood protection – have actually got worse since 2010.
Although it's going up, still less than a fifth of our energy
production comes from renewables. The government said it
would make our ageing, dirty coal plants so expensive to
run that they would close by 2025, but that is looking very
unlikely. That will make our Climate Change Act targets
very hard to hit.

Lots of people argue that we have to break our dependence on fossil fuels. That's why they say **fracking** – the
controversial method of releasing shale gas from the
ground – is a bad option, even if you don't consider the
potentially harmful side-effects. The supporters of fracking
(UKIP and, to some extent, the Conservatives) believe that
shale gas will reduce our energy bills. In August 2013,
David Cameron said 'fracking has real potential to drive
energy bills down'. There is not agreement on this though.
The exact amount of shale gas in the UK is not yet known –
more drilling and testing is required to ascertain that. This
sort of exploration is expensive and the cost of drilling a
well can easily be greater than the value of the gas you get
out. Nevertheless, fracking fans would point to its success
in America – it's been projected that by around 2020, in no
small part due to fracking, the United States will be the
largest global oil producer. The economic effect of that is
clear, and appealing.

Germany is often held up as an example of how green
energy should be done. Their *Energiewende* (energy trans-
formation) policy aims to have nearly all of their energy
coming from renewables by 2050, and is already seeing

results. In the first quarter of 2014, renewables accounted for 27 per cent of their electricity demand, and that peaked at a colossal 74 per cent in May due to favourable weather – windy and sunny. Although, that weather dependence is partly why some people are sceptical of wind and solar's ability to power a country – the output is variable, and therefore needs back up in the form of energy 'on demand'. As Paul Younger, Professor of Energy Engineering at the University of Glasgow, says, 'Nuclear generates steadily, 24/7 and we can increase generation from coal and gas as and when we need it. We desperately need not to lose sight of that.' Essentially, we don't want the lights to go out on a cloudy, still day. Another complaint about land-based wind farms is that they need to be vast to generate a significant amount of power, and that they are ugly, noisy and injure wildlife. However, the Department of Energy and Climate Change (DECC) Public Attitudes survey found that 67 per cent of the public support onshore wind farms.

There has been significant criticism of the Energiewende. It has promised environmental sustainability and economic growth but the cost of energy for German businesses has gone up by 60 per cent in five years. Many would argue that those increases will harm economic growth, not help it. The businesses' running costs are higher and so they are less competitive in the market. It also comes back to the question that people have asked here in the UK – how long are taxpayers going to be expected to fund these subsidies? It's also worth noting that the emissions per person in Germany are still higher than in the UK, and some people suggest they are actually rising.

It's not just about the UK though, because this is an issue that, more than anything else in the book, is truly global. We can't really look at the UK in isolation. It's everyone's

problem. We have spent years talking about tackling climate change and trying (and failing) to get everyone to sign
treaties and stick to targets, but the sad truth is that the
latest IPCC report shows that worldwide carbon emissions – mainly from burning coal, oil and gas – are still
rising. To tackle climate change, those emissions have to
fall to zero sooner rather than later. The EU has pledged to
cut its carbon emissions by 40 per cent by 2030. But the EU
is responsible for less than 10 per cent of global emissions,
so clearly it can't stop global warming on its own, but it has
hoped to set an example for the rest of the world. We need
those other countries to follow, but so far, in spite of our
best efforts, the Chinese and Indians and Americans
haven't signed up. In 2013, carbon emissions per head in
China were more than in the EU for the first time, and
China's got a lot of heads (over 1.3 billion). China is the
biggest emitter of greenhouse gases in the world. However,
there has been some promising movement. The US and
China recently announced that, after secret negotiations,
they have agreed their own deal on emissions. This is the
first time China has agreed to cap its emissions, which they
have pledged to do by 2030 or sooner. The US have committed to big reductions by 2025.

   One of the reasons that it's so significant that China has
set targets is that we buy a lot of stuff from there. That's
because a lot of our manufacturing industry – much of
which is polluting – has moved overseas. So when we buy
goods from places like China, the emissions associated
with their production get stuck on China's 'carbon books'.
That raises a fundamental question – in this global economy, who should be responsible for emissions? The
producer or the consumer? You could argue that the current system of 'climate accounting' is making our carbon

emissions figures look better, and China's worse ...
Wherever the emissions come from, they affect the entire
planet.

In December 2015 in Paris, everyone will have another
go at getting a legally binding universal agreement on climate, from all the nations of the world. This will mean
setting targets for reducing emissions, and agreeing to
improving aid for developing world countries to help them
meet the targets. Financial penalties may be imposed on
countries that fail to meet those goals.

If a global agreement isn't reached soon, then even if we
in the UK increase our efforts enormously, doing everything we can to prevent more warming, it won't be nearly
enough. In fact, it might be a colossal waste of money. That
is an understandable fear.

Meanwhile, the UK public are getting less enthusiastic
about saving the environment. Between 2000 and 2010, the
number of Brits who said they'd be up for paying higher
prices to limit global warming has slumped from 43 per
cent to 26 per cent. That's no surprise in times of economic
hardship – climate change prevention has to be thought of
in the long term, but when people are feeling poorer, they
tend to think in the short term. They don't want to pay
more for their electricity. They don't want to pay more for
anything. And assurances that renewable energy prices will
eventually drop are falling on deaf ears.

This reluctance to do what is necessary to hit the targets
set by the Climate Change Act is mirrored by a growing
number of politicians on the right of British politics (within
the Conservative Party and UKIP). At the time the Act was
signed, there was a real consensus from all the parties, but
that is disintegrating. Owen Paterson, the former Tory environment minister, believes that there are better ways of

meeting our clean energy requirements, and that we have
set ourselves unrealistic targets. He wants us to suspend the
Climate Change Act. David Davis, MP and former
Chairman of the Tory party, says, 'We should not sacrifice
Britain's economic recovery on the altar of climate change.'
Nigel Lawson, the former Conservative Chancellor, thinks
that 'the ordinary bloke has an instinctive sense that it
wouldn't be too bad if the weather warmed up'. The
Conservatives made no policy statements on climate
change at their most recent party conference, but David
Cameron did address the issue at the UN Climate Summit
in September 2014, saying, 'we must agree a global deal in
Paris next year. We simply cannot put this off any longer.'
He also said of the UK, 'We've legislated. We've acted.
We've invested.'

Labour has said, 'We will unlock investment in clean
energy by setting a firm 2030 decarbonisation target.'
What that target might be is anyone's guess. There have
been similar statements from the Lib Dems, too, who
claim to be 'the only party that can be trusted to deliver
green jobs and green growth in government'. UKIP make
no such promises – Nigel Farage has said, 'We may have
made one of the biggest and most stupid collective mistakes in history by getting so worried about global
warming.' They would repeal the Climate Change Act,
support fracking and 'abolish green taxes and charges in
order to reduce fuel bills'. As you'd expect, the Green
Party makes environmental policy a priority, promising to
'tackle climate change faster and more effectively' by
moving to renewable energy and leaving fossil fuels like
shale gas in the ground. They also talk about preparing to
'shield us from extreme weather events'. Which brings us
to the idea of adaptation.

It's almost certainly true that even if we miraculously managed to reduce our carbon emissions to zero tomorrow, the effects of climate change would still be felt for decades afterwards. In 2009, the Institution of Mechanical Engineers released a report in which they said that they 'recognise that global CO_2 emissions are not reducing and our climate is changing, so unless we adapt, we are likely to face a difficult future'. So how about just accepting these things are going to happen, and being well prepared? How much could we do? Well, we are in a relatively strong position because this sort of adaptation costs money, which is why the poorer, developing world is most vulnerable and will need financial help from us in the developed world. That seems fair enough, given that the developed world is responsible for the vast majority of the emissions that are causing this climate change.

Some of the things we would need to invest money in are better flood defences, including reinforcing our river banks. We would need to improve our personal water storage – so every property has a water butt. We could start using water-permeable paving to improve drainage. It's been suggested that we should replace the plants in our gardens with ones that require less water. Elsewhere in the world we would need to develop crops with greater drought tolerance, and better irrigation systems. None of this will be cheap, but it is all achievable and it's believed by many that this will, in the long run, save money and lives.

There are some more subtle examples of adaptation too, like the Confederation Bridge in Canada, which was built high enough to allow ships to pass under it even when sea levels have risen – WHICH THEY WILL.

It seems sensible that we should take action to adapt to

the unavoidable consequences of climate change, while simultaneously making every effort to get our carbon emissions down to zero. But the question remains: will the rest of the world follow? We will hopefully get the answer in Paris in 2015.

If you care about the future of our planet – VOTE.

15. Representation

Is Westminster representative?

In our democracy, the set-up is simple – we, the people, elect Members of Parliament (MPs) to represent us in Parliament. Those MPs then represent and look after our views and interests. At least, that's the idea. The wheels start to come off a bit if we don't vote, but let's put that to one side for now.

So who are these people that represent us? They are 650 MPs, one for each constituency in the UK. They sit in the House of Commons.

In terms of gender and ethnicity, the make-up of Parliament has never resembled the make-up of the UK better. That's not to say that it now resembles it well – it's just that in the past it was even worse. There are 148 female MPs and 27 Black and Minority Ethnic (BME) MPs out of the total 650. That's still overwhelmingly male and overwhelmingly white ('male, pale and stale', as the phrase goes). If the Commons was to be entirely representative of the wider British population, those numbers would need to be: 330 female MPs and 117 BME MPs.

These numbers are creeping up, slowly. But more will need to be done if we are ever to turn on Prime Minister's Questions (worth a little peek if you haven't seen it before) and see a room full of people that look anything like modern Britain. And yet I'm not sure that this is the most important representation problem that we have. I think the reason that Parliament feels so very distant to many people is because there isn't a large enough range of ages, or educational backgrounds, or accents, or career paths, or – arguably – opinions. Those are the things that make it difficult for us to relate to politicians, and perhaps why the reverse is true too. Perhaps the reason that people don't feel represented is not to do with the numbers of this sort of person or that sort of person, but that their outlook or opinions aren't represented. Of course this can be related to race and gender, but not exclusively.

When Nick Clegg came on *Free Speech*, he was asked by a young woman in the audience: 'Have you ever struggled? How can you know what the fair thing to do is?' Clegg was very honest about his upbringing – he was lucky and had a happy childhood, so no struggle there you might say – and he went on to talk about the challenge of representation. He said that he, like all the other MPs, is trying to represent his constituents not by pretending 'to be personally like all of the 60,000-odd folk', but by having the compassion and empathy to imagine what it's like to be somebody else. And perhaps there's something in that argument. We need politicians who can empathise. Who at least understand the opinions, needs and struggles of the electorate. And although we have more women and more black and ethnic minority people in Parliament than before, Michael

Meacher, a Labour MP since 1970, thinks the situation is worsening: 'Parliament is more unrepresentative of society than at any time in my political career.' Clegg puts it a bit more colourfully: 'Westminster on a Wednesday lunchtime [at Prime Minister's Questions] resembles *Downton Abbey* gone a bit loopy.'

So what's happening? Why aren't more *normal* people becoming MPs? Well, there are a whole load of obstacles and, unsurprisingly, the biggest is money. ConservativeHome did some research and found that the average cost (in travel, and lost earnings and campaigning, and God knows what else) of attempting to become an MP is around £34,000; £41,000 if you win! That's a lot of money. You also need to get selected to stand by your party – assuming that you aren't standing as an independent candidate – and they often 'try you out' in some seat that is both far from home and, worse, pretty much unwinnable. So you stand and probably lose. And you've also lost thousands of pounds. Then you repeat the exercise at the next election, hoping that someone high up in the party likes you enough to let you stand in a more winnable seat.

Sure, if you eventually win a seat and become an MP, you'll then be paid £67,000 a year (or £74,000 from May 2015, if the planned rise comes in), which is about three times the national average. But along the way you will have spent at least £41,000, depending on how many attempts you've made. It's clear that this is a risk that the wealthy are more likely to take.

Also, the time commitment is huge. Your party will have you campaigning all day long if they can, so you either need to have an employer who is prepared to give you that time off, or leave your job. Again, this is not really an option for people with normal incomes. Only 4 per cent of current MPs were manual workers (people doing physical labour, usually from poor backgrounds) before they entered Parliament. There were four times as many of those MPs in 1979. The employer issue begins to explain why an increasing number of politicians these days have come from political jobs – those employers are, of course, very understanding. Now, one in six politicians is a career politician – someone who has never worked in 'the real world'. We are seeing the professionalisation of politics.

Interestingly too, over half of MPs take a pay cut to become an MP. That can be looked at positively – presumably they are entering politics for the right reasons, not being motivated by money. But that in itself is a luxury that only the wealthy can afford. That they were previously earning over £67,000 a year shows just how many of our politicians come from high-earning professional backgrounds.

It's also often said that being an MP doesn't fit with having a family. Most non-London MPs will be away from home all week. A number of MPs have quit because they don't see their kids enough. The sacrifices and costs are great – both financial and emotional. MPs are put under an enormous amount of scrutiny by the media and opposition parties. Mistakes they may have made in the past are dredged up. But surely all normal people make mistakes? Should we be so judgemental? These are supposed to be representatives of the people, not beacons of perfection. You can certainly see why many good people would be put off. I'm not suggesting for a moment that I'd be a good MP, or that anyone would vote for me, but I know that I couldn't stand in any case – I wouldn't be comfortable or confident about the intense examination of my life that would follow. So you can also see why our politicians are viewed as out-of-touch members of the wealthy elite. And as long as it remains so tough to get into Westminster if you're not rich, then it's hard to see how we make our Parliament feel more representative of its people.

This is all a bit doom and gloom. Are we destined to be governed by rich white men for ever? Not necessarily. All of the major parties are aware of the problem. As I said before, it's not that our MPs have to look exactly like our population – but it would help. Labour is using **all-women shortlists** in their candidate selection process; 50 per cent of their target seats will be contested by women. These shortlists aren't universally popular, because some people feel that they are unfair on men, and that women shouldn't be given special treatment because it undermines equality. Nick Clegg supports all-women shortlists but his party, the Liberal Democrats, keep rejecting them. Clegg says that 'it divides Liberal opinion. Some people think it is tokenism and leads to a sense of unfairness.' Only 12 per cent of Lib Dem MPs are female, compared to 16 per cent of Tories and 34 per cent of Labour MPs. Those in favour of all-women shortlists think they can have a rapid and positive effect on the gender imbalance of our Parliament, and that until someone comes up with a better plan, they are worthwhile. The idea would be that once there was something approaching the 'right' number of women MPs, there would be no need for shortlists anymore. The status quo will have been reset. An interesting international example is Rwanda, which has a gender quota (30 per cent of all decision-makers must be women) written into its constitution. Currently, 64 per cent of parliamentary seats are occupied by women!

The Labour MP David Lammy is in favour of similar

shortlists to get more BME candidates: 'We need bold measures to tackle this problem, not just more tinkering around
the edges.'

Unfortunately, these measures probably won't have any
effect on the social and economic background of candidates. By and large we'll be getting rich women and rich
minority groups. Of course, there is a variety of ways that
people can get rich, and from entirely different circumstances, but it's possible to imagine a Parliament made up
of the exact same proportions as the wider population that
still isn't representative. After the expenses scandal, four
MPs and two peers were jailed. That meant that in 2011,
0.13 per cent of the general population was in jail, while
0.61 per cent of House of Commons members were locked
up. I'm pretty sure that that didn't mean prisoners felt over-
represented in Parliament.

There is another problem, too: **safe seats**. As I mentioned in the voting chapter, these won't necessarily stay
safe for ever. But they are seats where the result can be predicted with a very high degree of accuracy. This can be
because of the political leanings of the voters in the area or
sometimes the popularity of the current MP. In 2010, it
was estimated that nearly 400 of the 650 available seats
were safe. MPs in those seats often seem out of touch with
their constituents because they can afford to be – they are
so confident that they're going to win their seat anyway. So
the only way these individual MPs risk losing their seat is
if they fall out of favour with their party leaders.
Unsurprisingly then, what happens is that many MPs in
safe seats apparently care much more about pleasing their
party than about pleasing the people they are supposed to
represent. They answer up to their party bosses, rather
than down to their constituents. The situation's made

worse because every candidate will want to be given a safe seat, and rely on the party to assign them. When we vote for our MPs, those people on the ballot have already been selected for us by the parties who put them forward. It is a common frustration that many of the candidates aren't even from the area they're standing for, and have just been 'parachuted' in.

There is a way to avoid this though. You hold open primaries. An open primary is a sort of pre-vote – a vote before the vote to elect your MP. They are widely used in America. So there will be a list of candidates from each party, and we, the electorate in our constituency, will get to decide which of those candidates we want to stand for each party. All of a sudden, the parties can't just put their favourites up for election in safe seats. The candidates have to first win the approval of their constituency before they can stand for election. That means that the candidates have to answer to the people first, not the party. Local opinion becomes far more important. Some object to open primaries because they are more expensive, but the idea is that you will get a more representative House of Commons – because open primaries attract a much broader range of candidates, and people from the area – and more MPs who don't owe their position to the party leaders, but to the people.

The Conservative MP Dr Sarah Wollaston was a GP who won the first-ever open primary in Totnes in 2010. She is a firm believer in primaries, saying they would change Parliament for the better: 'You can bring people into politics from non-political backgrounds and bring their experience to bear.' Dr Wollaston is known for being independently minded and hard for her party leaders to control – and she believes that is why the coalition government has shelved plans for 200 open primaries in safe seats. They don't want outspoken MPs like Dr Wollaston. But maybe the public do.

If you care about being represented by people that will actually represent you – VOTE.

16. Public Finances

What exactly do people mean when they talk about 'the deficit' and 'the debt'?

Every year, the government collects in about £600 billion of our money. Income tax, value added tax (VAT), corporation tax, tax on beer and cider – the list of taxes is long. The government also spends a lot of money – around £700 billion, so rather more than it gets in, as I'll explain in a bit. During this election campaign the parties will argue about who is doing, or will do, a better job of looking after these public finances.

To explain these finances, I'll start simple and then I'm afraid it will get a bit complicated. Like with any household budget, there are two columns: 'ingoings' and 'outgoings'. The difference between the two tells us whether we're in the red (making a loss) or the black (making a profit). For some reason, the terms used for making a loss and making a profit are 'budget deficit' and 'budget surplus', respectively. If the government runs the country at a loss (so, spending more than is coming in), the deficit will build up and create an overall debt. This is the money that we owe, because we've had to borrow it. The deficit in the year 2013/14 was £98 billion. The overall debt, accumulated through a number of years of spending more than we were getting in, was £1.457 trillion in November 2014. The interest payments on that debt in 2013/14 were £48.7 billion – more than we spend on defence, schools or the police. It's like a credit card bill nightmare. We're paying a lot of interest, and we keep borrowing more.

A quick word about who we borrow money from – it's not quite as simple as us going in to the bank and saying, 'Hello, we need to borrow £91 billion this year, thanks', but the upshot is that we owe money to a combination of building societies, the Bank of England, insurance companies and pension funds. Many of those are based overseas. They are all doing fine out of it, because they're getting our interest payments, but eventually, they'll ask us to pay back what we owe. Gulp. Or they might lose confidence in our economy, and hike up the interest rates.

There are various ways in which the government can try to change the size of the ingoings and outgoings. Government outgoings can be divided into two main areas: day-to-day spending (called 'current spending') on running the country, and investment (called 'capital spending') in bigger, **infrastructure** projects, like building roads or hospitals or whatever. The day-to-day spending is on things like the NHS, the education system, welfare payments, defence, the cost of running the various government departments and, of course, interest payments on the national debt. When politicians talk about 'cuts to services', it is these areas they are talking about. If the country is running at a loss just taking into account current spending (the current budget deficit), then capital spending will obviously require us to borrow even more money, and have a larger deficit (the overall budget deficit). It might seem sensible to scale back capital spending, but often politicians and economists will argue that investment will lead to economic growth, so it will be worth it in the long run. In 2007, the Labour government borrowed £37.7 billion in total, and invested £28.3 billion of that into big projects. In 2013, the coalition government borrowed £91.5 billion, and invested £23.7 billion – a much smaller proportion of the borrowing, although a similar amount in actual cash.

Government ingoings, or income, comes from selling public property (like the Royal Mail) or, mainly, from taxation. Personal tax, VAT on goods sold, corporation tax, national insurance, council tax and so on. So they can increase the amount they get in either by increasing some or all of those tax rates, or by trying to encourage economic growth. If companies are doing well and expanding, they will be paying more corporation tax. They may create more jobs, which will increase the amount of income tax that the government receives. The people in those jobs will probably spend more money, meaning that the government will get more VAT. On top of that, if people are moving from unemployment to employment, they will receive less in benefits from the government, and that will reduce the outgoings column. And of course, **GDP** will be growing.

The opposite of that is also true. So when times are tough, in a **recession** say, there will be more people out of work, so the amount of tax the government receives will be lower, and the amount it spends on unemployment benefits will be higher. An increase in unemployment of 100,000 people is believed to cost the government £500 million a year. The government therefore has to either make spending cuts or borrow more, which means the deficit (borrowing) will be higher, which in turn means the overall national debt will get bigger.

Now, bear with me because this is the complicated bit. No need to get too bogged down with this stuff, but it's good to go through all of the terms we'll hear when the parties talk about their plans for the economy. So, the fluctuations in current spending – more borrowing when times are hard, less borrowing when times are good – can be taken off the accounts when we're working out the deficit (or the surplus) to give what is called the cyclically adjusted current budget deficit (I know), or 'structural deficit'. This is sometimes called the underlying deficit – it is the borrowing that we need irrespective of how the economy is performing.

So those are the (not-that-basic) basics. The economy will be a major focus for all of the parties in the run-up to the election. The Conservatives, Labour and the Lib Dems all agree that the amount of borrowing (the deficit) needs to be reduced. They all agree that we need to start trying to reduce the national debt. What they don't agree on is how those aims will be achieved, to what extent they need to be achieved, or how quickly they should be done.

The current government has set two targets already. The first target is to have the current budget (day-to-day spending) balanced – meaning, we are spending exactly what is coming in – or in surplus by 2017/18. The second target is to have the debt falling as a share of GDP between 2014/15 and 2015/16. We often measure the debt-to-GDP ratio because it's a useful way of comparing our situation to the situation in other countries. Clearly, if you want to reduce the debt-to-GDP ratio there are two broad options – you pay off some of the debt, or you increase GDP. By

November 2014, our debt-to-GDP ratio was 79.5 per cent. It has been going up, but the coalition is saying it will go down next year. The Treasury has done some sums and says that to meet these targets, any government would have to raise taxes or make spending cuts amounting to between £25 billion and £30 billion.

The Conservatives are adamant that their long-term plan is working and urging voters to 'stay on course to prosperity'. They accept that they will have to take 'difficult decisions' to reduce the deficit. They intend to have an overall budget surplus of £23 billion by the end of the next Parliament (2020), if the recovery is sustained. That means that we will be making more than we are spending on current *and* capital spending together. This is more ambitious than the current coalition government plans – the coalition just wants our revenue to cover current spending by 2017/18, meaning we would still be borrowing to pay for capital spending, and still be running a deficit. The Conservatives are aiming for no borrowing at all, meaning that we would be able to start repaying our debt (if we chose to).

Chancellor George Osborne has said that he will achieve this only by using spending cuts. He has also said that he will make tax cuts (lower taxes) of £7 billion, which Labour claims are 'unfunded' – meaning, where is he getting the money to do that? Nick Clegg says that only using spending cuts is 'wholly implausible'.

The Conservatives have pledged to protect spending on schools and the NHS, so their spending cuts will have to be made to other public services like the police, local government and so on. The Office for Budget Responsibility (OBR) has calculated that the real-terms (adjusted for inflation) spending per head in 2019/20 on the public sector, without education and the NHS, would be £1,290. That is 57 per cent less than in 2009/10, and would represent a substantial shrinking of the public sector. The Conservatives dispute that because they believe they can save money by making more cuts to the welfare system, and intend to get more money by going after tax dodgers aggressively.

The Conservatives say that they are cutting income tax for 25 million people, saving the average taxpayer £705 a year. They also say that as part of the coalition government they have cut '**red tape**' to allow small businesses to prosper without costly bureaucracy, which has created 1.7 million jobs. They have cut corporation tax from 28 per cent in 2010 to 21 per cent in 2014, which they say has allowed companies to grow. As mentioned in the Jobs and the Economy chapter, employment is at a record high and wages have started to rise quicker than inflation. George Osborne has welcomed 'encouraging signs that pay cheques are beginning to rise faster than inflation. If we want to keep Britain on this path then we need to keep working through our economic plan.'

The Conservatives will spend a lot of time explaining what a terrible mess a Labour government would make of the economy, and vice versa. I'll explain Labour's plans for the deficit and debt in a moment, but it is fair to say that they are less ambitious than the Conservatives. Osborne says that shows that Labour aren't serious enough about trying to reduce the national debt. David Cameron gave a speech in which he said, 'Ed Miliband would never clear the overall, headline budget deficit. He would run a budget deficit – permanently adding to debt – indefinitely. Every year. For ever.' Which is quite emphatic. The Conservatives also believe that Labour will increase taxes and therefore limit economic growth, and therefore jobs.

The Shadow Chancellor, Ed Balls, has said that Labour

will 'deliver a surplus on the current budget and falling national debt in the next Parliament'. They have not yet made any promises on how large the surplus will be, or how they'll achieve it. Balls is clear that the pace of their changes would depend on the state of the economy – wages, growth and so on. The Institute for Fiscal Studies (IFS) has compared the parties' targets and calculated that, if Labour just wanted the current budget deficit to hit zero by the end of the next Parliament, then it would have to cut spending by £9.3 billion from 2015/16. There are already plans laid out by the coalition to cut £8.7 billion in 2015/16.

So there is a big, big difference between what the Conservatives and Labour are aiming for. The Labour target is for the current budget only – so does not include capital spending. In the last year of the next Parliament, capital spending is currently projected to be £27 billion. Given that the Conservatives are saying they will have a £23 billion surplus by then, the total difference between the two parties' aims is £50 billion (£27 billion plus £23 billion). This is vast, by anyone's standards. Labour's plans will require £50 billion less in '**austerity** cuts'.

Ed Balls says that the Conservatives' plans are totally unrealistic and will mean that the standard of public services under them would simply not be good enough. His thoughts are echoed by the Lib Dems. Business Secretary Vince Cable, a member of the coalition government, said that he would 'really worry' that George Osborne's plans will 'destroy public services in the way that we know them'.

Balls has not come out and said this, but presumably Labour is giving itself the option to continue borrowing and investing, which it hopes will promote economic growth, and therefore reduce the debt-to-GDP ratio, but without the need for painful cuts. Labour points out that in 2010 the Conservatives pledged 'they'd balance the books by 2015. But they are on course to break this promise, with the deficit set to be £75 billion next year.' Labour says that every spending and tax commitment in their **manifesto** will be fully funded, which it says is untrue of the Conservatives'.

Labour's other main economic plans are to offer tax breaks for companies paying a living wage, to abolish **zero-hour contracts**, and to increase the minimum wage to £8 an hour by 2020. These are all measures that they believe will create 'stronger and more balanced growth to tackle the cost-of-living crisis'.

The Lib Dems' budget plans are a sort of halfway house between the Conservatives and Labour. They will balance current budget from 2017/18 onwards – exactly in line with the current coalition plans, and earlier than Labour – and reduce national debt year on year, when growth is positive. The IFS calculates that the Lib Dems' targets would require a spending cut of £8.6 billion between 2015/16 and 2018/19.

Both the targets chosen by Labour and the Lib Dems are, in theory at least, easier to hit. They should allow them to spend more, or have lower taxation levels, or both, than the Conservatives. But that would mean the debt would not be falling in absolute terms, and falling less quickly as a share of GDP (unless GDP suddenly rocketed up).

In 2010, the Green Party promised to halve the deficit by 2013, and say that they will be 'making a similar commitment this year in our election manifesto'. The Greens are opposed to austerity and the 'damaging cuts to public services'. They would fund their policies by raising taxes on wealthy corporations and individuals. They would also increase the minimum wage to a living wage.

UKIP's economic spokesperson, Patrick O'Flynn, has remarked that 'the brutal truth is that the government has comprehensively failed in its central mission to wipe out the deficit'. UKIP would make spending cuts by abolishing the Department of Energy and Climate Change (and all green subsidies) and the Department for Culture, Media and Sport. They also pledge to cut the foreign aid budget by £9 billion a year.

One of the most infuriating things about the economy is that when the parties sling accusations around, it is bloody difficult to follow what they're talking about, because the terms all get confused. Take two recent campaign posters from Labour and the Conservatives. Labour's poster says: 'The Tories want to cut spending on public services back to the levels of the 1930s'. That sounds pretty terrible – but is it true? Well, it certainly isn't true in absolute terms (which is what normal people tend to think in). The Conservatives' spending would still be higher than it was in 2007/8. However, Labour is using a figure for public spending as a proportion of GDP, which under the Conservatives would fall to 35.2 per cent by the end of the next Parliament. Data doesn't go back far enough to judge exactly how this figure compares to the 1930s. The OBR said, 'That would probably be the lowest in around eighty years.' This backs up Labour's claims, but ignores the fact that this proportion is roughly the same as it was in 1999, under Tony Blair's Labour government.

The Conservatives' poster was no better, frankly. The main image is of a road, representing the country's route to prosperity – which some are claiming is a German road! But never mind that, one of their claims is 'The Deficit

Halved'. Well, the borrowing in 2009/10 was £153 billion.
In 2013/14 it was £98 billion. Some quick maths will tell
you that is a reduction of just over a third. So where are the
Conservatives getting this 'halved' stat from? It's the same
trick as Labour used in their poster. They are talking about
deficit-to-GDP ratio. To be fair, it's true that that ratio has
been halved. But it's still misleading, because 'the deficit'
means the absolute amount (if it means anything) to normal
people, not a ratio which is mainly used by economists
and poster-makers trying to sound good.

Good luck with trying to follow the arguments over the
public purse – there are big differences between the parties'
approaches. Whoever's approach you like most – VOTE.

17. Drugs

Should all drugs be legalised?

'**D**rugs policy has been failing for decades.' Not my words, but the words of a junior politician in 2005. That politician is now our prime minister, David Cameron.

Cameron was a member of the Home Affairs Select Committee when it called for an international debate on the legislation of drugs. The *Independent* reported him as saying, 'Politicians attempt to appeal to the lowest common denominator by posturing with tough policies and calling for crackdown after crackdown.' Yet by 2012, in response to another Home Affairs Select Committee report, which suggested looking at decriminalisation, he said, 'I don't support decriminalisation. We have a policy that actually is working in Britain'. He and his government maintain that they will not change the drug laws, and that they have the right approach. Either he has changed his mind, based on new evidence, or he has succumbed to the pressure on politicians to look 'tough on drugs'. The very thing he was speaking about in 2005.

The illegal drug trade causes two big, distinct problems: firstly, it damages the health of the people who use the drugs and, secondly, it gives vast amounts of money (the drug trade was estimated to be worth $320 billion a year in 2005) to criminal gangs, who spread murder and corruption across the globe. In many cases, it also causes drug users to commit crime too. The War on Drugs, which has been waged for over forty years now, has tried to deal with these problems by going after the people who buy and sell drugs. Unfortunately, that hasn't worked as planned. However you look at the War on Drugs, it hasn't eliminated the problem. In a sense, it's failed on both counts; the gangs are still making money, and people are still taking drugs. Having said that, in the UK drug use has fallen and fewer young people admit to having tried drugs. Opponents of the current drug laws believe that to be due to the more responsible attitudes of young people and the police turning a blind eye, rather than the implementation of strict laws. In fact, a recent Home Office study that looked at eleven countries' drug policies concluded that 'looking across different countries, there is no apparent correlation between the "toughness" of a country's approach and the prevalence of adult drug use'.

After this report came out, towards the end of 2014, the Lib Dem MP Norman Baker said that its publication had been delayed by several months because the Conservatives did not 'like the independent conclusions' that challenged the 'lazy assumption' that harsher penalties are the answer. He went on to say that 'banging people up and increasing sentences does not stop drug use'. He resigned from his Home Office post shortly afterwards. The press office of the Home Office, the very government department that had authored the report which had concluded there was no obvious link between tougher sanctions and levels of drug use, released a familiar-sounding statement saying 'this government has absolutely no intention of decriminalising drugs. Our drugs strategy is working.' Given their confidence, it's hard to understand why they did the study at all ...

There are a number of alternatives to our drug laws and, usefully for the purpose of comparisons, many of these alternatives are currently being tried out in other countries. If you are interested in the idea of changing our drugs laws – and the evidence is many young voters are – there are lots of guinea pigs out there already. The two basic concepts are 'decriminalisation' and 'legalisation'. These sound very similar, but they aren't. Decriminalisation, as well as being a bloody mouthful, means that people possessing small amounts of drugs will not be arrested, or jailed. They may be given a fine (this is happening in Jamaica with cannabis), or made to attend rehab classes (this happens in Portugal). Campaigners say this approach would mean we wouldn't have to spend taxpayers' money on prosecuting and then imprisoning people who often seem more like victims than criminals. It would also free up police time and manpower to focus on more serious crime, drug-related and otherwise. Nick Clegg is a strong advocate of decriminalising drugs and believes that drug addiction needs to be seen as a health issue, not a criminal one. Supporters of this approach say the Portugal model is working fairly well – and the approach of treating addiction as a medical issue has meant less drug-related crime and disease. Although the level of drug use rose initially after decriminalisation, since then it has declined. However, the number of children in Portugal who have tried drugs since they were decriminalised has increased.

That mustn't be overlooked. It's also interesting that in 2012 the Czech Republic, which has very similar drug laws to Portugal, had the highest prevalence of cannabis use among young adults (15–34-year-olds) of thirty surveyed European countries.

To some, decriminalising feels like a bit of a cop-out. One problem is that while it might seem sensible and right to give casual drug users and addicts help and treatment rather than throwing them in jail, it doesn't tackle the problem of where the drugs are coming from. In Portugal, users may be getting treated better by the state but the cocaine they're using is still being produced by violent criminals in Colombia or wherever. That criminal monopoly will remain untouched, even if we do divert more money towards trying to bring down those gangs. In fact, simply decriminalising might actually work in the gangs' favour. They get to supply consumers who are no longer fearful of arrest.

Full legalisation would mean that drug users face no consequences – no fines, no compulsory help, nothing. But much more importantly, the supply of drugs would be legal. The growing, the shipping and the selling of drugs would become a legitimate business. Something that you'd imagine would appeal to governments about this is that as soon as a business is legitimate, it becomes taxable. Supporters of legislation argue that governments would stand to get a lot of tax revenue out of the drug trade and that some or all of that money could be invested in better health care for addicts. The money spent by law enforcement on trying to stop the illegal drugs trade would also be saved. The idea is that the violent drug gangs would be forced out of the marketplace, unable to compete. They argue that this is what happened after alcohol prohibition ended in America.

There is also the argument that it is better, if people are going to do drugs, for them to be doing drugs that are being quality-controlled, and supplied by reputable pharmaceutical companies and sold in dispensaries, for example. Those who disagree with this idea worry about the prospect of drugs being sold on the high street, and making the process – they argue – as casual as popping into Boots for an aspirin. However, campaigners argue that even selling drugs in Boots would be better than users buying drugs on the street, knowing nothing about the purity of the product, what it might be mixed with, how strong it is and so on. The unreliability of street drugs makes overdose and other health problems much more likely. Legalising drugs would sanitise the trade. Professor David Nutt, the government's former drug advisor, believes that the way to prevent harm is through education, saying, 'People have the right to know what they are taking.' In Amsterdam, where some drug use is legal, anyone can get their drugs tested to see if they are dangerous or impure. Anonymous testing is one way that a country without any relaxation of drug laws could protect users.

One problem that those who oppose changing the drug laws have with legalisation is that they believe it would normalise drugs and turn the state into 'drug dealers'. They point out that Colorado, where cannabis was decriminalised in 2014, has more cannabis shops than Starbucks cafes and that this sends the wrong signal to people. If legalisation normalises drug-taking, will that lead to a massive increase in drug use? Given that drug use is falling in the UK, would changing policy therefore be an irresponsible risk for the government to take? Does the government have a duty to protect its citizens or should we be allowed to make our own decisions? You'd assume that a big increase in the number of drug users would also see a big increase in the number of drug-related health problems, whether the drugs are pure or not, and this would put a further financial strain on the NHS. Which it hardly needs, as I've discussed in the NHS chapter.

Cocaine was legal until 1920 in the UK; cannabis was legal until 1928. Crucially, two drugs are still legal in this country — alcohol and tobacco. That complicates things even further. In various studies, most notably by Professor Nutt, alcohol and tobacco are found to be significantly more damaging to individuals and society as a whole than drugs like LSD, ecstasy and marijuana. In fact, Nutt believes that alcohol is more damaging to society than heroin. So supporters of changing the law argue — is there not a problem of inconsistency? Why persist with making a drug that is less harmful illegal, while allowing a more harmful one to be sold freely? If drugs are illegal on the basis that they are damaging the nation's health, then surely you have to make alcohol illegal. Excessive drinking is linked to 33,000 deaths a year. The annual cost to the NHS of drinking-related treatments is estimated at £3.5 billion. So why is virtually no one suggesting that we make alcohol illegal? Certainly prohibiting alcohol would mean the end of £10 billion a year in taxes ... And to be clear, MPs like a cheap drink — the alcohol in the bars at the Houses of Parliament is subsidised by the taxpayer (£2.90 a pint!). Which I can't say I'm that happy about.

So what we have is a situation where the public are warned of the dangers of drinking and smoking, and urged to do it 'responsibly'. I wonder if that wouldn't work with other drugs too: 'Snort Coke Responsibly'. Of course you might argue that two wrongs don't make a right — maybe alcohol and tobacco shouldn't be legal, but the impact on public health might be even worse if other drugs were legalised too. One idea, again a bit of a halfway house, would be to have a system of ranked regulation. Harmless drugs like caffeine sold over the counter to anyone; cannabis treated like alcohol and only sold to over 18s; heroin and cocaine only available on prescription to addicts. That could work.

America has been leading the War on Drugs for years, and it's interesting that several states have now legalised cannabis. Now they have, it's more likely that we might follow suit. Usefully, we have the luxury of waiting to see how things work out in those states. In Colorado, where marijuana has been sold over the counter to over 21s (like alcohol) since January 2014, there is no hard evidence of the effects of legalisation, mainly because it's not been in place long enough to do a comprehensive study. There are some anecdotal horror stories about kids in primary schools eating their grandparents' weed, but then overall crime is falling in Denver (the Colorado state capital). It depends who you talk to, and what side of the argument they're on. In time evidence will emerge, and the government would be well-advised to take notice of it. There is evidence that public opinion in the UK is shifting, so any government fear of alienating voters if they were to suggest a new approach could well be misplaced. A recent YouGov poll found that 71 per cent of the UK population think the War on Drugs has failed and 60 per cent would like to see a trial of the Portuguese model in some British cities.

David Cameron and the Conservatives are, so far, sticking to their tough approach to drugs. Ed Miliband seems to agree, saying that decriminalising drugs would send out the 'wrong message' to young people. He reprimanded one

of his Labour MPs for speaking out in favour of decriminalisation. However, there are rumblings within the party
that a change of direction might be wise. That hasn't happened yet, though. The Lib Dems want 'radical change' to
the UK drug laws. They want to stop sending people to jail
for personal drug use. The Lib Dems haven't said they
would decriminalise drugs – the police would still arrest
you and take you to court, but the punishment wouldn't be
prison. It may be fines, compulsory courses, or some kind
of community service. The Green Party wouldn't go that
far, but it would decriminalise cannabis and focus on tackling drug traffickers. Caroline Lucas, the Greens' only MP,
thinks that UK drug policy has been driven by a fear of the
tabloids. There is nothing on the UKIP website about a drug
policy, although Nigel Farage has tentatively voiced
approval of the Portuguese model, saying it 'does show us
that perhaps there is a better, more enlightened way to deal
with this'. UKIP would allow regular smoking back into
the pubs that wanted it.

If you think the War on Drugs is failing, or that it just needs
to be fought harder – VOTE.

18. Social Media

Will social media change politics?

Anyone who doubts the significance of social media in politics today should spare a thought for Emily Thornberry. Thornberry is a Labour MP who tweeted a picture of a house, during the Rochester by-election in November 2014, which had several England flags up and a white van outside. Her caption was simply 'Image from #rochester'. UKIP was likely to win the by-election, so was she suggesting that this was a typical UKIP voter? Was she implying anything negative about the flags? Crucially, only she knows the answers to those questions, but it nevertheless caused a huge outcry. The offending tweet was retweeted and spread at breakneck speed. Journalists, politicians and pretty much everyone else had a field day.

What the majority took from the tweet was that this MP, who lives in a nice expensive house in North London, was out of touch with and condescending towards a certain type of voter – the 'working man'. Not only that, but these are people that have traditionally voted Labour. In the end, it didn't really matter what she did or didn't mean. It only mattered that people were furious. The other parties seized the opportunity to occupy the moral high ground. UKIP, who went on to win the by-election, accused Thornberry of having 'sneered, and looked down her nose at a white van'. David Cameron said that her actions were 'completely appalling'. Presumably realising very quickly just how toxic this tweet was becoming to his party, Ed Miliband was apparently 'angrier than he had ever been', which is hopefully an exaggeration (or he might need to have a long, hard look at how he prioritises things). It was no surprise when Thornberry resigned from the shadow cabinet, saying that she apologised and had 'made a mistake'.

The point is: an MP lost her job over one, fairly innocuous tweet. There is a lesson in that. Social media's power is ever-growing, and politicians need to wise up and use it carefully. While Emily Thornberry's embarrassment should serve as a cautionary tale, politicians shouldn't be scared of social media, they should see it as an opportunity. Those who harness it in the right way stand to benefit hugely. It has the potential to provide direct engagement with us, the voters. Political discussion is happening online with or without the input of politicians. It makes sense that they should engage with social media to find out what their voters think about certain issues. They could then use these informal consultations to steer policy and decision-making. And perhaps more importantly, they could be responsive and engage with the public to help build their trust.

The old media model didn't allow that. What happened before was politicians told us what they were doing, and we listened. Political interaction was a one-way street. It felt like we had no means of giving feedback until a general election. Now we do have those means, and we can and should be involved in conversations about politics. Back in 2010, Nick Clegg spoke about how social media will allow politicians to 'connect with the next generation of voters'. That's absolutely right. Over half of British adults now regularly use social media, and of every hour we spend online, 13 minutes are spent on social media. That's more than on anything else, including checking the news. Twitter and Facebook provide a huge amount of political information and are becoming very important news sources, especially for young people. This means that they can be used to increase people's political knowledge and interest (I wish I could have fitted this book into 140 characters). If politicians are serious about engaging young people in **democracy**, this is where they should be focusing their attention.

Some clever people have argued that social media is great for sharing information and coordinating like-minded people, but that it won't force change itself. They believe that change still has to be achieved through action 'in the real world'. For example, when a hashtag trends on Twitter, what impact does that have? It raises awareness, certainly, but can it go any further than that? And what does it tell you about a debate or issue if one side of the argument is more popular on Twitter? At the moment, some would say that all it tells you is exactly that: it is more popular on Twitter. For now, Twitter users in the UK are not representative of the UK as a whole, especially in terms of age. That might change with time, as current users get older and retain their social media presence. Although Carl Miller of the **think tank** Demos states that 'Social media generally hates politicians and the mainstream business-as-usual political class.' In which case, it may never be representative.

A couple of interesting recent examples were the social
media presence of the two sides of the Scottish referendum campaign and the hashtag #CameronMustGo. During
the course of the referendum campaign, the Yes camp had
more followers on Twitter and more likes on Facebook than
the No camp (likes on Facebook in particular are believed
to indicate genuine support). In the months leading up to
the referendum, the top independence hashtag #VoteYes
got 1.1 million mentions on Twitter, nearly five times as
many mentions as the top union hashtag #BetterTogether
(224,000 mentions). And yet when it came to the vote itself,
the No campaign won, 55 per cent to 45 per cent. So the
picture painted by Twitter was very different to the one
unveiled at the ballot boxes. I suspect that what you see on
social media is a vocal, engaged minority. The undecided
and less-engaged majority remain silent. Either because
they're not on social media at all, or because they just
wouldn't post anything about their politics.

The #CameronMustGo hashtag trended for several
weeks – much longer than you would expect something
like that to last. In fact, it only stopped trending because of
the way trending topics are identified, which is not just to
do with number of mentions but also with how new it is.
Therefore if a hashtag continues to dominate in numbers
for a period of time, it will at some point no longer be new
enough to trend (Twitter apparently brought that in to prevent Justin Bieber from trending all day every day). The
#CameronMustGo hashtag was started by a Labour sup-
porter called Jon Swindon because he felt that the
mainstream media weren't providing enough of a dissent-
ing voice. It caught the imagination of Twitter users in a big
way. The hashtag accompanied a whole variety of complaints about Cameron, although they mainly focused on

the coalition government rather than him personally. A lot of the tweets contained facts about broken promises and ways in which the government is failing people. Critics pointed out that many of these 'facts' were incorrect, and that is fair, but the interesting thing about Twitter is that if you tell someone that what they've tweeted is wrong or inaccurate, they will usually take it down or modify it. Twitter has a kind of self-moderation.

I think the way to read these tweets is similar to how we read newspapers, in print or online. I always try to keep in mind that when I read certain papers, they will favour certain parties. For example, the *Telegraph* traditionally sympathises with the Conservatives, the *Guardian* is left wing, the *Mirror* is Labour-friendly, and so on. That inevitably means that what they report, and how they report it, will be influenced by their political agenda. For that reason, on Twitter I follow a range of politicians and journalists from different parties and papers – it can be a bit confusing at times, but I think it's good to get a sense of what they are all saying. And not saying.

What is exciting about the #CameronMustGo hashtag is that it has got lots of people talking about politics. It's provided a platform for people to vent frustration and anger, collectively. Social media campaigns like this are, in a way, uncharted territory so it raises a lot of questions, most of which we can't answer yet. Questions like: will this convert into anything meaningful? I think we can safely assume that Cameron isn't going to resign because of a hashtag. However, if some of that online fury is translated into votes in May then perhaps it is significant. I don't say this because I support the hashtag, but I genuinely hope that all of those people who got involved with it do go out and vote, because if they don't they will

have wasted their time. Of course, an even more perti-
nent question is whether these 1 million odd mentions are
simply giving visibility to a group of dissatisfied voters
that already existed, or is this something new? If it's just a
load of people who would never have voted for Cameron
anyway, that's less interesting. But if it's got new people
involved, people who hadn't thought about how they
were going to vote, or were undecided, then it might be
very powerful. Like I say, we just don't know at the
moment.

Italian politics has thrown up an example of social
media's influence. Beppe Grillo was a comedian with a
huge Twitter and Facebook following and who also wrote
the most popular blog in Italy (it's hard not to immediately
think of Russell Brand in the UK). Grillo used that following to build support for his anti-corruption Five Star
Movement, which ran in the 2013 Italian elections and won
25 per cent of the votes. He managed that without doing
mainstream media interviews and without any funding
from big business. Italy was ripe for this kind of campaign
because the Italian people were fed up with the politicians
of their Establishment. Maybe the UK is ready for something like that, too. Our anti-establishment vote seems to be
going to UKIP at the moment, but it is in almost every way
a traditional party. UKIP's party chairman, Steve Crowther,
said, 'I have no Facebook page, Twitter account or
Instagram thingy. It's lovely.' And his social media advice
to the party is 'just don't'. There may well be space for an
alternative voice, and Grillo has shown that social media
can provide the platform.

Another instance in which social media has been shown
to have a real world effect was in the 2010 US election.
Scientists from the University of California and Facebook

showed that a non-partisan 'get out the vote' message, showing users' pictures of friends who had voted, generated an additional 340,000 votes across the US. That is, in percentage terms, a tiny amount – but in some close-run states it could have affected results. There is no reason to think that a similar effect on voter turnout wouldn't be seen if, for example, a voting-related hashtag was trending on Twitter throughout the day on the 7th of May.

I've written before about how I think politicians should use social media, and how bad British politicians tend to be at it. Far too many of them use social media like old media – broadcasting information to us, without engaging afterwards. A Nottingham University study into the types of tweets that MPs were writing found that only 28.7 per cent were part of conversations – using the @ function. That is far too low. Social networks demand many-to-many interaction; social media is about talking and listening. The days of passive consumption are gone – that's not what people expect any more. Of course, the volume of correspondence that MPs get is overwhelming, and it's obviously not possible to respond to every tweet. But people should understand that.

I would not for one second say that being a politician on Twitter or Facebook is a walk in the park, because it isn't. For starters, the traditional barriers of authority and hierarchy haven't just been lowered – they are non-existent. And what that means is that anyone with a public profile knows that when they post a tweet or comment, the first however many replies will probably be abusive. A cursory glance at the responses to any of David Cameron's tweets will show you that. Politicians and their aides need, first of all, to develop a thick skin and, second of all, to work out how to moderate and manage responses, particularly those that are critical, off-topic or abusive. With abuse it's best to simply ignore it, but it's also vital to distinguish between trolling and a difference of opinions. Politicians should certainly not block or delete comments simply because someone disagrees with them.

The trickiest part of social media for UK politicians seems to be the human element; coming across as 'real people'. They need to lose a level of formality on social media. Carl Miller of Demos comments 'Twitter and Facebook really value independent voice, familiar intonation and personality.' So politicians have to show some personality. That also means striking a balance between posting about their public life and interests and their private ones. Authenticity is absolutely vital because when something is forced, other users spot it immediately.

Barack Obama is a master of this. All of his social media output fits with his public persona. We know that he's funny, so he can get away with being funny. We know that he's a family man, so he can get away with being a bit cutesy. Compare that to when David Cameron posted a picture of himself on the phone to Obama, with the caption 'I've been speaking to @barackobama about the situation in Ukraine'. This created a tidal wave of mockery across the internet, with everyone from Sir Patrick Stewart (speaking into a packet of wet wipes) to JME (speaking into a chip and pin machine) getting involved. Cameron's photo felt staged and it felt like he was showing off ('Guys, look at me, I'm chatting to Obama!'). And it served no purpose. If you say you've been speaking to someone, people do not need visual confirmation. They know what a person on the phone looks like.

Social media will become ever-more influential on politics. It allows connection in a way that just wasn't possible

ten years ago. The current parties need to embrace it –
because emerging parties and candidates will.

If you think of a good hashtag to show that you've voted, let
me know. And then VOTE.

19. The EU

Should we leave the EU?

The European Union (EU) is a union (hence the name) of twenty-eight European (hence the name) countries, each of which has to pay money to be a member (although some get more out than they put in). It's basically a club, and the 'membership fees' have been rising. The answer to the question 'How much do we pay?' depends on who you ask – Nigel Farage says £55 million a day, or about £20 billion a year, while Nick Clegg claims it's more like half of that. Fullfact.org did a calculation to show that the net contribution in 2012 was £33 million a day, or £12 billion for the year. This takes into account what we get back from the EU (which was about £8 billion, for various things). The ONS says that the UK's net contribution was £8.5 billion in 2012, and £11.3 billion in 2013. Some would say any of those figures are quite steep. In October 2014, the UK was told to pay another £1.7 billion to the EU, because its economy has done better than expected in the last four years. This backdated payment caused widespread outrage, although defenders of the EU argued that if our economy had done less well than expected, we would have got money back from the EU.

The idea of the union is that collectively the nations are stronger. Within the EU there is a 'single market', which means there are, in theory at least, no barriers to trade with any of the member states. It's an economic union whereby we buy and sell each other's stuff. Effectively, each country can stick to what it's good at, and sell it to all the other members, and then buy in everything else. The ultimate aim is that goods, money, services and people can all move around more freely and we are all richer as a result. The countries are all still independent, but they have handed over power to the EU in certain areas. This is something that makes Eurosceptics – those who want us to leave or seriously reform the EU – unhappy. They argue that the EU has become too powerful.

There are various parts of the EU, carrying out various functions. The European Council (made up of the head of state or head of government from each country – so the prime minister, in our case) decides on the 'general direction' of the EU. The European Commission (with a representative from each member state) proposes EU laws and checks that they're being obeyed. The Council of Ministers (made up of one government minister from each member state, but changes according to what is being discussed) considers and approves the European Commission's proposals. The European Parliament, which is made up of 751 members, of which 73 are from the UK, also considers proposed laws. In this parliament, UKIP have 23 Members of the European Parliament (MEPs), ahead of Labour and the Conservatives, who have 18 each. Together, with the European Court of Justice, the European Bank and the Court of Auditors, these bodies run the EU.

The extent of EU influence over UK laws and regulations is a matter of debate. No one agrees as to how far it reaches. It would obviously be useful to know exactly what proportion of our laws are being decided in Brussels (the unofficial 'capital' of the EU). The House of Commons Library looked into this and said that between 1997 and 2009 it is 'possible to justify any measure between 15 per cent and 50 per cent or thereabouts, depending on the approach'. During a televised debate on the subject, Nick Clegg said that 7 per cent of UK legislation is based on EU law. Nigel Farage said that the figure is actually 75 per cent. They can't both be right.

The reason for such a huge discrepancy – aside from the fact that Clegg and Farage were trying to make very different points – is that there are lots of different types of legislation. If you want to come up with a lower estimate, only include some of those types. If you want a higher estimate, include all of them. Often, the EU's influence on a law is indirect, so you can argue it either way. Also, some regulations made in the EU apply to the UK but are essentially irrelevant to us – for example, regulations relating to olive growing. We don't grow many olives (yet!). UKIP would argue that whatever the actual number of laws set by the EU, it is too high.

One of the big debates in the lead-up to this general election is whether the UK should stay in the EU, or get out. The term you'll read in the papers for this is 'Brexit', the British exit from the EU. It's hard to say whether the benefits of EU membership outweigh the costs. Both sides make compelling arguments. As it stands, we are signed up to various agreements on various things, such as fishing regulations, health and safety, agricultural policy, etc. etc. If we leave the EU, we would be taking back control of all of

these things, making our own rules and setting up new
agreements. No EU laws would take precedence over UK
laws. UKIP is adamant that we have to leave the EU,
because it doesn't think reform is realistic, and some members of the Conservative party agree. I'll look at this
reasoning first.

Eurosceptics say that the considerable amount of money
we'd save from not paying our EU membership could be
reinvested into our own UK priorities. They say that the
UK would also be able to buy things from outside of the EU
more cheaply than we currently do – for example, food
imported from outside the EU would be cheaper. There is a
thing called the Common Agricultural Policy, which means
that the EU pays money – taken out of its membership
fees – to farmers directly and towards rural development. It
is the most expensive part of the EU budget. UKIP says that
it would continue to subsidise British farmers with some of
the money saved on membership.

Eurosceptics believe that we can govern ourselves better
than a committee of representatives from twenty-seven
other countries can. Nigel Farage says that it is 'our
birthright' to do so. People who want to leave the EU point
out that if the UK strongly disagrees with a law that is about
to be passed by the EU, it has no power to overrule that law.
They believe that is unfair and wrong. UKIP says that it
would review 'all legislation and regulations from the EU,
and remove those which hamper British prosperity and
competitiveness'. Another point they make is that taking
back power from Europe will allow us, the voters, to recon-
nect with our **democracy**. Farage has warned that if we
don't leave the EU, things might get ugly. During the debate
over the EU with Nick Clegg, he said: 'If you take away
from people their ability, through the ballot box, to change

their futures, because you've given away control to others, people tend to resort to unpleasant means.'

Much like the number of laws coming from the EU, no one can quite agree on the financial implications of leaving. We know that our exports to the EU in 2013 were worth £151 billion. Our imports – the stuff we bought from Europe – were worth £218 billion. So we buy more than we sell, which makes us a net importer. A study suggested that in 2011, 4.2 million UK jobs were directly or indirectly related to EU exports. The total income from those jobs was around £211 billion, or £3,500 per person in the UK. Membership of the EU gives us free access to 500 million consumers – that's a lot of people to sell to. UKIP says that if we leave the EU it's not as if we're suddenly going to stop trading with those countries, so we won't lose out. It says that because we buy a lot from EU countries (more than we sell to them) it will be in their interests to continue doing business with us. UKIP says that it would absolutely still want to trade and cooperate with Europe, and would try to set up our own **free trade agreements**.

Farage points out that Switzerland, Norway and Iceland, none of which are EU members, have managed to do that and still trade with Europe. He thinks that the argument of the pro-EU camp, that we would be unable to negotiate favourable free trade agreements with European and non-European countries, is defeatist and suggests a lack of faith in Britain. He also argues that having to conform to another country's trading standards (which you have no influence over) when you sell to them is not a problem – when a business sells to a new territory, it simply adapts accordingly. Eurosceptics also believe that we would be freer to negotiate trade deals outside of the EU. Iceland is a small country which has its own free trade agreement with

China, one of the world's largest economic powers. UKIP would want to use the UK's membership of the World Trade Organisation to arrange free trade agreements with fast-growing export markets like China, Singapore, Brazil, Russia and India.

Eurosceptics say that the amount of '**red tape**' and regulation imposed by the EU makes things extremely expensive for smaller businesses here in the UK. They argue that leaving the EU would actually free those business up and create more jobs. One study from a Eurosceptic thinktank concluded that one million jobs would be created by leaving.

Another concern raised by those who are pro-EU is that the UK would be a much less attractive proposition for investors. But research company Capital Economics quoted a survey in 2013 that showed that over 65 per cent of non-European investors would actually find it a more attractive place to do business if the UK was out of the EU.

UKIP has also focused on freedom of movement. In the Immigration chapter, I explained which contributing parts of net migration we have control over – currently, only non-EU immigration. That's because one of the fundamental principles of the modern EU is freedom of movement for its citizens. David Cameron wants to try and negotiate a compromise, so that the UK can exert some control over the level and type of EU immigration. That may prove tricky. UKIP argues the only way we can guarantee full control over our border is by exiting the EU.

I've talked in more detail about this in the Immigration chapter, but to summarise – UKIP would argue that when we have unemployment and pressure on public services like the NHS, which we do, we can't afford to have mass uncontrolled immigration, because we need to focus first on getting unemployed UK citizens access to those services, and into work. UKIP also says that immigration has squeezed wages for working-class people. The UK would save some money on welfare and benefits if EU immigration was significantly reduced. At times it feels like leaving the EU and controlling immigration levels are one and the same thing but, while immigration is part of the EU question, it is not the whole story by any means.

Another reason that UKIP wants us to leave the EU is so that the UK can withdraw its financial support for renewable energies and escape the carbon emission targets set by the EU (as well as repealing our own Climate Change Act). They think those measures are misguided, reasoning that the extra cost on electricity bills, caused by green subsidies, is damaging to business, and that is why many industries have left the UK. Farage says that 40 per cent of the cost of running an average factory goes on energy bills. He also notes that India and China are expanding economies using a lot of coal power, and the US is **fracking** to release shale gas, which is reducing their energy bills. UKIP believes we should be fracking in the UK to reduce our energy bills too.

So that's the case for leaving the EU. As you can imagine, pro-EU parties like the Lib Dems and Labour see it very differently. They argue that we do a lot of trade with the EU, so why risk jeopardising any of that, or any of those jobs, by leaving? They say that the safer thing to do is stay, and know that we can maintain that level of trade. They also argue that if we did manage to leave and still managed to maintain that level of trade with the EU, we would then still be subject to the EU's trade legislation, and also export tariffs (making our goods more expensive for the EU buyers). International car companies like Nissan that have set up in the UK with a view to exporting to the EU might well think twice about staying here. So basically, we'd be playing by the same rules, but would no longer get a say in setting those rules. There will be no one at the negotiating table to make sure that our interests are being protected. David Cameron put it like this: 'If we weren't in there helping write the rules they would be written without us . . . and we wouldn't like the outcome.' That is what they would argue happens to Norway and Switzerland – they have no power over the legislation that affects their trade with the EU. Not only that, but they still have to pay money to some EU programmes and grants – basically the price of doing business with the EU. Norway, for example, paid €400 million to the EU in 2007.

Most of the parties that believe we should stay in the EU also believe that the EU needs to be reformed. They argue that we can only reform it from within. David Cameron is committed to trying to renegotiate the terms of Britain's membership. He wants deregulation (which basically means getting rid of expensive red tape) to address the 'pointless interference, rules and regulations that stifle growth, not unleash it'. He also wants some powers to be returned from Brussels to the UK and other member states, and a degree of control over EU immigration. Eurosceptics say that attempting to reform the EU is pointless, because it just won't happen. So far David Cameron has made a bit of progress – he managed to cut the EU budget, and overruled (vetoed) a treaty.

People who want us to stay in the EU also argue that as part of the EU, we are part of a big trading bloc. The EU accounts for about 20 per cent of global **GDP**, which means it gets taken seriously. They argue that if we go it alone, our global influence would almost certainly decline. We might find ourselves on the fringes when it comes to sorting out trade agreements, and we'll have much less of a say over the big transnational issues like security and the environment. There is a funny quote from the *Global Times*, a Chinese government-controlled newspaper, about the perception of the UK: 'The Cameron administration should acknowledge that the UK is not a big power in the eyes of the Chinese. It is just an old European country apt for travel and study.' Thanks for that, guys.

Those who are pro-EU also say that being a member has helped to make the UK one of the leading locations for overseas investment, because of our direct access to a market of 500 million people, and the whole EU economy. Part of the attraction for multinational firms to set up in the UK is that our EU status allows them to trade freely with all of the member states. That's a very appealing prospect. They fear that if we pull out, we may be less attractive to those firms; if it's a straight choice between, say, setting up in the UK that doesn't have such direct access to the EU, and France, which does, then we might end up losing out. They worry that millions of jobs might be lost if global manufacturers decide to move to EU countries where labour is also cheaper. That may especially apply to our car industry (which is predominantly foreign-owned) and aerospace engineering.

The Confederation of British Industry surveyed its members in 2013 and found overwhelming support for Britain to stay in the EU among both big and small businesses: 78 per cent wanted to stay versus only 10 per cent wanting to quit. Three-quarters thought leaving would have a negative impact on foreign investment in the UK. The pro-EU parties would say that the Eurosceptic argument that we need to focus on building trade agreements outside of the

EU is right – but that it's not an either/or situation. They think we can stay in the EU and also negotiate agreements outside of it. That is currently happening with the **Transatlantic Trade and Investment Partnership** (TTIP) deal, which is being negotiated between the EU and the US. I'll talk more about that shortly.

Another pro-EU argument is that we live in a global society, which has global problems. Problems that cross borders, like terrorism, climate change and criminal activity. They say that we need to cooperate with other countries to tackle these problems, not isolate ourselves by leaving the EU. The European Court of Human Rights and Interpol (which facilitates international police cooperation) are outside of the EU, though, so we could still be involved with them if we left. There are also many British citizens (in 2011, The Migration Observatory calculated just over one million) living outside of the UK in the EU. What would happen to these citizens if we withdrew from the EU? The rights of these citizens to work and live (and claim benefits) in the EU would depend on what sort of deal the UK was able to strike when it left. Pro-EU commentators think it's likely that it would be much harder for UK citizens to go and work in the EU, which means our freedoms would be diminished. A lot of workers' rights are protected by EU law. Things like the forty-eight hour working week, four weeks' paid holiday and the anti-discrimination law all exist because of the EU. If we left the EU, any new UK-specific workers' rights would be entirely dependent on the government at the time.

Because of its relevance to international trade, it's worth mentioning the TTIP negotiations that I touched upon above and in the NHS chapter. The idea is that the TTIP deal will make trade between the US and the EU much easier and cheaper. The UK government claims it could bring £10 billion a year into the UK economy and that American goods like cars and clothes would be cheaper for consumers. They also say it would be better going the other way, too – UK businesses will find it easier to export to the US. One of the aims of the deal is to bring in common standards for products, so businesses won't have to do different, and expensive, sets of tests to sell to different places. Currently, the US and EU regulators have different standards on things like safety testing for medicines and cars.

There is significant opposition to TTIP, chiefly because of something called 'investor-state dispute settlements' (ISDSs). These are being discussed, and would potentially allow companies to sue foreign governments if they feel that they have been unfairly treated. Opponents of TTIP say that this would affect our government's ability to do what is right for its citizens. For example, if the government decided to introduce a new health regulation that meant a product was no longer legal in the UK, the manufacturer of the product could sue the government for loss of revenue. Many people are especially worried about this happening to the NHS, although the government has made assurances that the NHS will not be threatened. Environmental campaigner George Monbiot calls TTIP a 'monstrous assault on democracy'. He and others believe that ISDSs would effectively give large corporations the power to trample over democratic decision-making, because the government would be scared of getting sued.

Another concern about TTIP is that it may lower our food standards, because in the US they have less strict regulations on the use of pesticides and genetically modified (GM) crops. The US may end up selling cheaper products with poorer standards to the EU. In the cosmetics industry,

Europe also has stricter safety regulations – a substance
has to be proved safe before it can be used. In the US, any
substance can be used until proven to be unsafe.

David Cameron is firmly behind TTIP, saying it will provide 'two million extra jobs, more choice and lower prices
in our shops'. Labour is also in favour of TTIP although, as
discussed in the NHS chapter, it would ensure that the
NHS is exempt. The same is true of the Lib Dems. UKIP of
course wants the UK out of the EU, so would want any
trade deal with the US to be negotiated solely by the UK.
However, UKIP has, along with Labour and the Lib Dems,
said it will fight to keep the NHS out of any TTIP deal. The
Green Party is the only party totally opposed to TTIP.
Natalie Bennett says, 'Chicken carcasses washed in bleach,
hormone-stuffed beef and open season on pollution are not
things we want to import from the US.'

The Conservatives have traditionally been split on the
EU, and remain so today. David Cameron wants to stay in
and improve the terms of the UK's membership. He has
promised a public referendum by 2017 on EU membership,
by which time he hopes to have successfully reformed the
EU. Ed Miliband has said that there is an 'overwhelming
economic case' for EU membership, and Labour would
only hold a referendum if there was a proposal for more
powers to be transferred to the EU. Like Cameron, Miliband
believes that reforms need to happen in the EU. The Lib
Dems have a similar position to Labour on the subject –
Nick Clegg is a long-term advocate of the EU, but wants to
reform it. UKIP would call an immediate referendum to
allow the British public to decide whether they wanted to
stay in the EU or get out. The Green Party would stay in the
EU but believes that the 'present EU structures are fundamentally flawed', so would look to reform it quite

considerably. Caroline Lucas, the Greens' former leader, has come out in favour of a referendum and said that the EU needs to 'urgently change direction, away from an obsessive focus on competition and free trade, and towards placing genuine cooperation and environmental sustainability at its heart'.

If you want in or out, or just want to make sure you get your say – VOTE.

20. Inequality

Are we living in a fair society?

I think we need to work out what is meant by a 'fair society'. Do we mean a society where the wealth is shared out equally? Do we mean a society where everyone has equal opportunities to succeed? Do we mean both? Maybe it doesn't matter because neither is true of the UK or, arguably, anywhere in the world. There is global wealth inequality and global opportunity inequality. The numbers in the UK are pretty stark. According to the Equality Trust, the 100 wealthiest people have as much money as the poorest 18 million.

You might have thought that the financial crisis of 2008 would have hit the people at the top mainly, the people most likely to have money invested in things like shares, but this hasn't been the case. In 2007, the richest 10 per cent controlled 52 per cent of the nation's wealth. Now they control 54 per cent. Oxfam's head of inequality, Emma Seery, says, 'economic recovery following the financial crisis has been skewed in favour of the wealthiest'. Britain is the only leading economy in the world that has seen inequality increase this century. I could keep listing statistics like that all day, but you probably get the picture. The UK has serious inequality. A recent ComRes poll found that for 20 per cent of voters, 'reducing inequality' is their top priority. That puts it fourth behind the NHS, immigration and **cost of living**.

Not everyone thinks inequality is a bad thing though. Boris Johnson, the Conservative Mayor of London, gave a speech in which he described greed as a 'valuable spur to economic activity'. Some economists will agree, saying that in developed countries high levels of inequality tend to go hand in hand with stronger economic growth. It's certainly true that global wealth – all of the money in the world – has doubled since 2000. So their point is if there's more money to go round in general, then the fact that the people at the top are getting even richer isn't a problem. There is, they argue, a 'trickle down' effect that means that the people at the bottom will also get more money, just not as much more. But that can still be enough to pull them out of poverty. There is a difference between worrying about people living in poverty and 'hammering the rich'. According to a YouGov poll last year, 56 per cent of the British public would prefer to see more equality even if the total amount of wealth was reduced. But you can imagine a situation in which the whole economy is suffering – where the poor people are becoming a bit poorer and the rich people are becoming a lot poorer. Technically, you could view inequality as having been reduced here, but its reduction would have benefited no one. When you look at it like this, then, it is not necessarily inequality that is the enemy. If there was evidence of a situation in which the rich got richer and inequality rose, but in which at the same time poverty fell, then perhaps inequality could be looked at as a good thing.

If we look at the global situation, it seems pretty positive. In 1990, 36 per cent of the world's population were living in extreme poverty. By 2011, that had reduced to 15 per cent. In rapidly developing economies like India and China, poverty rates are falling rapidly. Fans of **capitalism** would point to this as evidence that the free market is actually reducing worldwide inequality.

In June 2014, David Cameron claimed that 'inequality [in the UK] is at its lowest since 1986'. Using an Office for National Statistics measure of income inequality, that was true in 2011/12. However, it had risen again in 2012/13, and the Institute for Fiscal Studies expects it to keep rising into 2015/16. The overall level of poverty in the UK has remained broadly unchanged in recent years, although the breakdown of those people in poverty has changed. The poverty rate among pensioners is at an all-time low, while poverty among working-age adults with no children is as high as it's ever been. Also, because real-term wages have been falling, the poverty line (which is set at 60 per cent of the average wage) has also fallen. So someone who was classified as in poverty in 2010, say, may be in exactly the same position now, but no longer classified as being in poverty.

As discussed in the Jobs and the Economy chapter, economic growth is not necessarily being felt by the people on the lowest incomes. Many are feeling left behind as the economy has started to grow again but their income hasn't. There are different types of inequality. That disparity in pay is income inequality. If you just compare simple wages, the inequality is huge. It might be more reasonable to

compare 'final income' though – that takes into account
benefits received, and taxes paid, and so on. Inequality by
that measure is much less. There is also consumption to
look at. Widespread access to affordable consumer goods is
unprecedented now, which you could say represents a high
degree of equality.

The third type of inequality is in wealth: although
income from working is the main way that most people get
money, rich people are also more likely to have wealth in
the form of 'capital'. Capital is held in assets – things that
you own that have value, things like houses, shares in companies, savings and so on. Economist Thomas Piketty,
author of the hugely successful *Capital in the Twenty-First
Century*, states that capital grows more quickly than
income. So basically, if you're lucky enough to own a house
(especially in London), it will probably earn more money
than you do from working. That means it is incredibly hard
for poor people to bridge the gap because the gap is widen-
ing more quickly than they can earn money to close it.

Bill Gates, the Microsoft billionaire, has criticised
Piketty's analysis, saying that he hasn't mentioned any of
the factors that reduce inequality. Gates is talking about
things like the spending habits of the rich – when they buy
a fantastically expensive car, say, it's taxed and they are
putting money back into the system – and philanthropy.
The rich do give a lot of money away. And taxes obviously
redistribute wealth. Gates also points out that the majority
of individuals on the *Forbes* 400 list (a list of the richest
people in America) are 'self-made'. That's true globally, too.
Of all the billionaires in the world, only 13 per cent inherited their money, and 21 per cent are adding to existing
fortunes. The rest have presumably come from more
modest backgrounds.

That should be quite inspiring – the thought that if you work hard, you might rise up and earn millions one day. On that basis, Boris Johnson thinks that inequality is essential to create 'the spirit of envy'. That's fine, but unfortunately in the UK people at the bottom are getting stuck at the bottom, so whether they are looking up and enviously thinking 'I want some of that money' or not is irrelevant. Duncan Exley of the Equality Trust **think tank** says, 'We have a situation where jobs are created but they are entry-level jobs that aren't going to go anywhere.' There isn't enough career progression. This is having a devastating effect on **social mobility**. People in the UK are finding it increasingly difficult to climb up the income ladder. Presumably, as a country we are missing out on a lot of potential because of that.

A person's background has a huge effect in the UK too, and it's not like that everywhere. For example, a child from a poor family in Denmark is three times more likely to do better than her parents than an equivalent child in the UK. That's another type of social mobility – the opportunity to rise up above your background. In the UK, a child of a professional or managerial dad is twenty times more likely to end up in a high-status job than the child of a working-class dad. The Heritage Foundation believes that a two-caste system is forming in the US: in one caste, already rich children are raised by university-educated parents. In the other, poor children are raised by lone parents with only basic qualifications. The playing field doesn't appear to be level.

Even if you think that you personally aren't being affected by the inequality in this country, because you were lucky and born into a relatively well-off family, or have managed to get a good job – you probably are being affected. The Equality Trust did a study to show how much the gulf between the rich and poor is costing the UK economy. It's £39 billion – £39 billion! That's because – they argue – inequality is causing lower healthy life expectancies (which costs the NHS a lot of money), poorer mental health (again, the NHS bears the brunt) and higher crime levels (increasing prison costs). Reducing inequality, by adjusting income levels and the distribution of wealth, would hopefully create a better, healthier society.

One other effect of inequality that is especially relevant to the theme of this book – get out and vote – is the control it gives the rich over how our country is run. The **Occupy movement** protests against what they see as the wealthiest 1 per cent controlling the other 99 per cent through the power of their wealth. There's an old saying, 'money is power'. Many on the left and right argue that anything that challenges what the elite want can be beaten down or discredited or ignored because the elite have the money, status and contacts to lobby against those challenges. Lobbying is the practice of trying to influence the opinions of MPs and members of the **House of Lords**. Lobbyists are individuals or organisations who are paid by, for example, big businesses to affect the decisions of government. There are lots of ways in which they attempt to do that, including manipulation of the press; trying to steer any given debate onto ground that suits them; funding seemingly independent think tanks which will produce favourable reports; and hinting at future employment opportunities for MPs. This is often done out of public view. Lobbying works best when no one sees it operating. It seems reasonable that the more money an individual or corporation has, the better the lobbying they'll be able to finance. And that's why some argue the rich (and that might include everyone from banks to big renewable energy companies) end up having a much bigger say in our **democracy**. A way of changing this would be to limit the scale of political donations from private companies. That might make our democracy seem a bit fairer. In the meantime, one thing that we must do is exert our influence, by voting. If we vote, at least we get the people that we want in Parliament. And they won't all be susceptible to the invisible hand of lobbyists.

So what can we do to reduce inequality? Or rather, what could the government and politicians be doing? The most common solution is to redistribute some wealth – not all of it, by any means – so that the poorest are less poor, but the overall economy doesn't suffer. That sounds straightforward enough but it's a big ask and there isn't a consensus on how it should be done. But it does seem that there are a number of measures that could be taken. The first is to look at our taxation system. There is a common and entirely reasonable belief that the rich pay more tax than the poor. That just seems right, doesn't it? And it's true in absolute terms (in the UK the top three thousand pay more income tax than the nine million lowest paid) – but not in relative terms. In fact, when taking into account all taxes, the poorest 10 per cent of households pay 43 per cent of their income in taxes, while the richest pay 35 per cent. That's because while taxes like income tax and national insurance are 'progressive' (they go up as you earn more), indirect taxes on consumers like VAT, sales tax and duties on things like fuel and alcohol are not. They are fixed, so it doesn't matter how much you earn, you will pay the same amount of tax. That means poorer people will effectively be hit harder.

Council tax is bizarrely structured too, so that according to the Equality Trust the bottom 10 per cent of households will pay 'more than four times as much of their income in council tax as the top 10 per cent'. That's all happening while billions of pounds of tax money is being lost through tax avoidance and evasion by the wealthy. The OECD (Organisation for Economic Co-operation and Development) recommends that governments everywhere make sure that the rich are paying their 'fair share' of tax. That can be achieved by raising some tax rates for high earners and clamping down on tax avoidance schemes and loopholes. However, in a different report the OECD also warns that redistribution (higher taxes for the rich, more benefits for the poor, higher wages for the poor) can be counter-productive for economic growth. It's a balancing act. The government also needs to make sure that when it allocates benefits, they are going to the right people.

Some commentators are starting to argue that because the largest inequality is found in 'wealth', that's where any tax increases should be focused. So rather than increasing income tax, taxes on property and consumption should be hiked for the rich. This could be achieved by revamping the council tax system, and taxing the purchases of luxury goods. The additional tax revenue could then be used to reduce the income tax of the poorest individuals.

Inheritance is another thorny problem for those worried about inequality. It's understandable that some people are opposed to the idea of taxing the wealth of the dead. They want to be able to pass on what they've amassed to their children. David Cameron has said that he will raise the **inheritance tax** threshold from £325,000 to £1 million, because he believes in 'people being able to pass things down the generations. I think you build a stronger society.' Piketty argues that instead you could say that money gained, whether from income or the luck of being born into a wealthy family, should be taxed the same. Why not just get rid of inheritance tax altogether and just treat any lump sum from an inheritance like regular income – and tax it as such? Piketty believes that would keep a check on inequality. People would, as they do now, try and get round this by 'gifting' the money or assets before they die, but we could introduce legislation to prevent this. Opponents of this concept would say it's unfair, because the money is getting 'double taxed' – once when the person is alive, and once when the person dies. That's true, but it is different people who are being taxed. No single person is getting taxed twice. And if this can help redistribute wealth, then maybe it is worth it.

Clearly wages are a big issue here too. As discussed in the Jobs and the Economy chapter, real wages have been falling for a long time, while profits for shareholders and pay for executives have been going up. For those worried about inequality, something has to be done about that. There are a few options, from raising the minimum wage to making companies publish details of their highest and lowest salaries (in the hope they will be shamed into paying more to the lowest). The left-of-centre think tank New Economic Foundation (NEF) has published a report that details several ways to bring down inequality. As well as having fairer taxes and reducing the wage gap within companies, they also recommend focusing on creating good quality jobs right across the UK, because currently the jobs market is skewed too heavily towards London and the South-East. The NEF also identifies the problem of social mobility within work – it thinks that we need to invest much more in skills and training to make sure that people can rise up and get better jobs, rather than being marooned at the bottom with no way out.

The Labour Party says it is very keen to try and address

inequality. According to the IFS, last time Labour was in government (1997–2010) there was a small increase in income inequality. Ed Miliband said in 2012, 'I will never accept an economy where the gap between rich and poor just grows wider and wider.' Labour is adamant that inequality is bad for the rich as well as for the poor. Miliband would bring back the 50p tax rate on income over £150,000 (the highest rate is currently 45p). He would introduce the 'mansion tax' on properties worth over £2 million. And he would have a repeat of Labour's tax on bankers' bonuses, which would be used to fund its Jobs Guarantee for young people who've been out of work for a year.

The Conservatives are taking a markedly different approach. They are capping benefits, cutting some benefits for young people and making cuts to public services. David Cameron has spoken about cutting £25 billion from public spending in the first two years of a new government and says they'll meet that cost with no tax increases. For the Conservatives, the priority is securing a strong economy with good growth that should help create jobs, improve wages and lift people out of poverty. Chancellor George Osborne had been trying to appeal against an EU ruling on a cap for bankers' bonuses, although he dropped this challenge in November 2014. His reasoning for wanting to block it was that if you put a cap on bankers' bonuses, then they will just pay themselves more as a salary.

The Lib Dems are closer to Labour on this issue, in that they want to build a 'fairer society'. They would introduce a mansion tax and increase the income tax allowance, which would help everyone, but especially poorer people. Like the Lib Dems, UKIP would raise the income tax allowance. But it would also cut the top rate of tax to 40 per cent, which means the richest are paying less tax. And it would get rid of inheritance tax entirely. UKIP would introduce a benefits cap, too. It's surprising that most of their policies in this area seem to favour the wealthy, given that 80 per cent of UKIP supporters apparently think the gap between rich and poor should be reduced.

The Green Party is fully opposed to inequality. It plans to tax the richest 1 per cent on their assets – which the Greens believe would affect about 300,000 people worth in excess of £3 million each. They would introduce a 'living wage', which would hopefully reduce the pay gap between the top and the bottom, and they'd cap bankers' bonuses.

If you care about where all the money goes – VOTE.

21. Celebrity Involvement in Politics

Is Russell Brand a good thing or a bad thing?

Celebrities are arguably more prominent in society now than they have ever been, and Russell Brand is one of many who have got involved with politics and campaigns. Brand is everywhere at the moment. He has a huge audience on YouTube, his appearances on *Question Time* and *Newsnight* divide people, and it seems that everyone is talking about him. Nick Robinson, the BBC's political editor, allegedly called him a 'sanctimonious twat' after Brand refused to be interviewed for a radio show about **democracy**.

The influence of celebrities on politics has been studied a number of times. One such study in the US looked at Jennifer Aniston's support of the Democrats and Peyton Manning's (a famous American footballer, who I've never heard of) support of the Republicans. It found that when people dislike a celebrity and learn that that celebrity has supported a party financially, they then like the party less. The opposite is also true, but apparently to a lesser extent – if people like a celebrity who is supporting a party, they may feel slightly more positive towards the party. It also seems that if people dislike a party already and a celebrity comes out in support of that party, people will then like the celebrity less. All quite obvious really and suggests that, in general, celebrities aligning themselves with parties in public is a big risk for both the parties and the celebrities. In 1996, when Geri Halliwell described Margaret Thatcher as 'the first Spice Girl', I don't think it did either of them any favours. When Thatcher died, Halliwell tweeted in praise of her and then quickly deleted the tweet.

Single-issue campaigns are much easier and safer for celebrities to get involved with, because they can be separate from party politics. Celebrity involvement can push an issue onto, or higher up, the agenda of politicians and the public. They have the ability to spread a message far and wide, help raise a lot of money and get media attention for a cause. That's exactly what Russell Brand is trying to do, although he isn't just championing a single cause. He is supporting several different causes, and also bringing attention to a number of wider problems that he believes exist in our democracy. He is absolutely not supporting a political party, or politicians. On the contrary, he is pretty dismissive of all of them, saying 'I regard politicians as frauds and liars.' Which is fairly unequivocal.

But if Brand is dismissive of politicians, the public seems pretty dismissive of him. In a YouGov poll in late 2014, only 13 per cent of the British public thought that Brand was making a 'positive contribution to politics', while 46 per cent thought that he was making a 'negative contribution to politics'. Why is that? And are they right?

Let's have a look at Brand's 'contribution to politics' in this country. He got behind an existing campaign being run by residents of the New Era estate in East London, who were facing eviction as the new owners – US investors Westbrook Partners – planned to more than double their rents. The organisers and Brand protested outside the UK offices of Westbrook, and took a petition to 10 Downing Street. That petition was signed by 300,000 people and I'm sure many of those signatories were people who were directed to the cause by Brand. At the time of writing, the US investors have apparently bowed to pressure and are about to sell the estate to a social-housing provider, Dolphin Square Charitable Foundation, so the residents should be able to afford to stay in their homes. Now, Brand wasn't running the campaign, but there can be no question that his involvement brought attention to the case. Some commentators have been worried about the effect that a campaign like this will have on business confidence, and whether it will dent housing firms' eagerness to invest, but whatever you think about it, for the residents it was undoubtedly a positive outcome. Protest organiser Lindsey Garrett said Brand 'gave us a bigger voice. And rather than taking over, he gave us a much bigger audience to speak to.'

That's just one example of Brand's political activity. What is arguably more important to me, though, is that he is triggering conversation and interest around other areas of politics. He is highlighting what he sees as big problems: the huge inequalities in our society, media monopolies, the problems of sustainable food production, and much more. In his book *Revolution*, Brand wrote about debt cancellation. The cancellation of personal debt, through debt amnesties, is something that happened routinely in the past – the first ever legal contract, discovered in modern-day Iraq and dating back 4,400 years, was for the cancellation of debt. It's an idea that Brand got from David Graeber, an eminent anthropologist and activist, who I suspect few of us had come across before. Graeber points out that the bailout of UK banks during the financial crisis was just one massive debt cancellation. Mainstream economists will tell you that cancelling personal debt would bring down the banking system and the global economy. I have no idea. Perhaps that's right, but the point is that Brand is bringing these concepts – concepts that we wouldn't hear about otherwise – to our attention. Good on him.

So why do so many think that he is having a negative contribution? Clearly, there are people who find him annoying and grating. This is always a danger for celebrities. Because many of them have found fame through their personalities, it is easy to attack them on that basis, rather than on the basis of what they say. There are those who question whether Brand, a man who has considerable personal wealth, can be genuine in his support for the poor. (Though the same arguments aren't made about millionaire 'philanthropists'.) All of this should be irrelevant anyway. Brand being annoying has nothing to do with the issues that he is trying to talk about. Does it even matter if he is 'genuine'? I think we are guilty of, in footballing terms, 'playing the man, not the ball'. Instead of having a pop at him personally, we should be responding to what he is saying.

The papers are also guilty of misrepresenting some of what Brand stands for. To read many of them, you would believe that he had only said, 'I will never vote and I don't think you should, either', and left it at that. This is obviously the opposite of what this book is trying to say, because I am convinced, along with many others, that

voting is the primary way that we can change things we
don't like. However, Brand didn't just say 'don't vote' without any qualifications. In the same *New Statesman* editorial
he wrote: 'I don't vote because to me it seems like a tacit act
of compliance ... As far as I'm concerned there is nothing
to vote for.' After being widely criticised, Brand explained
himself again, this time on his YouTube channel: 'If there
was someone worth voting for, I'd vote for it, and I'd
encourage other people, if they think that there is a political party that represents their views; if they think there are
politicians that are speaking on their behalf, by all means
vote for them.' Some might argue that his opinion on it has
shifted – I don't have a problem with that. Brand just
doesn't want to support the existing political class. That
actually fits well with what I think – and besides if you,
like Brand, don't feel represented by any of the parties or
candidates, you can still make your dissatisfied voice heard
by spoiling your ballot, and hence Voting for no one. Or
you can get involved with a protest movement. Or, as mentioned in the first chapter on voting, you can join an
existing party and try and change it from within, or start
your own party. All are equally valid forms of political
engagement. Nevertheless, some of the media has run with
this 'don't vote' narrative and used it as a way to try and
demonstrate that he is irresponsible and poisoning the
minds of would-be voters. When actually what he is trying
to do is make people think.

Rod Liddle, the former editor of BBC Radio 4's *Today*
programme, wrote a piece about Brand in the *Spectator*.
Liddle was dismayed that the editor of *Newsnight*, BBC's
flagship political show, was so pleased with the 10 million
or more hits it received for an interview between Brand
and Jeremy Paxman. His conclusion was that, 'regardless of

how many people agree with you on YouTube, Alastair Darling [the Labour MP and Chair of the Better Together campaign] is much, much more important than Russell Brand'. This appears to be an expression of what many political commentators and journalists feel: Brand shouldn't be allowed to talk about politics. Politics is for people like them, who have edited political shows, and written about politics for years. Liddle would presumably much prefer that *Newsnight* did an interview with Alastair Darling that was watched by a vanishingly small number of people. Why is that? Because they would be the right sort of people, and it would be the right sort of interview? Quality not quantity? If that's the case, I find it deeply offensive. And so should you. First of all, it's possible to have both quality and quantity. Second of all, politics isn't the domain of some exclusive group. Politics is for all of us. That's the reason I'm writing this book.

I'm quite sure that some people will take exception to me, a TV presenter, writing a book about politics. I don't doubt that the likes of Liddle have written far better books about politics. What I would say, though, is that a different group of people will hopefully read this book to those who would read a book by Liddle. And it's the people who will read/are reading (hello!) this book that I'm trying to help. I realise that Liddle would get little or nothing from this book, but it's not for him. I'm hopeful that some people will be able to get enough useful information from this and that it will make them feel confident in making a decision on who to vote for.

However – and this is really key – this is just for people who would like to be a bit more informed, for themselves. I think it's preferable to be informed, sure, but it is not necessary in order to have an opinion and have your say at the

ballot box. Everyone gets a vote. When people worry about
the 'informed-ness' of the electorate, I worry about what
they want. A test to determine who is informed enough?
Who would set that test? Someone like Liddle? No thanks.
It's too reminiscent of Louisiana in the early 1960s, when
many would-be voters were made to take a tricksy, pseudo-
intelligence test dressed up as a literacy test. And the tests
were used, not explicitly but undeniably, to exclude black
people, and occasionally the poorest white people, from
voting. Exclusion of any form is unacceptable. I'll say it
again – politics is for all of us.

Another criticism that I have read of Brand – and I've
been spoilt for choice, since so many have lined up and
taken a shot – is that somehow, by writing a book that is
getting read by people (the shame!), he is depriving better
political writers of an audience. Presumably the audience
is too busy reading Brand's book to read anything else. This
logic is so dumb, and snotty, I hardly know where to start
in dismantling it. Brand is bringing a whole new audience
to the subject, an audience who probably wouldn't read
Noam Chomsky or David Graeber. But maybe, after being
introduced to them by Brand, they will seek them out. So if
anything, the opposite is true. Brand may well be bringing
these (admittedly all left-wing) experts a bigger audience.

On *Question Time*, an audience member (who turned
out to be the brother of a UKIP MEP) challenged Brand to
stand – to run to be an MP. Brand said that he wouldn't for
fear of 'becoming one of them'. Although it may have been
a consequence of being put on the spot, that was a disap-
pointing response. Not because I think he needs to stand –
he seems to be getting pretty good results from outside the
system – but because of the reason he gave. It had occurred
to people before that Brand might become our version of

Beppe Grillo, the Italian comedian who proved that it is possible to make that transition from comedian to politics when he ran in the 2013 Italian elections and won a staggering 25 per cent of the votes. Grillo did so by making a genuine connection with the people who are, in Brand's words, 'utterly disenchanted by politics'. Whatever you think of Brand's politics, I personally believe that his passion is genuine (I should point out that I barely know him, so could be wrong). But he seemed to be saying that he would be corrupted if he were to be elected. That suggests to me that he thinks no one is able to resist the corrupting influence of power, in which case the outlook is bleak. I choose not to believe that. I choose to believe that there are many, many politicians who are motivated by the same things that Brand says he's motivated by. It's those politicians that we should be trying to elect to power.

I'm not defending Brand because I agree with everything he says – or because I think he has all the right answers to the problems he is talking about. On the contrary, I'm unconvinced by some of his answers but I don't know if that matters. He is asking questions, about stuff that matters to all of us. Stuff that, actually, no one else was talking about before – at least not in full public view. To think that he is having a negative contribution to politics because you disagree with his politics is missing the point. If a politician or journalist or whoever strongly disagrees with something that Brand says, and writes a compelling piece about why he is wrong – that's fantastic, isn't it? That the conversation is being had? I think we should be grateful that he is using his profile and reach to try and do something good.

In other comedians-in-politics news, Eddie Izzard has said he will run for London Mayor before 2020, and Al

Murray's Pub Landlord character is standing for Parliament in South Thanet against candidates including Nigel Farage.

Russell might not say this himself, but if you care about any of the things he is talking about – VOTE.

22. Alternatives to Our Democracy

How does our voting system *actually* work?

There are many forms of **democracy**. What we have in the UK is a 'representative democracy'. There is also a form called 'direct democracy'. I don't have enough space to go through all of the democratic alternatives, but I'll outline a few options, including 'direct democracy' and something called 'bi-representative democracy'. (It's interesting, trust me.) Let's start with what we have, though. In our representative democracy we choose people, by voting, to represent us in Parliament. The idea is that we then trust these MPs, our representatives, to vote on laws and policies. We entrust them to look after our best interests and try to reflect our will (or at least the will of the majority). They are not there to act with self-interest. However, MPs are often susceptible to the instructions of their party leaders, and to the lobbying of corporations and special interest groups who want them to vote on issues in Parliament in a particular way. Once we have elected them, we have no way of holding MPs to account if they don't behave as they promised they would. Or at least, not until the next general election. We have to leave it to their judgement to debate and decide what to do.

It's clearly important to look at how exactly we choose these people. The voting system that we use is called **First Past the Post** (FPTP). Every eligible person in the UK gets one vote, which they use to choose the candidate in their area that they want to represent them as a Member of Parliament. In each of the 650 constituencies, the candidate with the most votes in the constituency wins. It's simple and it's quick and it's cheap to run. However, it does have its problems and its critics. It's believed to encourage 'tactical voting'. Tactical voting is where a person doesn't vote for their favourite candidate, but rather votes against the candidate they dislike the most. As discussed in the Voting chapter, I'm sceptical of tactical voting because I feel it puts some people off voting at all. Many people also argue that FPTP tends to shut out smaller parties, favouring the two largest (Labour and the Conservatives). You can see this in the results of the 2010 election. The Lib Dems won 23 per cent of the overall votes, but only 8.8 per cent of seats (57 seats), whereas the Labour party won 29 per cent of the overall votes, and 39.7 per cent of seats (258 seats). It's understandable why smaller parties such as the Lib Dems would consider this unfair.

Another serious complaint about FPTP is 'wasted votes'. Wasted votes are votes that end up counting for nothing – that is, any vote for any candidate other than the candidate who wins. There are always some wasted votes in elections, but the problem is especially bad with FPTP. At the 2010 election, more than half of all votes (52.8 per cent) were for losing candidates. This means that many MPs, and often the government, were not voted for by a majority of the electorate, which raises the question: what right do they have to govern? Even in 2001, when Tony Blair and Labour won a very comfortable majority of seats (Labour got 412 seats to the Conservatives' 166), they only got just over 40 per cent of the vote – so nearly three-fifths of voters did not want a Labour government. And that doesn't even take into account the people who didn't vote at all (which was over 40 per cent of the electorate that year).

When going into coalition with the Conservatives in 2010, the Lib Dems insisted on a referendum (a public vote, usually on a single issue) to change the general election voting system from FPTP to something called the Alternative Vote (AV). Using AV, voters get to rank candidates in order of preference and can rank as many of the candidates as they like. If no one candidate has 50 per cent or more of the first preference votes, then the candidate with the fewest of these gets eliminated, and their second choices are allocated to the remaining candidates. This continues until someone has over 50 per cent of the votes. The good thing about AV is that it is said to improve the legitimacy of MPs because they have to have majority support, and it also helps smaller parties convert votes into seats – which is why the Lib Dems favoured it. However, AV is slow to process, complicated and tends to lead to more coalition governments, which we haven't had many of in the UK. In May 2011, the UK public voted against AV, so we still have FPTP. The rejection of AV probably means another referendum on our voting system is unlikely in the near future.

However, it's still worth talking about Proportional Representation (PR). This is very commonly used as the basis of voting systems across the world. PR aims to make the number of seats won directly reflect the proportion of votes won. For example, in a perfectly proportional vote, if a party got 20 per cent of the vote they would also get 20 per cent of the available seats. In the UK we use a form of PR, the **Closed Party List**, in our European Parliament elections. Supporters argue there are far fewer 'wasted votes' with PR and it's generally much fairer to smaller parties that struggle under FPTP. Because of that, people have suggested that it creates a greater effective choice for voters who will feel that they can vote for anyone, not just one of the larger parties. The fact that an overall majority is less likely with PR can be argued as a good thing or a bad thing. A good thing because more parties will be involved in a coalition or **minority government**, and have a say in policymaking. A bad thing because those governments are generally weaker than majority ones, and can have problems passing legislation (I looked at this question in the Coalition chapter). In the Closed Party List, voters just vote for the party, not a specific candidate. This is criticised because it removes the link between an MP and their constituency. As I discussed in the Representation chapter, though, this link often feels absent anyway.

So that's how we vote our elected representatives in to Parliament, but there are democratic alternatives to just having elected representatives making decisions on our behalf. In a 'direct democracy', the public participates in the decision-making process. Essentially, they get to vote on everything. There are degrees of direct democracy. In its purest form, you would have no elected officials, just people working for a kind of admin board, running the votes and counting them up and then acting upon the decisions that the public take. That's quite hard to imagine working in practice. The entire population will surely not be available all day, every day to consider, debate and then vote on laws. However, direct democracy can work in tandem with representative democracy. You could structure it so that, for example, only the most important decisions are made by a public vote. The remaining decisions, the day-to-day running of things, would still be carried out by a parliament of elected MPs. Those in favour of direct democracy say that it gives the electorate real power.

Something like this happens in Switzerland. There, the public are allowed to vote on laws which the parliament has passed. In effect, they can overrule their parliament's decisions. For pretty much every law their parliament passes, the Swiss public can trigger a referendum on it if 50,000 people – about 1 per cent of the population – sign to say they want one. This actually happens very rarely. Opponents of direct democracy would argue that's because when push comes to shove, the public just aren't interested or informed enough. It might be that, or it might be that politicians know that the public will be 'marking their work', and so are making sure that they do a good job of representing the will of the people already.

There is also the possibility of introducing 'citizens' initiatives'. These would be laws proposed by the public, not by MPs. Again, a certain level of support would be required for these proposed laws to be voted upon. In the UK we have a very watered-down version of this. Since 2011, there has been a government website (http://epetitions.direct.gov.uk) that invites people to try and gain support for their own petitions. If a petition gets 100,000 or more signatures it *could* be debated in the House of Commons. So no guarantee that it will – MPs still have the final say on whether the issue gets discussed. It certainly doesn't guarantee any sort of public vote. But, weak as it is, it is nevertheless a form of direct democracy.

The main political parties in the UK are very unlikely to want direct democracy to in any sense replace representative democracy – you could argue that any amount of direct democracy weakens the power of Parliament. Some would obviously say that that is a good thing. But given that there isn't going to be any political support for direct democracy to take hold of our system, how could it ever happen? Would there need to be a revolution? No, not necessarily. One way would be if a new party, whose sole policy was to use direct democracy, formed and then stood for election. A party actually exists already called the UK's People's Administration Direct Democracy Party, although they don't appear to have much popular support. The idea, though, is that if (and it's a fairly big if) they got into power they would then run the country by allowing the public to create and vote upon all policies. Of course, if they then lost the next election, we would presumably go back to square one.

There are many concerns about direct democracy, but one – that it would be too expensive to run loads of votes – has diminished over the years. Back in 2012, the Labour MP Kevin Brennan said, 'Technologically it is now possible. We could function as a direct democracy. The cost of obtaining people's views on a range of different subjects is minuscule compared to any other time in history.' It seems sensible to take advantage of the fact that we can gauge the public's opinions so quickly and easily through social media and consultation pages on websites. However, it would require a lot of time from the public themselves – how many people would be willing to take part in votes every other day of the week?

There are two other serious objections to direct democracy that still seem valid. The first is that there is a chance that the pubic may vote for something that would be genuinely bad for the country. If you allow the government to stop that happening, then you undermine the whole notion of direct democracy. So you would have to let it go ahead, and then deal with the consequences. When stuff goes wrong at the moment, we can blame the government. In this system, we would have to blame ourselves. Peter Kellner of YouGov says, 'It is like a court case in which the jury and the defendants are the same people.' Minority rights may also be eroded by the majority – in California in 2008 the Californian people voted against gay marriage. That is an inherent danger of direct democracy. The second major objection is that these public votes could be unduly influenced by interested parties. A group of people who feel strongly about a vote, for or against, may have too much of an impact on the result, especially if voter turnout was generally low. There is also the concern that the wealthy would have more money and resources for campaigning and lobbying, and be able to get the vote to go their way. Obviously, this happens already – politicians are lobbied the whole time. What would be difficult is ensuring that the public are given unbiased information about the issue, especially as trust continues to decline in the media.

There is a campaign running currently regarding the possible expansion of a London airport. Gatwick Airport wants an additional runway, and so does Heathrow. Both airports are spending vast sums of money on advertising and marketing, making their cases. Environmentalists believe that these campaigns are 'subverting democracy' because they are making the debate about a choice between expansion plans, rather than whether expansion should be happening at all. So the worry is that this sort of thing would happen on all public votes in a direct democracy, and the side with the most money and marketing clout would have an unfair advantage.

As a side note, an interesting solution has been proposed to one of the problems of financial influence over political power. As it is, almost all of the major political parties are funded, in part, by private donors. This means two things – the more money a party has, the more it will be able to spend on campaigns and favourable coverage. Also, the more money an individual donor gives, the greater their influence is likely to be on the party. If I want a party to act a certain way and I give them a vast donation, the party is more likely to listen to me. For example, opponents of Labour say that because the party gets lots of money from the trade unions it is biased towards their agenda, and opponents of the Conservative Party say that the large donations it gets from financial services companies mean it is biased towards their agenda. To counter that, some argue that all political parties should be funded not by private entities and individuals, but solely by the taxpayer. The amount the parties get in each region would be proportional to the number of votes they get in that region, as opposed to the number of seats in Parliament. That would probably help smaller parties like UKIP and the Greens.

Those against this idea would point out that the opposition parties already get state funding – this is called 'Short Money', and it is roughly proportional to the number of seats the party has in Parliament. For example, the Labour party has received £6,684,794.15 for the year 2014/15. In addition to that, the parties fund themselves through a combination of large corporate and private donors, and smaller donations from the public. If you go onto the party websites you'll see that all of them have the option to donate on the front page. You could argue that if you no longer allow these donations from the public, it will make the parties more complacent, not less. Also, additional state funding to make up the difference – more taxpayer money going to political parties – is unlikely to meet with public approval.

Going back to the structure of our democracy in the UK, an even more radical departure would be a 'bi-representative democracy'. In this system, Parliament would be made up of elected politicians – MPs like we have now – but also members of the public. You would choose these members of the public randomly, exactly like jury service. This is, like direct democracy, another way of giving power to the people. Suddenly, we would have the 'normal people' in Parliament that many crave. The typical fear of this system is that the non-elected would be incompetent and unqualified to make decisions of national significance. Yet we trust people on juries to make pretty big, life-changing decisions, and jurors tend to take their job very seriously. Also, supporters of the idea point out, it's not as if MPs have detailed knowledge in every area of government; they can jump from post to post in government because they are surrounded by staff, researchers and professionals within individual departments that provide them with assistance. That could be the same with these 'citizen politicians'.

Any member of the public selected to go into Parliament would just serve a fixed length of time – they would not be worried about trying to get re-elected. They wouldn't have to bother with party politics or media appearances. This would presumably allow them more time and freedom to dedicate to making decisions for the common good. Any laws would be passed by the combined efforts of the elected members (MPs) and the non-elected members (the public). The best of both worlds. Currently, the public are suspicious and untrusting of politicians and what they do, so it might be useful for members of the public to actually witness and take part in politics. It would be interesting for the public to see at first hand the complexities of politics. Conversely, politicians would see at first hand that citizens are capable of making rational decisions about complex issues. Both the public and politicians would benefit. The divide between the political class and the people would be much less defined, and that is surely a good thing.

The Green Party is a supporter of 'direct participation', believing it to be the 'highest form of democracy'. So they would presumably bring in initiatives, triggered by the public, and referenda on various issues. UKIP would also bring in the 'Citizen's Initiative', allowing the public to vote on whatever they chose. Both UKIP and the Greens are in favour of recall too, which gives the public the power to get rid of MPs during a parliamentary term, rather than having to wait until a general election. This is another form of direct democracy, in that it gives more power to the people. In terms of voting systems, the Tories want to keep First Past the Post because it 'guarantees strong stable government' (and favours them). In 2011, Ed Miliband was in favour of Alternative Vote but over 100 Labour MPs were opposed to it, believing that FPTP gives them a better chance at elections. In 1997, Labour promised a referendum on Proportional Representation but that never happened. The Lib Dems say they would introduce PR for local elections. The Green Party would introduce the Additional Member System at the general election. This is basically a combination of FPTP and PR – each voter gets a vote for their local candidate (which would be FPTP), and a vote for the national party (which would be PR).

If you want our democracy to function in the best way possible – VOTE.

Glossary

Abstention: When an eligible or registered voter chooses not to vote on election day.

All-women shortlists: Originally enforced to increase gender equality in Parliament, this is a political strategy mandating that only women can be elected in certain constituencies.

Asylum seekers: Non-UK residents whose request for legal status as a refugee is awaiting official approval from the government.

Austerity: Policies implemented by the government in an attempt to reduce overall spending during times of economic hardship.

Bedroom tax: This is the common name for the Under-Occupancy Charge. It means that the amount of housing benefit paid to working-age claimants will be reduced if their home has a 'spare' bedroom or bedrooms.

Benefits trap: This occurs when welfare benefits from the government outweigh the benefits of a paid job.

Carbon capture and storage: A method of capturing carbon dioxide from emission sources, such as fossil fuel power plants, and storing it at sites capable of stopping its release into the atmosphere.

Capitalism: An economic system defined by free enterprise, where trade and the production of goods are controlled by private business owners rather than the government.

Claimant Commitment: This sets out what the claimant has agreed to do to prepare for and look for work, or to increase their earnings if they are already working. To claim Jobseeker's Allowance or Universal Credit you have to accept your Claimant Commitment.

Closed Party List: A voting system where, instead of voting for individual candidates, you vote for a party. This is a form of proportional representation.

Cost of living: The cost of sustaining a certain level of living, through spending on basics like housing, food and energy.

Deficit: This is the amount that financial outflow (costs) exceeds inflow (revenue).

Democracy: A form of government by the whole (eligible) population of a state, usually through elected representatives.

Financial crash: When financial assets (things like stocks and shares, bonds and loans) lose nominal value, sending banks and financial companies into panic. This will often coincide with a recession.

First Past the Post: A voting system used in the UK general election. Each constituency elects a Member of Parliament by having voters choose only one candidate, and then selecting the individual with the most votes.

Food banks: Charitable organisations that distribute food, free of charge, to people who are struggling to buy it themselves.

Fracking: A process of extracting gas and oil by drilling through shale rock and then blasting it with a high-pressure water mixture to release the natural resources inside.

Free trade agreements: Agreements where two or more countries reduce their individual trade barriers in order to improve relations with each other and increase opportunities for their own exports.

Frontline jobs: Generally taken to mean the staff who deal with the customer on a day-to-day basis, i.e. not management. So in the case of the NHS, all of those workers who provide patient care are considered 'frontline'.

G20: This is a group of twenty major world economies – made up of nineteen countries, including the UK, and the EU. Government and central bank representatives from each economy meet up and discuss ways to promote global financial stability and growth.

Globalisation: An ongoing process that is making the world more interconnected, through increased international trade of goods and services, and cultural exchange.

Green belt: Originally, green belt areas were protected areas of non-urban land on the edge of towns and cities (hence 'belt') to prevent urban sprawl. Now, under the green belt policy, designated areas of land within urban environments are preserved for forestry, agriculture and natural wildlife.

Green jobs: Jobs in sustainable and environmentally friendly industries.

Gross Domestic Product: A measurement used to determine a state's current economic situation.

House of Lords: The second chamber of Parliament, the House of Lords combines efforts with the House of Commons to approve laws. Its members also consider and debate public policy, and scrutinise the work of the government. Members are not elected by the public.

Infrastructure: The organisation and internal structure necessary for a society to function, physically, economically and socially.

Inheritance tax: If you inherit someone's estate (property, money, other assets) then you have to pay a 40 per cent tax on it (the first £325,000 is exempt).

Intergovernmental Panel on Climate Change (IPCC): Acting as a scientific body under the UN, the IPCC is the leading organisation for the assessment of global climate change.

LibLabCon: A derogatory term for the main political parties in the UK (Liberal Democrats, Labour and Conservatives), which implies that all three are the same.

Manifesto: A political party's statement declaring their beliefs, policies and overall goals. This is especially important during or before an election campaign.

Marginal seats: Constituencies or seats with a small majority, making them vulnerable and likely to change allegiance (or 'swing') during elections.

Minority government: This occurs when the governing political party does not have the majority of seats in Parliament, and so depends on the support of other parties.

Occupy movement: A global movement that fights against perceived inequalities in the world, both financial and economic.

Privatisation: In politics, privatisation involves transferring the ownership of property or business from the government to the private sector.

Recall: A recall bill is currently being examined in the House of Lords (update here: http://services.parliament.uk/bills/2014-15/recallofmps.html). If it's passed, then an MP could be recalled if they are convicted of a serious offence, or if they are suspended by the House of Commons for at least twenty-one sitting days. If either of these things happen, and a recall petition is signed by 10 per cent of voters in the appropriate constituency, the MP will be forced to step down.

Recession: A prolonged period of negative economic growth. In the UK, a recession is defined as two consecutive three-month periods (quarters) where real GDP (inflation-adjusted) falls.

Red tape: Formal regulations and bureaucratic procedures whose complexities often prevent intended change or progress.

Repatriation: The return of someone or something back to its country of origin, such as deporting a non-UK citizen back to their home country.

Safe seats: Positions (seats) in Parliament where a change in party during election time is highly unlikely.

Social democrat: Associated with left-wing politics, social democrats advocate a more socialist form of government that upholds citizens' rights and the equal distribution of wealth.

Social mobility: The upward or downward movement of people (families, individuals, groups) through a society. This often involves a change in social status. 'Rags to riches' is a form of upward social mobility.

Stamp duty: If you buy any type of property in the UK, you're charged a stamp duty, or stamp duty land tax (SDLT). The rate of this tax changes depending on the purchase price and whether or not the property is residential.

Thatcherite: A term denoting supporters of Thatcherism, the ideology put forth by Conservative leader Margaret

Thatcher that supported the small state and free markets through increased privatisation and individual freedom in financial and social decisions.

Think tank: An expert organisation formed to provide opinions, advice and ideas about national issues. Often, these bodies are funded and aligned with certain political parties or ideologies.

Transatlantic Trade and Investment Partnership: A trade agreement currently being negotiated between the EU and US, designed to reduce regulations and barriers, such as tariffs (these are taxes on imports or exports), in order to promote trade between the two economies.

Universal Credit: A benefit for those out of work or on low income, providing support specially tailored to each individual's specific situation.

Zero-hour contracts: An employment contract in which the employer is not obliged to provide their employee with any minimum working hours and, likewise, the worker is not obliged to accept any of the hours offered.

References

Intro

'He writes that the places where he sees the highest turnout': Bruno Kaufman, 'The Swedish Way to Boost Voter Turnout', in *Time*, 5 November 2014. http://time.com/author/bruno-kaufmann/

'He suggests that this commonly voiced notion': Dave Meslin, 'The Antidote to Apathy', TEDxToronto October 2010. http://www.ted.com/talks/dave_meslin_the_antidote_to_apathy

'you have an understandably high turnout around 93 per cent': International Institute for Democracy and Electoral Assistance, 'Voter Turnout Data for Australia', 5 October 2011. http://www.idea.int/vt/countryview.cfm?CountryCode=AU

1. Voting

'At the last general election in 2010, 76 per cent of over-65s voted': The Intergenerational Foundation, 'Voting and Representation', *Youth Manifesto 2015*, 2014. http://www.if.org.uk/wp-content/uploads/2014/06/manifesto-2015-factsheet-1.pdf

'the UK has one of the largest differences in voter turnout': European Social Survey 2010, 'Did you vote at the last national election?', in Institute for Public Policy Research, *Divided Democracy*, p.9, fig. 1.4, November 2013. http://www.ippr.org/assets/media/images/media/files/publication/2013/11/divided-democracy_Nov2013 _11420.pdf

'average weekly wages of workers aged 18–21 have fallen by nearly 20 per cent': The Intergenerational Foundation, 'Why the Treasury should be concerned about intergenerational justice', p.11, fig. 3, *2014 Budget Submission*, 12 February 2014. http://www.if.org.uk/wp-content/uploads/2014/02/Improving-fairness-between-the-generations-in-the-UK-tax-system.pdf

'over-55s are on average about £1,300 worse off': European Social Survey, 2010 http://www.ippr.org/assets/media/images/media/files/publication/2013/11/divided-democracy_Nov2013_11420. pdf

'really healthy for politics': Jamie Merrill, 'Natalie Bennett: Green on the outside but red in the centre', *Independent*, 12 October 2014. http://www.independent.co.uk/news/people/natalie-bennett-green-on-the-outside-but-red-in-the-centre-9789266.html

'would you vote for this party if you thought they had a chance of winning': YouGov, 'If candidates from the following parties were standing in your constituency and had a chance of winning, how likely would you be to vote for them?', 18–19 November 2014. https://yougov.co.uk/news/2014/11/20/greens-would-soar-if-voters-thought-they-could-win/

'Studies suggest that around 190 seats': David Cowling, 'Election 2015: The political battleground', BBC News website, 24 February 2014. http://www.bbc.co.uk/news/uk-politics-25949029

'Another report by the Intergenerational Foundation concludes': The Intergenerational Foundation, *Politicians Beware: Younger voters may bite back*, January 2015. http://www.if.org.uk/wp-content/ uploads/2015/01/Politicians-Beware-Younger-Voters-May-Bite-Back.pdf

2. Party Differences

'ComRes recently did a survey': ComRes poll asked voters to place parties on the left-right political spectrum for the *Independent on Sunday/Sunday Mirror*, December 2014. http://blogs.independent.co.uk/wp-content/uploads/2014/12/cr4.jpg

'The website politicalcompass.org shows the positions of the major UK parties': http://politicalcompass.org/ukparties2010

'New Labour's shift to the centre had the effect of moving "the electorate to the right"': Anushka Asthana, 'New Labour pushed Britain's beliefs to the right, says academic', *Observer*, 24 January 2010. http://www.theguardian.com/politics/2010/jan/24/new labour-moves-uk-rightwing 'a functioning National Health Service, free education and an affordable home': 'What We Stand For', Green Party website. http://green party.org.uk/values/

3. The Rise of UKIP

'we paid £11.3 billion in 2013': UK official transactions with institutions of the European Union, Office of National Statistics, 'The Pink Book 2014, Part 3: Geographical Breakdown', 31 October 2014. http://www.ons.gov.uk/ons/rel/bop/united-kingdom-balance-of-payments/2014/rpt-the-pink-book-2013—part-3—geographical-breakdown.html?format=print

'estimate membership is worth between £62 billion and £78 billion every year': CBI, *Our Global Future*, 7 November 2013. http://www.cbi.org.uk/media/2451423/our_global_future.pdf

'exiting the EU would save us £8 billion annually': 'What a UKIP Government will do', UKIP website. http://www.ukip.org/policies_for_people

'Farage himself famously described their 2010 election manifesto': 'Nigel Farage: Ukip's controversial politicians have all defected from the Conservatives', *Telegraph*, 24 January 2014. http://www.telegraph.co.uk/news/politics/ukip/10594525/Nigel-Farage-Ukips-controver sial-politicians-have-all-defected-from-the-Conservatives.html

'In 2006 David Cameron wrote them off': 'UKIP demands apology from Cameron', BBC News website, 4 April 2006. http://news.bbc.co.uk/1/hi/4875026.stm

'Farage has bemoaned FPTP': Rowena Mason, 'Ukip could be in 2015 Coalition Government', *Telegraph*, 7 January 2013. http://www.telegraph.co.uk/news/politics/ukip/9784758/Ukip-could-be-in-2015-Coalition-Government.html

'Also, it's interesting that Farage has said that Ed Miliband': Gareth Platt, 'The Nigel Farage Interview', *International Business Times* UK website, 17 November 2014. http://www.ibtimes.co.uk/nigel-farage-interview-ukip-leader-rochester-immigration-putin-future-nhs-1475214

'a conviction politician, I'm not doing this for a career': 'I am odd (for a politician)', BBC news website, 7 January 2013. http://www.bbc.co.uk/news/uk-politics-20931123

'pass the parcel with your government for ages': James Chapman, 'Kingmaker Clegg wins the TV war of words', *Daily Mail*, 16 April

2010. http://www.dailymail.co.uk/news/election/article-1266285/ Leaders-debate-Historic-Brown-Cameron-Clegg-lock-horns.html

'UKIP is a libertarian, non-racist party seeking withdrawal from the European Union': Alex Wickham, 'Is UKIP abandoning its commitment to the libertarian right?', Breitbart website 7 October 2010. http://www .breitbart.com/london/2014/10/07/when-did-ukip-become-an-enemy-of-the-right/

'Farage himself would favour decriminalising some drugs': 'Farage backs decriminalisation of drugs', Politics Home website, 4 April 2014. http://www.politicshome.com/uk/story/41353/

'The academic Matthew Goodwin has studied the rise of UKIP': Nick Robinson, 'UKIP: How far could they go?', BBC News website, 10 October 2014. http://www.bbc.co.uk/news/uk-politics-29571412

'proportion of UKIP voters who were previously Labour voters' ; '43 per cent of voters as a whole are termed working class': Peter Kellner, 'UKIP's support is changing', Guardian, 17 November 2014. http://www.theguardian.com/commentisfree/2014/nov/17/ukip-support-british-politics-voters-labour-party

'a bit more sceptical than men': Gareth Platt, 'The Nigel Farage Interview', International Business Times UK website, 14 November 2014. http://www.ibtimes.co.uk/nigel-farage-interview-women-just-dont-get-ukip-1474920

'Now, the same tabloid newspapers that have spent more than twenty years': Matthew Goodwin, 'Why Ukip's scandals don't seem to be hurting its popularity', Guardian, 15 December 2014. http://www. the guardian.com/commentisfree/2014/dec/15/ukip-scandals-popularity-voters

'would feel more comfortable that my money would return value': Kashmira Gander, 'Nigel Farage caught on video suggesting the NHS should be run privately', Independent, 12 November 2014. http://www. independent.co.uk/news/uk/politics/nigel-farage-caught-on-video-suggesting-the-nhs-should-be-run-privately-9857389.html

'Steve Crowther then explained that the "shambolic" nature': Oliver Wright, 'Nigel Farage says "wag tax" is dead', Independent, 28 September 2014. http://www.independent.co.uk/news/uk/politics/f arage-uturns-on-25-luxurygoods-tax-days-after-it-was-announced-9760578.html

'safety net for the needy, not a bed for the lazy': 'What a UKIP Government will do', UKIP website. http://www.ukip.org/policies_ for_ people

4. Benefits

'around 13 million people living in poverty': 'Monitoring Poverty and Social Exclusion', Joseph Rowntree Foundation/New Policy Institute, 2014. http://www.jrf.org.uk/sites/files/jrf/MPSE-2014-FULL.pdf

'there is a definition of an "'absolutely poor person'"': Martin Ravallion et. al., 'Dollar a Day Revisited', *The World Bank Economic Review*, 26 June 2009. http://wber.oxfordjournals.org/content/23/2/163

'What is usually meant by poverty in the UK context': 'What is meant by poverty?' Joseph Rowntree Foundation. http://www.jrf.org.uk/sites/files/jrf/poverty-definitions.pdf

'Sleeping off a life on benefits': George Osborne's conference speech October 2012, quoted in *New Statesman*, 8 October 2012. http://www.newstatesman.com/blogs/politics/2012/10/george-osbornes-speech-conservative-conference-full-text

'In 2012 a YouGov poll showed that 74 per cent of us': Peter Kellner, 'Charity Ends At Home', YouGov website, 27 February 2012. https://yougov.co.uk/news/2012/02/27/charity-ends-home/

'69 per cent believed that the welfare system': 'Public attitudes to poverty and child poverty', Britain Thinks website. http://britainthinks.com/sites/default/files/Poverty%20&%20Child%20poverty%20presentation%20Final.pdf

'The Trades Union Congress did a poll in 2012': 'Support for benefit cuts dependent on ignorance', TUC website, 4 January 2013. http://www.tuc.org.uk/social-issues/child-poverty/welfare-and-benefits/tax-credits/support-benefit-cuts-dependent

'the largest budget of any government department': Joseph O'Leary, 'The Welfare Budget', Full Fact website, 20 June 2014. https://fullfact.org/economy/welfare_budget_public_spending-29886

'In 1987, 55 per cent supported higher spending on welfare': 'British Social Attitudes Survey 30', fig. 2.3, NatCen Social Research, 2013 edition. http://bsa-30.natcen.ac.uk/read-the-report/spending-and-welfare/welfare-benefits.aspx

'no robust evidence linking food bank usage to welfare reform': Chris Green, 'Anger as Employment Minister Esther McVey denies food bank use is linked to welfare reforms', *Independent*, 14 May 2014. http://www.independent.co.uk/news/uk/politics/anger-as-employment-minister-esther-mcvey-denies-food-bank-use-is-linked-to-welfare-reforms-9372032.html

'83 per cent of Trussell Trust food banks surveyed said that welfare sanctions': 'Latest Foodbank figures top 900,000', The Trussell Trust website. http://www.trusselltrust.org/foodbank-figures-top-900000

'The National Audit Office found a mere 17,850 people': Comptroller and Auditor General, 'Universal Credit: Progress Update', National Audit Office, 26 November 2014. http://www.parliament.uk/documents/commons-committees/public-accounts/Universal-Credit-progress-update.pdf

'The latest target is to have 500,000 people claiming UC by 2016': Comptroller and Auditor General, 'Universal Credit: Progress Update', National Audit Office, 26 November 2014. http://www. parliament. uk/documents/commons-committees/public-accounts/Universal-Credit-progress-update.pdf

'A minister who has dealt with Duncan Smith on the reform ': Isabel Hardman, 'Can Iain Duncan Smith force Labour to continue his welfare reforms?', Spectator, 25 November 2014. http://blogs. spectator.co.uk/coffeehouse/2014/11/can-iain-duncan-smith-force-labour-to-continue-his- welfare-reforms/

'789,000 sanctions were imposed in the year': 'Benefit sanctions figures published', press release, HM Government website. https://www.gov.uk/government/news/benefit-sanctions-ending-the-something-for-nothing-culture—2

'An Oxfam report found that between October 2012 and June 2014': Howard Reed, 'How effective are benefits sanctions?', Oxfam, 12 December 2014. http://policy-practice.oxfam.org.uk/publications/how-effective-are-benefits-sanctions-an-investigation-into-the-effectiveness-of-337096

'A government-commissioned review found that communications with claimants': Matthew Oakley, 'Independent review of the operation of Jobseeker's Allowance sanctions', July 2014. https://www.gov.uk/government/uploads/system/uploads/attachment_data/ file/335144/jsa-sanctions-independent-review.pdf

'so no out-of-work household can claim more in benefits than the average family earns in work': 'Our long-term economic plan', Conservative Party website. https://www.conservatives.com/Plan/CapWelfareReduceImmigration.aspx

'no strings attached and with no questions asked': 'Clegg hits back at bishop's welfare reform criticism', BBC News website, 20 February 2014. http://www.bbc.co.uk/news/uk-politics-26277152

'safety net for the needy, not a bed for the lazy': 'What We Stand For', UKIP website. http://www.ukip.org/issues

5. Broken Promises

'parties keep 67 per cent of their campaign promises": Francois Petry and Benoıt Collette, 'Measuring How Political Parties Keep Their Promises', in Louis M. Imbeau (ed.), *Do They Walk Like They Talk?* (Springer, 2009). http://www.academia.edu/8311153/_Measuring_ How_Political_Parties_Keep_Their_Promises_A_Positive_Perspective_ from_Political_Science._With_Benoît_Collette._In_Louis_Imbeau_ed._ Do_They_Walk_Like_They_Talk_Speech_and_Action_in_Policy_Proce sses._New_York_Berlin_Springer_2009_65-82

'We have no plans to introduce top-up fees': Hansard House of Commons transcript, UK Parliament website, 26 July 2000. http://www.publications.parliament.uk/pa/cm199900/cmhansrd/ vo000726/debtext/00726-03.htm#00726-03_spmin15

'their behaviour has fallen below the standards expected of an MP': 'Reforming the constitution and political system', HM Government website, 20 February 2013; updated 9 December 2014. https://www. gov.uk/government/policies/reforming-the-constitution-and- political-system/supporting-pages/recall-of-mps

'arguments against recall are that by-elections are expensive': 'Small Data: How much do by-elections cost?' BBC News website, 13 October 2014. http://www.bbc.co.uk/news/blogs-magazine-monitor- 29540785

'My final thought about how we might be able to reduce the amount of promise-breaking comes from the economist Robin Hanson': Robin Hanson, 'Yes, Tax Lax Ideas', Overcoming Bias blog, 14 March 2009. http://www.overcomingbias.com/2009/03/yes-tax-ideas.html

6. Immigration

'Tory leader Michael Howard made a speech about immigration': 'Tory leader attacks asylum system', BBC News website, 10 April 2005. http://news.bbc.co.uk/1/hi/uk_politics/vote_2005/frontpage/ 4428517.stm

'a UCL report found that migrants from the EU': Centre for Research & Analysis of Migration, 'Positive economic impact of UK immigration from the European Union', UCL Press Release, 5 November 2014.

http://www.cream-migration.org/files/Press_ release_FiscalEJ.pdf

'They claim that immigrants might actually have cost around £140 billion': 'Immigrants have cost the taxpayer over £140 billion since 1995', Migration Watch website, 13 March 2014. http://www.migrationwatchuk.org/press-release/380

'net immigration in the tens of thousands': Net migration to UK hits 260,000, *New Statesman*, 27 November 2014. http://www.newstatesman.com/politics/2014/11/net-migration-uk-hits-260000-smashing-david-camerons-promise-cut-it-tens-thousands

'the number of people who come in from the EU': 'Net migration to the UK was 260,000 in the year ending June 2014', Office for National Statistics, 27 November 2014. http://www.ons.gov.uk/ons/rel/migration1/migration-statistics-quarterly-report/november-2014/ sty-net-migration.html

'Theresa May talked about a Migration Advisory Council report': 'Home Secretary speech on "An immigration system that works in the national interest"', UK Government website, 12 December 2012. https://www.gov.uk/government/speeches/home-secretary-speech-on-an-immigration-system-that-works-in-the-national-interest

'no statistically significant impact of migration on employment': 'Are wages going down because of immigration?' Full Fact website, 17 November 2012. https://fullfact.org/factchecks/immigration_ jobs_wages-28674

'According to the ONS 236,000 people in the UK': 'Low pay, April 2014', Office for National Statistics, 19 November 2014. http://www.ons.gov.uk/ons/rel/ashe/low-pay/april-2014/stb-2014-low-pay-estimates.html

'parties all recognise that the 954,000 so-called NEETS': James Mirza Davies, 'NEET: Young people not in education, employment or training', UK Parliament website, 20 November 2014. http://www.parliament.uk/business/publications/research/briefing-papers/SN06705/neet-young-people-not-in-education-employment-or-training

'the UK has a "talent mismatch" of 9.6 out of 10': Alan Tovey, 'Fear of immigration holding back UK's economic recovery', *Telegraph*, 25 September 2014. http://www.telegraph.co.uk/finance/jobs/ 11119852/Fear-of-immigration-holding-back-UKs-economic-recovery.html

'an estimated 11 per cent of the NHS workforce are immigrants': Harroon Siddique, 'Figures show extent of NHS reliance on foreign nationals', *Guardian*, 26 January 2014. http://www. theguardian. com/society/2014/jan/26/nhs-foreign-nationals-immigration-health-service

'A report in 2013 estimated that we will need an extra 7 million migrants': 'UK needs seven million more migrants', *Huffington Post* UK website, 18 July 2013. http://www.huffingtonpost.co.uk/ 2013/07/18/uk-migrants_n_3615076.html

'there are some things that matter more than money': John Harris, 'It's Not About the Money', *Guardian*, 10 January 2014. http:// www.theguardian.com/commentisfree/2014/jan/10/farage-political-nose-gdp-immigration

'the type of language used when the media covers immigration': 'Migration in the news', The Migration Observatory, 8 August 2013. http://www.migrationobservatory.ox.ac.uk/reports/migration-news

'31 per cent of headlines about asylum are negative': Article 19, 'What's the story?' Article 19 website, 13 May 2003. http://www.article19. org/data/files/pdfs/publications/refugees-what-s-the-story-.pdf

'In 2010, of 17,790 who applied for asylum in the UK': Refugee facts and figures, British Red Cross website. http://www.redcross. org.uk/en/What-we-do/Refugee-support/Refugee-facts-and-figures

'the challenges of cohesion and integration are among the greatest we face': David Cameron, 'What I learnt from my stay with a Muslim family', *Observer*, 13 May 2007. http://www.theguardian.com/ commentisfree/2007/may/13/comment.communities

'separation means isolation and you can't succeed in Britain if you are isolated': Ed Miliband, 'Building a Britain that works together', Labour website, 14 December 2012. http://archive.labour.org. uk/building-a-britain-that-works-together

'thought that just over 24 per cent of the UK population is made up of immigrants': Alberto Nardelli and George Arnett, 'Today's Key Fact: You are wrong about almost everything', *Guardian*, 29 October 2014. http://www.theguardian.com/news/datablog/2014/ oct/29/ todays-key-fact-you-are-probably-wrong-about-almost-everything

'62 per cent of the German people think that immigration is an opportunity': German Marshall Fund, 'Transatlantic Trends key Findings 2013', 2013. http://www.gmfus.org/wp-content/blogs. dir/1/files_mf/1376944979TT2013_complete_web.pdf

'since 2005 they have run compulsory "integration courses" for new immigrants':Ipsos MORI, 'Perceptions and Reality: Public attitudes to immigration in Germany and Britain', 26 November 2014. https://www.ipsos-mori.com/researchpublications/publications/1712/Perceptions-and-Reality-Public-attitudes-to-immigration-in-Germany-and-Britain.aspx

'benefits of having talented people, and having a welcoming policy': Joseph Watts, 'Boris Johnson: Being xenophobic is human', *London Evening Standard*, 3 December 2014. http://www.standard.co.uk/news/politics/boris-johnson-being-xenophobic-is-human-and-its-up-to-politicians-to-praise-immigrants-9899619.html

'new citizen test with British values at heart': 'Capping Welfare and reducing Immigration', Conservative Home website. https://www.conservatives.com/Plan/CapWelfareReduceImmigration.aspx

7. Coalition Government

'the probability of another hung parliament after this general election': Chris Hanretty et al., 'Presenting a new model for forecasting the 2015 general election', LSE blog, 1 September 2014. http://blogs.lse.ac.uk/generalelection/presenting-a-new-model-for-forecasting-the-2015-general-election/?utm_content=bufferfba 61&utm_medium =social&utm_source=twitter. com&utm_campaign =buffer

'Cameron said he wanted to "put aside party differences"': 'David Cameron's full speech', *Telegraph*, 11 May 2010. http://www.telegraph.co.uk/news/politics/david-cameron/7712954/David-Camerons-speech-full-text.html

'Clegg hoped the arrangement was "the start of the new politics"': 'Nick Clegg's speech in full', *Guardian*, 12 May 2010. http://www.theguardian.com/politics/2010/may/12/nick-clegg-speech-full-text

'Leader of the Opposition, Conservative Margaret Thatcher, proposed': Margaret Thatcher Foundation website. http://www.margaretthatcher.org/document/103983

'The two parties are currently feuding over plans for the economy': 'Coalition divisions deepen as PM attacks Lib Dems' economic policy', ITV News website, 7 December 2014. http://www.itv.com/news/update/2014-12-07/clegg-tories-of-kidding-themselves-on-the-economy/

'recent polling has suggested that the Lib Dems will do better in this election under FPTP': Mike Smithson, 'If the LDs hold onto as many seats as the latest polling suggests ...' Political Betting blog, 28 November 2014. http://www1.politicalbetting.com/index.php/archives/2014/11/28/if-the-lds-hold-on-to-as-many-seats-as-the-latest-polling-suggests-then-clegg-should-thank-no2av/

'UKIP have said they will "do a deal with the devil"': Jason Cowley, 'Nigel Farage: I'd do a deal with Labour', *New Statesman*, 12 November 2014. http://www.newstatesman.com/politics/2014/11/nigel-farage-i-d-do-deal-labour

'half of their members say they would prefer to ally in some way with Labour': Stephen Tall, 'Hung Parliament: what Lib Dem members think will happen', Liberal Democrat Voice website, 6 October 2014. http://www.libdemvoice.org/hung-parliament-what-lib-dem-members-think-will-happen-and-what-you-want-to-happen-42775.html

'Latest polling suggests that the SNP might take 45 out of 59 seats': Tom Clark, 'Labour set for a bloodbath in Scotland in general election, poll says', *Guardian*, 26 December 2014. http://www.theguardian.com/uk-news/2014/dec/26/labour-bloodbath-scotland-general-election-2015-snp-westminster

'David Cameron has apparently been "courting" the DUP': Nicholas Watt, 'Prime minister "wooing" Democratic Unionists', *Guardian*, 8 May 2014. http://www.theguardian.com/politics/2014/may/08/david-cameron-hosts-dup-mps-in-lavish-downing-street-reception

8. The Housing Crisis

'then a chicken would now cost £51': Lee Boyce, 'The £51 chicken and an £88k salary', This Is Money website, 17 October 2013. http://www.thisismoney.co.uk/money/mortgageshome/article-2462753/How-items-cost-risen-line-house-prices.html

'four out of five homes for sale in England are unaffordable': 'Over 80% of homes on the market unaffordable for first-time buyers', Shelter website, 25 June 2014. http://england.shelter. org.uk/ news/june_2014/over_80_of_homes_on_the_market_unaffordable_for_first_time_buyers

'a quarter of under-35s are still living in their childhood bedrooms': 'Large increase in 20- to 34-year-olds living with parents since 1996', Office for National Statistics, 21 January 2014. http://www.ons.gov.uk/ons/rel/family-demography/young-adults-living-with-parents/2013/sty-young-adults.html

'there simply aren't enough homes': 'Building The Homes We Need', KPMG/Shelter, 29 April 2014. http://www.shelter.org.uk/__data/assets/pdf_file/0019/802270/Building_the_homes_we_need_-_a_programme_for_the_2015_government.pdf

'in the 1960s and 1970s we regularly churned out in excess of 300,000 a year': 'Housing starts at six-year high, but completions fall', BBC News website, 20 February 2014. http://www.bbc.co.uk/news/business-26271803

'the houses that are being built are small': Miranda Prynne, 'British Homes are the smallest in Europe', *Telegraph*, 18 June 2014. http://www.telegraph.co.uk/property/10909403/British-homes-are-the-smallest-in-Europe-study-finds.html

'a spiral of increasing house prices and rents': 'Building The Homes We Need', KPMG/Shelter, 29 April 2014. http://england.shelter.org.uk/professional_resources/policy_and_research/policy_library/policy_library_folder/report_building_the_homes_we_need

'the average private rent will rise from £132/week': 'Soaring Rent Rises to Leave Nearly 6 Million Private Renters Living in Poverty by 2040', Joseph Rowntree Foundation, 17 November 2014. http://www.jrf.org.uk/media-centre/soaring-rent-nearly-6million-private-renters-poverty-2040-6591

'associations have built an average of only 18,800 new homes a year': 'Mobilising across the nation to build the homes our children need', The Lyons Housing Review, 16 October 2014. http://www.yourbritain.org.uk/uploads/editor/files/The_Lyons_Housing_Review_2.pdf

'after their budget was cut by over 50 per cent in 2010': 'UK Social Housing: Sector Outlook, Third Quarter, 2012', Barclays Bank PLC, September 2012. http://www.prsjobs.com/File.aspx?path=ROOT/Documents/social_housing_outlout.pdf

'an increased budget for central government capital grant': 'Building The Homes We Need', KPMG/Shelter, 29 April 2014. http://www.shelter.org.uk/__data/assets/pdf_file/0019/802270/Building_the_homes_we_need_-_a_programme_for_the_2015_government. pdf

'admit that only 24 per cent of the green belt within the M25': 'The London (Metropolitan) Green Belt: Key Facts', Campaign to Protect Rural England, January 2010. http://www.cpre.org.uk/ resources/ housing-and-planning/green-belts/item/1958-the-london-metro politan-green-belt

'adamant that planning regulations have to be relaxed': Kristian Niemietz, 'The Cost of Living Debate 2014', IEA website, May 2014.

http://www.iea.org.uk/multimedia/video/kristian-niemietz-the-cost-of-living-debate-2014

'a plot of land the size of one-and-a-half football pitches': Alex Morton, 'Why aren't we building enough attractive homes?', Policy Exchange, September 2012. http://www.policyexchange.org.uk/images/ publica tions/why%20arent%20we%20building%20enough%20attractive% 20homes.pdf

'less than 7 per cent of the UK land is classified as urban': UK National Ecosystem Assessment report, 2011. http://news.bbc. co.uk/1/shared/bsp/hi/pdfs/28_06_12_uk_national_ecosystem.pdf

'There are people on incomes of £60,000 or £70,000 living in council homes': 'How many council tenants earn more than £60,000?' Channel Four website, 7 January 2014. http://blogs.channel4.com/ factcheck/factcheck-council-house-tenants-earn-60000/17393

'one third of MPs are private landlords': Carole Cadwalladr, 'When we pay rent to our MPs', *Guardian*, 17 July 2013. http://www.the guardian. com/commentisfree/2013/jul/17/when-we-pay-rent-to-our-mps

'Andrew Charalambous said that they favour building on brownfield sites': 'Andrew Charalambous: "Vote purple, keep Britain green"', UKIP website, 26 September 2014. http://www.ukip.org/andrew_ charalambous_vote_purple_keep_britain_green

9. Devolution

'total public spending per person in Scotland is significantly higher': 'Devolution: what's the Barnett Formula?' BBC News website, 30 October 2014. http://www.bbc.co.uk/news/uk-29477233

'36 per cent of the English population thinks that the Barnett Formula is too generous': 'British Social Attitudes Survey 31', NatCen Social Research, 2014 edition. http://www.bsa-31.natcen.ac.uk/ read-the-report/scotland/what-if-scotland-votes-'no'.aspx

'The Smith Commission report was prepared after the referendum': The Smith Commission Report, 27 November 2014. https://www. smith-commission.scot

'the SNP argues it doesn't go far enough': 'That isn't home rule – it's continued Westminster rule', ITV News website, 27 Novembe 2014. http://www.itv.com/news/border/2014-11-27/that-isnt-home-rule-its-continued-westminster-rule/

'Now the millions of voices of England must be heard': 'In full: David Cameron statement on the UK's future', BBC News website, 19 September 2014. http://www.bbc.co.uk/news/uk-politics-29271765

'It is completely wrong that a bill which imposes higher charges': Tim Yeo, Hansard Commons transcript, UK Parliament website, 27 January 2004. http://www.publications.parliament.uk/pa/ cm200304/cmhansrd/vo040127/debtext/40127-37.htm

'a report to show what effect removing Scottish MPs votes': Richard Keen, 'England, Scotland, Wales – MPs and voting in the House of Commons', UK Parliament website, 5 December 2014. http://www.parliament.uk/business/publications/research/briefing-papers/ SN0 7048/england-scotland-wales-mps-voting-in-the-house-of-commons

'Michael Kenny, an authority on "Englishness"': 'Let England Shake', *The Economist*, 27 September 2014. http://www.economist.com/news/britain/21620243-scotlands-independence-referendum-has-opened-cracks-united-kingdom-let-england-shake

'When one part of the union is 84 per cent': Nicholas Watt, 'Tory reform plans are lethal cocktail – Gordon Brown', *Guardian*, 14 October 2014. http://www.theguardian.com/politics/2014/ oct/14/ tory-reform-plans-lethal-cocktail-end-uk-gordon-brown

'serious devolution of powers and budgets': Daniel Martin, 'Osborne tells the North, "You need mayors like Boris"', *Daily Mail*, 24 June 2014. http://www.dailymail.co.uk/news/article-2666510/Osborne-tells-North-You-need-mayors-like-Boris-Chancellor-says-cities-offered-devolution-powers-agree-figures.html

'would give a £79 billion a year boost': 'Give cities more power to boost growth', BBC News website, 22 October 2014. http://www.bbc.co.uk/news/business-29707917

10. The NHS

'a complete and uncontrolled dictator': Andy McSmith, 'The Birth of the NHS', Any McSmith, *Independent*, 28 June 2008. http://www.independent.co.uk/life-style/health-and-families/ features/the-birth-of-the-nhs-856091.html

'41 million people are still uninsured': Sabrina Tavernise, 'Number of Americans without health insurance falls', *New York Times*, 16 September 2014. http://www.nytimes.com/2014/09/16/us/ number-of-americans-without-health-insurance-falls-survey-shows.html?_r=2

'the NHS came top of a Commonwealth Fund study': 'UK NHS named best healthcare system by the Commonwealth Fund', NHS Confederation website, 1 July 2014. http://www.nhsconfed.org/resources/2014/07/uk-nhs-named-best-healthcare-system-by-the-commonwealth-fund

'When the NHS was founded in 1948, the life expectancy for men was 66': Andy McSmith, 'The birth of the NHS', *Independent*, 28 June 2008. http://www.independent.co.uk/life-style/health-and-families/features/the-birth-of-the-nhs-856091.html

'Today those figures are 78.7 and 82.6': '8 facts about life expectancy', Office for National Statistics, 21 March 2014. http://www.ons.gov.uk/ ons/rel/lifetables/national-life-tables/2010—-2012/sty-facts-about-le.html

'In 2012/13, it was nearly £2,000 per head': 'Key statistics on the NHS', NHS Confederation website, 10 November 2014. http://www.nhsconfed.org/resources/key-statistics-on-the-nhs

'the NHS in England will face a £30 billion shortfall in its budget': 'The NHS belongs to the people', NHS England website, 11 July 2013. http://www.england.nhs.uk/2013/07/11/call-to-action/

'a poll showed that two thirds of us are unwilling to pay more tax': Two thirds of voters oppose new NHS tax, Reform website, 3 September 2014. http://www.reform.co.uk/publication/two-thirds-of-voters-oppose-new-nhs-tax/

'no more of the tiresome, meddlesome, top-down re-structures': George Eaton, 'The pre-election pledges that the Tories are trying to wipe from the internet', *New Statesman*, 13 November 2013. http://www.newstatesman.com/politics/2013/11/pre-election-pledges-tories-are-trying-wipe-internet

'The Health and Social Care bill': Health and Social Care Act, 2012. http://www.legislation.gov.uk/ukpga/2012/7/contents/enacted

'taken a job as an advisor with a private firm': 'Stephen Dorrell MP faces calls to resign over conflict of interest', *Telegraph*, 1 December 2014. http://www.telegraph.co.uk/news/politics/conservative/11264425/Stephen-Dorrell-MP-faces-calls-to-resign-over-conflict-of-interest.html

'Elizabeth Wade, the deputy director of policy at the NHS Confederation': James Chapman et al., 'Burnham on back foot in war on NHS', *Daily Mail,* 5 January 2015. http://www.dailymail. co.uk/news/article-2897699/Labour-accused-scaremongering-claiming-NHS-sunk-Tories-win-general-election.html

'Andy Burnham, Labour's Shadow Health Secretary, say this': Rowena Mason, 'Put more money in or face public backlash, says NHS chief', *Guardian*, 5 January 2015. http://www.theguardian.com/society/2015/jan/05/put-more-money-in-or-face-public-backlash-says-nhs-chief

'in 2012 private firms were taking £8.7 billion of that': Randeep Ramesh, 'NHS funding of private sector rose by £3bn', *Guardian*, 22 May 2013. http://www.theguardian.com/society/2013/may/22/nhs-funding-private-sector-study

'soon after Circle took charge its patient ratings were some of the highest in the UK': Peter Cambell and Sophie Borland, 'Transformed: the failing NHS Trust', *Daily Mail*, 23 February 2013. http://www.dailymail.co.uk/news/article-2283150/Hinchingbrooke-Hospital-The-failing-NHS-trust-taken-private-firm-Circle.html

'Circle have said they are planning to pull out of their contract': Charlie Cooper, 'Circle Holdings pulls out of NHS contract', *Independent*, 9 January 2015. http://www.independent.co.uk/news/business/news/circle-holdings-pulls-out-of-nhs-contract-hours-before-hospital-it-ran-was-rated-inadequate-9968997.html

'a toxic mix of cuts and privatisation': 'MPs back bill designed to limit NHS "privatisation"', BBC News website, 21 November 2014. http://www.bbc.co.uk/news/health-30137368

'Cameron "It's in the public sector, it will stay in the public sector"': David Cameron Press Conference G20, Brisbane, HM Government website, 16 November 2014. https://www.gov.uk/government/speeches/david-cameron-press-conference-g20-brisbane-australia

'often quoted that one in four of us will have mental health issues': Jamie Horder, 'How true is the one-in-four mental health statistic?', *Guardian*, 24 April 2010. http://www.theguardian.com/commentisfree/2010/apr/24/one-in-four-mental-health-statistic

'Leading mental health organisations estimate that two thirds of people': 'A manifesto for better mental health', Rethink, 22 August 2014. http://www.rethink.org/media/1146436/a%20manifesto%20for%20better%20mental%20health.pdf

'mental illness costs the country around £70 billion every year': Larry Elliott, 'Mental Health issues cost UK £70bn a year', *Guardian*, 10 February 2014. http://www.theguardian.com/society/2014/feb/10/mental-health-issues-uk-cost-70bn-oecd

11. Leadership

'in the words of psychology writer Michael Bond, we are led by "instinctive biases": Michael Bond, 'How to pick a leader', *Prospect Magazine*, 18 March 2010. http://www.prospectmagazine.co.uk/science-and-technology/how-to-pick-a-leader

[Farage] 'These men are utterly hopeless, dull as bloody ditchwater': Macer Hall, 'Farage slams main party leaders', *Express*, 10 October 2014. http://www.express.co.uk/news/politics/520956/Ukip-leader-Rivals-as-dull-as-ditchwater

'Psychologists such as Professor Gad Saad believe factors like that': Professor Gad Saad, 'How do people choose their political leaders?', *Psychology Today*, 30 December 2012. http://www. psychology today.com/blog/homo-consumericus/201209/how-do-people-choose-their-political-leaders

'Research published in 2009 also suggests that the faces of candidates strongly influences voters': Christopher Olivola and Alexanader Todorov, 'The Look of a Winner', *Scientific American*, 5 May 2009. http://www.scientificamerican.com/article/the-look-of-a-winner/

'Children aged 5–13 were able to predict Obama's win in 2008': John Antonakis and Olaf Dalgas, 'Predicting Elections: Child's Play!', *Science*, vol. 323, 27 February. 2009. http://www.uvm.edu/~pdodds/ teaching/courses/2009-08UVM-300/docs/others/2009/antonak is2009a.pdf

'fleeting judgements about someone's competence to lead based on their face': Alexander Todorov et al., 'Inferences of Competence from Faces Predict Election Outcomes', *Science*, vol. 308, 10 June 2005. https://psych.princeton.edu/psychology/research/todorov/pdf/Todorov_Science2005.pdf

'Recent polling suggests that only 13 per cent of the British public': Joe Murphy, 'Only 13% of people believe Ed Miliband can be PM', *London Evening Standard*, 12 November 2014; updated 13 November 2014. http://www.standard.co.uk/news/politics/blow-for-ed-miliband- as-poll-reveals-just-13-per-cent-think-he-could-be-pm-9855880.html

'look at the "likeability" of Miliband, Cameron and Clegg': Paul Whiteley, 'Voter survey shows Miliband panic is overblown', The Conversation website, 8 November 2014. http://theconversation.com/voter-survey-shows-miliband-panic-is-overblown-33975

'Labour is the most liked party, but Ed Miliband still hasn't convinced the public': 'Labour are the most popular party, but their

leader lags behind', Ipsos MORI, 17 September 2014. https://
www.ipsos-mori.com/researchpublications/researcharchive/3450/
Labour-are-the-most-popular-party-but-their-leader-lags-behind.aspx

12. Jobs and the Economy

'July to September quarter in 2014 it grew 0.7%': 'Quarterly National
accounts Q3 2014', Office for National Statistics, 23 December 2014.
http://www.ons.gov.uk/ons/rel/naa2/quarterly-national-accounts/q3-
2014/stb-quarterly-national-accounts—q3-2014.html

'Are you better off than you were four years ago?': Ronald Reagan's
speech, 28 October 1980: see YouTube.com. https://www.youtube.
com/watch?v=loBe0WXtts8

'the figures are now below 2 million': Department for Work and
Pensions, 'Final 2014 employment figures show all time record number
of people in jobs', HM Government website, 17 December 2014;
updated 18 December 2014. https://www.gov.uk/government/
news/final-2014-employment-figures-show-all-time-record-number-of-
people-in-jobs

[Cameron] 'an important moment for our country': 'Fall in jobless
total slowing down', Daily Mail, 17 December 2014. http://
www.dailymail.co.uk/wires/pa/article-2877025/ Government-hopes-
good-jobs-news.html

[Paul Johnson] 'given economic performance, employment is
amazingly high': Paul Johnson, 'IFS launches election 2015 website',
Institute for Fiscal Studies website, 12 January 2015. http://www.ifs.
org.uk/publications/7516

'was down to 754,000 by October 2014': 'Youth unemployment
statistics', UK Parliament website, 17 December 2014. http://www.
parliament.uk/business/publications/research/briefing-papers/
SN05871/youth-unemployment-statistics

[David Kern] 'still nearly three times the rate of unemployment as a
whole': 'BCC: Labour market improves but youth unemployment is far
too high', British Chambers of Commerce, 19 March 2014.
http://www.britishchambers.org.uk/press-office/press-releases/bcc-
labour-market-improves-but-youth-unemployment-is-far-too-high.html

'around 700,000 young people have never had a job': 'Economic
recovery not enough to solve youth unemployment', IPPR, 13 August
2014. http://www.ippr.org/news-and-media/press-releases/ economic-
recovery-not-enough-to-solve-youth-unemployment

'86 per cent of people getting a job (with the same company or elsewhere) after completion': Key facts about apprenticeships, HM Government website. https://www.gov.uk/government/publications/key-facts-about-apprenticeships

'95 per cent of the rise in employment last year was due to "full-time" jobs': 'Final 2014 employment figures show all time record number of people in jobs', HM Government website, 17 December 2014; updated 18 December 2014. https://www.gov.uk/government/news/final-2014-employment-figures-show-all-time-record-number-of-people-in-jobs

'the employment growth is being driven mainly by the London jobs market': Tom Clark, 'Self-employment surge across UK hides real story behind upbeat job figures', *Guardian*, 6 May 2014. http://www.the guardian.com/society/2014/may/06/self-employment-uk-job-figures-analysis

'since 2007 the average self-employed wage has fallen by a massive 20 per cent': 'Self-employed see a plunge in earnings', Resolution Foundation, 6 May 2014. http://www.resolutionfoundation.org/media/press-releases/self-employed-see-plunge-earnings-even-numbers-surge/

'84 per cent of the self-employed claimed they were more satisfied': 'Self-employed: £74 a week poorer but happier and more fulfilled finds RSA report', RSA, 28 May 2014. http://www.thersa. org/about-us/media/press-releases/self-employed-74-a-week-poorer-but-happier-and-more-fulfilled-finds-rsa-report See also: http://www.the guardian.com/business/2014/may/28/self-employed-greater-job-satisfaction-rsa-report

'report which says that one in twelve workers are now in "precarious employment"': Yvonne Roberts, 'Low pay and zero-hours contracts rise dramatically, figures show', *Guardian*, 13 December 2014. http://www.theguardian.com/uk-news/2014/dec/13/zero-hours-contracts-low-pay-figures-rise

'at the start of 2014 there were 1.4 million zero-hour contracts': 'Zero hours contracts: Analysis of Employee Contracts that do not Guarantee a Minimum Number of Hours', Office for National Statistics, 30 April 2014. http://www.ons.gov.uk/ons/rel/lmac/contracts-with-no-guaranteed- hours/zero-hours-contracts/art-zero-hours.html

'on average the unemployed have £174 left every month': 'Unemployed have more disposable income', Scottish Friendly

website 1 December 2014. http://www.scottishfriendly.co.uk/news/
2014/unemployed-have-more-disposable-income-than-part-time-
and-zero-hour-workers

'focused on Sports Direct, the high street retailer, as a "bad place to
work"': Christopher Hope, 'Ed Miliband says "Victorian" Sports Direct
is a "bad place to work"', *Telegraph*, 14 November 2014. http://www.
telegraph.co.uk/news/politics/ed-miliband/11232442/ Ed-Miliband-
says-Victorian-Sports-Direct-is-a-bad-place-towork.html

'the most severe squeeze on real earnings since Victorian times': 'UK
workers suffering the most severe squeeze in real earnings since
Victorian times', TUC website, 12 October 2014. http://www.
tuc.org.uk/economic-issues/labour-market-and-economic-reports/
economic-analysis/britain-needs-pay-rise/uk

'British workers that suffered the biggest fall in real wages': Angela
Monaghan, 'British workers suffer biggest real wage fall of major G20
countries' *Guardian*, 4 December 2014. http://www.the guardian.
com/business/2014/dec/04/british-workers-suffered-biggest-real-
wage-fall-major-g20-countries

'average real earnings are rising, after six consecutive years of decline':
'UK Labour Market, December 2014', Office for National Statistics, 17
December 2014. http://www.ons.gov.uk/ons/rel/ lms/labour- market-
statistics/december-2014/statistical-bulletin.html#tab-6—Average-
Weekly-Earnings

James Knightley 'going to be seeing quite a pickup in real take-home
pay': Angela Monaghan, 'Pay rise for British workers after six years of
falling wages', *Guardian*, 17 December 2014. http://www.the guardian.
com/money/2014/dec/17/pay-rise-british-workers-six-years-falling-
wages

'according to the ONS it's been averaging 1.4% between 2009 and
2014': 'Annual Survey of Hours and Earnings, 2014 Provisional
Results', Office for National Statistics, 19 November 2014. http://
www. ons.gov.uk/ons/rel/ashe/annual-survey-of-hours-and-earnings/
2014-provisional-results/stb-ashe-statistical-bulletin-2014.html

'according to the Shadow Chancellor Ed Balls working people are
now £1600 worse off': 'Some figures from the Autumn statement',
Full Fact website, 3 December 2014. https://fullfact.org/article/
economy/autumn_statement_2014-37183

'consistently higher growth rates, and in April 2014 earnings for this
group grew by 4.1 per cent compared with April 2013': Annual Survey

of Hours and Earnings, Office for National Statistics, 19 November 2014. http://www.ons.gov.uk/ons/dcp171778_385428.pdf

[Christina McAnea] 'Our members' pay has been frozen or held down for the past five years': 'UNISON NHS members in England set to strike in new year', UNISON website, 19 November 2014. http://www.unison.org.uk/unison-nhs-members-in-england-set-to-strike-in-new-year

'calculated according to the basic cost of living in the UK': What is the Living Wage? Living Wage Foundation website. http://www.livingwage.org.uk/what-living-wage

'average annual price hike of 3.7 per cent since 2003': 'Variation in the inflation experience of UK Households 2003–2014', Office for National Statistics, 15 December 2014. http://www.ons.gov.uk/ons/ mrel/elmr/ variation-in-the-inflation-experience-of-uk-households/2003-2014/index.html

13. Big Business

'eight of the fifty largest economic entities in the world': 'Top 175 Global Economic Entities, 2011', D. Steven White website, 11 August 2012. http://dstevenwhite.com/2012/08/11/the-top-175-global-economic-entities-2011/

'The social responsibility of business is to increase its profits': Milton Friedman, 'The Social Responsibility of Business Is to Increase its Profits', *The New York Times Magazine*, 13 September 1970. http://www.colorado.edu/studentgroups/libertarians/issues/friedman -soc-resp-business.html

'Tax Research UK that estimates the tax gap in 2013/14 to be around £120 billion': 'The tax gap is £119.4 billion and rising', Tax Research UK website, 22 September 2014. http://www.taxresearch.org.uk/ Blog/2014/09/22/new-report-the-tax-gap-is-119-4-billion-and-rising/

'in 2012/13 it was more like £34 billion': Measuring Tax Gaps 2014 Edition, HMRC, 16 October 2014. https://www.gov.uk/government/ uploads/system/uploads/attachment_data/file/364009/4382_Meas uring_Tax_Gaps_2014_IW_v4B_accessible_20141014.pdf

'DWP's estimated cost of benefit fraud': Fraud and Error in the Benefit System, Department for Work and Pensions, 6 November 2014. https://www.gov.uk/government/uploads/system/uploads/attachment_ data/file/371459/Statistical_Release.pdf

'does not do enough to tackle companies which exploit international tax structures to minimise UK tax liabilities': Finbarr Bermingham, 'HMRC not doing enough to stop corporate tax avoidance', *International Business Times* website, 18 November 2014. http:// www. ibtimes.co.uk/hmrc-not-doing-enough-stop-corporate-tax-avoidance-say-mps-1475301

'tax collection is very complicated and HMRC is understaffed': Finbarr Bermingham, 'HMRC not doing enough to stop corporate tax avoidance', *International Business Times* website, 18 November 2014. http://www.ibtimes.co.uk/hmrc-not-doing-enough-stop-corporate- tax-avoidance-say-mps-1475301

[Osborne] 'to tackle non-compliance': Ann Gripper, 'Budget 2014: George Osborne's statement in full', *Mirror*, 19 March 2014. http:// www.mirror.co.uk/news/uk-news/budget-2014-george-osbornes-statement-3260473

[Serwotka] 'making it harder to chase down these wealthy individuals': Rajeev Syal, 'Tax clampdown under threat', *Guardian*, 26 March 2014. http://www.theguardian.com/politics/2014/mar/26/tax-clampdown-under-threat-revenue-customs-job-cuts

[Gauke] 'since 2010/11 the percentage tax gap [as a proportion of GDP] has stayed lower': 'HMRC publishes 2012 to 2013 tax gap', HM Government website, 16 October 2014. https://www.gov.uk/government/news/hmrc-publishes-2012-to-2013-tax-gap

[Cameron] 'to damn well pay': Louise Eccles and Liz Hull, 'You'll damn well pay, PM warns firms', *Daily Mail*, 30 October 2014. http://www.dailymail.co.uk/news/article-2815017/You-ll-damn-pay-PM-warns-firms-exploit-tax-loopholes-Cameron-vows-clamp-companies-funnel-billions-offshore-tax-havens.html

[Osborne] 'a great deal for Britain': Simon Goodley, 'George Osborne waters down flagship controversial tax break', *Guardian*, 11 November 2014. http://www.theguardian.com/politics/2014/nov/11/george-osborne-patent-boxes-tax-break

'it needs to be the policy makers that change things': Simon Neville, 'Starbucks completes £20 million tax payment', *Independent*, 1 December 2014. http://www.independent.co.uk/news/business/news/ starbucks-completes-20-million-tax-payment-as-coffee-chain-seeks-to-put-scandal-behind-9896360.html

'taxing companies on where sales are made': Michael Udell and Aditi Vashist, 'Sales Factor Apportionment of Global Profits', District

Economics Group, 14 July 2014. http://www.districteconomics.
com/papers/USsalesfactorapportionment.pdf

'The High Pay Centre has looked at how much the bosses of those
companies are paid': 'FTSE 100 bosses now paid an average 130
times as much as their employees', High Pay Centre website, 18
August 2014. http://highpaycentre.org/blog/ftse-100-bosses-now-
paid-an-average-143-times-as-much-as-their-employees

'78 per cent of the public would be in favour of a maximum limit':
'Reform Agenda: How to make top pay fairer', High Pay Centre, 14
July 2014. http://highpaycentre.org/blog/reform-agenda-how-to-
make-top-pay-fairer

'simply making companies disclose their pay ratios': Andrew Simms
and David Boyle, 'The Ratio', New Economics Foundation website, 3
July 2011. http://www.neweconomics.org/public ations/entry/the-ratio

'equitable distribution of resources, wealth, opportunity and power':
Green Party economic policy, Green Party website. http://policy.
greenparty.org.uk/ec.html

14. Climate Change

'bring high risks of severe, widespread and irreversible impacts': 'IPCC,
2013: Summary for Policymakers' in IPCC, *Climate Change 2013: The
Physical Science Basis* (Cambridge University Press, 2014).
http://www.ipcc.ch/pdf/assessment-report/ar5/wg1/ WG1AR5_SPM_
FINAL.pdf

'Science has spoken. There is no ambiguity in the message': Alister
Doyle, Publication of UN report, Reuters, 2 November 2014.
http://www.reuters.com/article/2014/11/02/climatechange-report-
idUSL6N0SS0B820141102

'government thinks that by 2080, flooding damage could cost the
country up to £27 billion': Oliver Bennett and Sarah Hartwell-
Naguib, 'Flood Defence Spending in England', House of Commons
Library, 17 November 2014; updated 19 November 2014. http://www.
parliament.uk/business/publications/research/briefing-papers/
SN05755/flood-defence-spending-in-england

'By the 2050s, anywhere between 27 million and 59 million people':
Naomi Hicks and Dr Nicola Ranger, 'What are the potential impacts of
climate change for the UK?' Grantham Research Institute and Duncan
Clark, *Guardian*, 8 October 2013. http://www.theguardian.com/
environment/2013/oct/08/potential-impacts-climate-change-uk

'in 2008, we passed the Climate Change Act': The Climate Change Act 2008: Committee on Climate Change website. http://www.theccc.org.uk/tackling-climate-change/the-legal-landscape/ global-action-on-climate-change/

'The first coal-fired power station using large scale CCS in the EU': Yorkshire CCS plant: Update, White Rose website, 23 December 2014. http://www.whiteroseccs.co.uk

'vital to limit climate change': 'Fast-track carbon capture and storage pilot projects after "lost decade" of delay', UK Parliament website, 21 May 2014. http://www.parliament.uk/business/committees/committees-a-z/commons-select/energy-and-climate-change-committee/news/carbon-capture-storage-substantive/

'increased the cost of the average gas/electricity bill by £45 in 2013': Ben Spencer, 'Green subsidies on energy bills set to rise by four times by 2030', Daily Mail, 10 December 2014. http://www.dailymail.co.uk/news/article-2867965/Green-subsidies- energy-bills-set-rise-four-times-2030-175-added-average-cost-funding-wind-solar-power.html

[Robinson] 'More subsidies are likely to be needed': Tom Bawden, 'New era of cheap oil "will destroy green revolution"', Independent, 12 December 2014. http://www.independent.co.uk/environment/new-era-of-cheap-oil-will-destroy-green-revolution-9922217.html

[Cameron] 'greenest government ever': James Randerson, 'Cameron: I want coalition to be the "greenest government ever"', Guardian, 14 May 2010. http://www.theguardian.com/environment/2010/may/14/cameron-wants-greenest-government-ever

'no satisfactory progress has been made in any of the ten environmental areas': Andrew Grice, 'MPs give Government a red card on green issues', Independent, 16 September 2014. http://www.independent.co.uk/incoming/mps-give-government-a-red-card-on-green-issues-9734393.html

'Less than a fifth of our energy production is coming from renewables': Department of Energy and Climate Change, 'Energy Trends Section 6: Renewables', HM Government website, December 2014. https://www.gov.uk/government/uploads/system/uploads/attachment_data/file/386 837/6_Renewables.pdf

'ageing, dirty coal plants so expensive to run that they would close by 2025': Tom Bawden, 'UK Carbon Emissions', Independent, 10

November 2014. http://www.independent.co.uk/news/uk/politics/ uk-carbon-emissions-the-stench-of-missed-targets-as-coalitions-green-credentials-are-torn-up-and-thrown-out-9850180.html

'first quarter of 2014, renewables accounted for 27 per cent of their electricity': Stefan Nicola, 'Renewables Meet Record 27 Percent of German Electricity Demand', Bloomberg, 9 May 2014. http://www.bloomberg.com/news/2014-05-09/renewables-meet-record-27-percent-of-german-electricity-demand.html

[Younger] 'Nuclear generates steadily, 24/7 and we can increase generation from coal and gas as and when we need it': 'Security or insecurity of energy supply', Utilities Scotland website, 2 December 2014. http://utilitiesscotland.com/2014/12/02/security-or-insecurity-of-energy-supply/

'survey found that 67 per cent of the public support onshore wind farms': Department of Energy and Climate Change, 'DECC Public Attitudes Tracker – Wave 10', HM Government website, 12 August 2014. https://www.gov.uk/government/uploads/system/uploads/attachment_data/file/342426/Wave_10_findings_of_DECC_Public_Attitudes_Tracker_FINAL.pdf

'cost of energy for German businesses has gone up by 60 per cent in five years': Matthew Karnitschnig, 'Germany's expensive gamble on renewable energy', *Wall Street Journal*, 26 August 2014. http://www.wsj.com/articles/germanys-expensive-gamble-on-renewable-energy-1409106602

'carbon emissions per head in China were more than in the EU': Matt McGrath, 'China's per capita carbon emissions overtake EU', BBC website, 21 September 2014. http://www.bbc.co.uk/news/ science-environment-29239194

'China has agreed to cap its emissions': Lenore Taylor, 'China and US make carbon pledge', *Guardian*, 12 November 2014. http://www.theguardian.com/environment/2014/nov/12/china-and-us-make-carbon-pledge

'number of Brits who said they'd be up for paying higher prices to limit global warming': Randeep Ramesh, 'Public support for tackling climate change declines dramatically', *Guardian*, 7 December 2011. http://www.theguardian.com/environment/2011/dec/07/public-support-climate-change-declines

'We should not sacrifice Britain's economic recovery on the altar of climate change': Alex Stevenson, 'Climate Change Blues', politics.co.uk website, 16 October 2014. http://www. politics.co.uk/ comment-analysis/2014/10/16/climate-change-blues-the-tories-green-retoxification-confirm

[Cameron] 'we must agree a global deal in Paris next year. We simply cannot put this off any longer': 'UN Climate Summit 2014', HM Government website, 23 September 2014. https://www.gov.uk/ government/speeches/un-climate-summit-2014-david-camerons-remarks

[Farage] 'We may have made one of the biggest and most stupid collective mistakes in history by getting so worried about global warming': Nigel Farage confronts Barroso on global warming scam, 11 September 2013. https://www.youtube.com/watch? v=EFpza QPKC54

'recognise that global CO_2 emissions are not reducing': Sarah Mukherjee, 'CO_2 reduction treaties useless', BBC News website, 13 February 2009. http://news.bbc.co.uk/1/hi/uk/7888994.stm

15. Representation

[Meacher] 'Parliament is more unrepresentative of society': Tim Wigmore, 'Parliament must shed privately-educated and Westminster bubble MPs to win voters' trust', New Statesman, 7 August 2014. http://www.newstatesman.com/politics/2014/08/parliament-must-shed-privately-educated-and-westminster-bubble-mps-win-voters-trust

'average cost ... of attempting to become an MP is around £34,000': 'The costs of being a candidate', Conservative Home website, 1 August 2006. http://conservativehome.blogs.com/goldlist/2006/08/the_costs_of_be.html

[Clegg] 'It divides Liberal opinion. Some people think it is tokenism': 'Lib Dem All-Women shortlists warning', Sky News website, 9 May 2014. http://news.sky.com/story/1258488/lib-dem-all-women-shortlists-warning-by-clegg

'An interesting international example is Rwanda': 'Rwanda', Quota Project website, 7 April 2014. http://www.quotaproject.org/uid/countryview.cfm?CountryCode=RW

[David Lammy] 'We need bold measures to tackle this problem': 'David Lammy latest MP to call for all-minority ethnic shortlists', Labour List website, 1 August 2014. http://labourlist.org/ 2014/08/david-lammy-latest-mp-to-call-for-all-minority-ethnic-shortlists/

'saying they would change Parliament for the better': Nigel Morris, 'Has Tories' independent-minded MP put the party off open primaries?', *Independent*, 21 January 2012. http://www. independent. co.uk/news/uk/politics/has-tories-independent minded-mp-put-the-party-off-open-primaries-6292653.html

16. Public Finances

'government collects in about £600 billion of our money': Simon Rogers, 'Tax receipts since 1963', *Guardian*, 18 March 2013. http://www. theguardian.com/news/datablog/2010/apr/25/tax-receipts-1963

'The government also spends a lot of money – around £700 billion': Phillip Inman and George Arnett, 'Budget 2014', *Guardian*, 21 March 2014. http://www.theguardian.com/news/datablog/2014/mar/21/ budget-2014-tax-spending-visualised#_

'The deficit in the year 2013/14 was £98 billion': Fraser Nelson, 'Why is David Cameron now misleading voters about the deficit?' *Spectator*, 15 December 2014. http://blogs.spectator.co.uk/ coffeehouse/2014/12/shamefully-david-cameron-is-now-misleading-voters-about-the-deficit/

'£1.457 trillion in November 2014': 'Summary of public sector finances November 2014', Office for National Statistics, 19 December 2014. http://www.ons.gov.uk/ons/rel/psa/public-sector-finances/november-2014/sum-public-sector-finances—november-2014.html

'interest payments on that debt in 2013/14 were £48.7 billion': Matthew Keep, 'Public sector borrowing, debt and debt interest payments: historical statistics' House of Commons Library, SN/EP/5745, 19 December 2014. http://www.parliament.uk/briefing-papers/sn05745.pdf

'In 2007, the Labour government borrowed £37.7 billion in total': Richard Anderson, 'UK debt and deficit', BBC News website, 21 February 2014. http://www.bbc.co.uk/news/business-25944653

'increase in unemployment by 100,000 people is believed to cost the government £500 million': 'The economic recovery and the budget deficit', HM Government website. http://www.parliament.uk/ business/publications/research/key-issues-for-the-new-parliament/ the-public-finances/the-economic-recovery-and-the-deficit/

'By November 2014, our debt-to-GDP ratio was 79.5 per cent': 'Summary of public sector finances November 2014', Office for National

Statistics, 19 November 2014. http://www.ons.gov.uk/ons/rel/psa/public-sector-finances/november-2014/sum-public-sector-finances—november-2014.html

'to meet these targets, any government would have to raise taxes or make spending cuts': Patrick Wintour and Nicholas Watt, 'Treasury asks top civil servants to find £30bn in public service cuts', *Guardian*, 10 November 2014. http://www.theguardian. com/politics /2014/nov /10/treasury-civil-service-spending-cuts-plan-general-election

'Clegg says that only using spending cuts is "wholly implausible"': Patrick Wintour, 'Ed Balls: Labour will back coalition charter on tackling deficit', *Guardian*, 15 December 2014. http://www. the guardian.com/politics/2014/dec/15/ed-balls-labour-back-coalition-charter-deficit

'spending per head in 2019/20 on the public sector': Anthony Reuben, 'Headline numbers', BBC News website, 3 December 2014. http://www.bbc.co.uk/news/business-30318870

'encouraging signs that pay cheques are beginning to rise faster than inflation': 'George Osborne response to labour market statistics', Politics Home website, 12 November 2014. http://www.politicshome. com/uk/article/108153/george_osborne_response_to_labour_market_statistics.html

'The Institute for Fiscal Studies (IFS) has compared the parties' targets': Rowena Crawford et al.,'How do the parties fiscal targets compare?' Institute for Fiscal Studies, 19 September 2014. http://www.ifs.org.uk/publications/7373

'capital spending is currently projected to be £27 billion': Robert Peston, 'The £50bn gap between Tories and Labour', BBC News website, 4 December 2014. http://www.bbc.co.uk/news/business-30339240

17. Drugs

[Cameron] 'Drugs policy has been failing for decades': Marie Woolf, 'Tory contender calls for more liberal drug laws', *Independent*, 7 September 2005. http://www.independent.co.uk/news/uk/politics/tory-contender-calls-for-more-liberal-drug-laws-6143525.html

[Cameron] 'I don't support decriminalisation': Helene Mulholland, 'David Cameron rejects call for royal commission on drugs', *Guardian*, 10 December 2012. http://www.theguardian.com/politics/2012/dec/10/david-cameron-rejects-royal-commission-drugs

'the drug trade was estimated to be worth £320 billion a year': 'World Drug Report 2005', United Nations Office on Drugs and Crime. https://www.unodc.org/unodc/en/data-and-analysis/WDR-2005.html

'Looking across different countries, there is no apparent correlation': Ian Dunt, 'The Home Office admits it: Tough enforcement does not lower drug use', politics.co.uk website, 30 October 2014. http://www.politics.co.uk/blogs/2014/10/30/the-home-office-admits-it-tough-enforcement-does-not-lower-d

[Norman Baker] 'banging people up and increasing sentences does not stop drug use': Patrick Wintour and Alan Travis, : 'UK government's drug laws survey was suppressed', *Guardian*, 30 October 2014. http://www.theguardian.com/politics/2014/oct/30/government-drug-laws-survey-suppressed-lib-dem-minister-norman-baker

[Home Office] 'this government has absolutely no intention of decriminalising drugs': 'UK government's drug laws survey was suppressed', *Guardian*, 30 October 2014. http://www.theguardian.com/politics/2014/oct/30/government-drug-laws-survey-suppressed-lib-dem-minister-norman-baker

'the highest prevalence of cannabis use amongst young adults': 'Country Overview', European Monitoring Centre for Drugs and Drug Addiction. http://www.emcdda.europa.eu/publications/country-overviews/cz#gps

[Professor Nutt] 'People have the right to know what they are taking': 'Professor David Nutt Talks Drugs Live', Mixmag website, 25 September 2012. http://www.mixmag.net/words/features/professor-david-nutt-talks-drugs-live

'more cannabis shops than Starbucks': 'Cannabis in Colorado', Julie Bindel, *New Statesman*, 27 February 2014. http://www.newstatesman.com/lifestyle/2014/02/cannabis-colorado-ups-and-downs-legalising-highs

'alcohol and tobacco are found to be significantly more damaging': Professor David Nutt et al., 'Drug harms in the UK: a multicriteria decision analysis', *The Lancet*, vol. 376, 6 November 2010. http://www.thelancet.com/journals/lancet/article/PIIS0140-6736(10)61462-6/abstract

'Excessive drinking is linked to 33,000 deaths': Alcohol and sensible drinking, patient.co.uk website. http://www.patient.co.uk/health/alcohol-and-sensible-drinking

'annual cost to the NHS of drinking-related treatments': 'Alcohol

Treatment in England 2013–14', Public Health England, October 2014. http://www.nta.nhs.uk/uploads/adult-alcohol-statistics-2013-14-commentary.pdf

'prohibiting alcohol would mean the end of £10 billion a year in taxes': 'HMRC Tax & NIC Receipts', HMRC, 19 December 2014. https://www.gov.uk/government/uploads/system/uploads/attachmen t _data/file/388910/20141210_Novreceiptsbulletin.pdf

'recent YouGov poll found that 71 per cent of the UK population think the War on Drugs has failed': YouGov/*Sun* survey results, YouGov, June 2012. http://d25d2506sfb94s.cloudfront.net/ cumulus_uploads/document/prr2r9pht5/YG-Archives-Life-Sun-Drugs-090712.pdf

18. Social Media

[UKIP accused Thornberry of having] 'sneered, and looked down her nose at a white van': 'Labour's Emily Thornberry quits over "snobby" tweet', BBC News website, 21 November 2014. http://www.bbc. co.uk/news/uk-politics-30139832

'angrier than he had ever been': Steven Swinford and Christopher Hope, 'Labour front-bencher Emily Thornberry sacked', *Telegraph*, 20 November 2014. http://www.telegraph.co.uk/news/politics/labour/ 11244687/Labour-front-bencher-Emily-Thornberry-sacked-over-prejudiced-flag-tweet.html

[Clegg] 'connect with the next generation of voters': Allegra Stratton, 'Nick Clegg woos younger vote', *Guardian*, 20 January 2010. http://www.theguardian.com/politics/2010/jan/20/nick-clegg-twitter-facebook-youtube

'Over half of British adults now regularly use social media': Carl Miller, 'Only social media can fix the crisis of modern politics', *Wired*, 12 February 2014. http://www.wired.co.uk/news/archive/ 2014-02/12/the-coming-storm

[Carl Miller] 'Social media generally hates politicians': Charles Morris, 'Which party is winning the social media war?', May 2015 website, 29 October 2014. http://may2015.com/featured/which-party-is-winning-the-war-on-social-media/

'top independence hashtag #VoteYes got 1.1 million mentions on Twitter': Danny Sullivan, 'Twitter says #voteyes beats #bettertogether', Marketing Land website, 18 September 2014. http://marketingland. com/twitter-scotland-vote-100751

[Crowther] 'I have no Facebook page, Twitter account or Instagram thingy. It's lovely': 'Twitter ye not, says Ukip chairman', *Express*, 21 December 2014. http://www.express.co.uk/news/politics/548102/Ukip-chairman-Steve-Crowther-urges-party-members-not-to-use-social-media

'showed that a non-partisan "get out the vote" message': Zoe Corbyn, 'Facebook experiment boosts US voter turnout', *Nature*, 12 September 2012. http://www.nature.com/news/facebook-experiment-boosts-us-voter-turnout-1.11401

'study into the types of tweets that MPs were writing found': James Donald, 'MPs and Twitter', Ballots & Bullets blog, 26 July 2013. http://nottspolitics.org/2013/07/26/mps-and-twitter-what-are-mps-tweeting-about/

19. The EU

'Nigel Farago says £55 million a day': 'Is our EU membership fee £55 million?' Fullfact website, 27 March 2014. https://fullfact.org/economy/cost_eu_membership_gross_net_contribution-30887

'possible to justify any measure between 15 per cent and 50 per cent': Vaughne Miller, 'How much legislation comes from Europe?', House of Commons Library, UK Parliament website, 13 October 2010; updated 13 July 2011. http://www.parliament.uk/business/publications/research/briefing-papers/RP10-62/how-much-legislation-comes-from-europe

'During a televised debate on the subject, Nick Clegg said': *The European Union: In or Out?* BBC Two, 3 April 2014.

'our exports to the EU in 2013 were worth £151 billion': 'UK Overseas Trade Statistics with EU, January 2014', HMRC, 18 March 2014. https://www.gov.uk/government/uploads/system/uploads/attachment_data/file/292757/OTS_EU_Jan14.pdf

'4.2 million UK jobs were directly or indirectly related to EU exports': British Jobs and the Single Market, Centre for Economics and Business Research, 31 March 2014. http://www.cebr.com/reports/british-jobs-and-the-single-market/

'study from a Eurosceptic thinktank concluded that one million jobs': Hugo van Randwyck, 'EFTA or the EU?', The Bruges Group website, 21 March 2011. http://www.brugesgroup.com/eu/efta-or-the-eu.htm?xp=paper

'non-European investors would actually find it a more attractive place': Justin Chaloner et al., 'Nexit: Assessing the Economic Impact of the Netherlands Leaving the European Union', fig. 80, p. 109, *Capital Economics*, 6 February 2014. http://www.pvv.nl/images/Rapport_NExit_full_ENG.pdf

'Norway, for example, paid €400 million to the EU in 2007': 'Literature review: Economic costs and benefits of EU membership', HM Government website. https://www.gov.uk/government/uploads/system/uploads/attachment_data/file/220969/foi_eumembership_literaturereview.pdf

[Cameron] 'pointless interference, rules and regulations that stifle growth not unleash it': 'PM's Speech at the Lord Mayor's Banquet', HM Government website, 14 November 2011. https://www.gov.uk/government/speeches/prime-ministers-speech-at-the-lord-mayors-banquet

'the UK is not a big power in the eyes of the Chinese': 'China won't fall for Cameron's "sincerity"', *Global Times*, 3 March 2013. http://www.globaltimes.cn/content/829371.shtml

'overwhelming support for Britain to stay in the EU among both big and small businesses': '8 out of 10 firms say UK must stay in EU', CBI/YouGov, 12 September 2013. http://www.cbi.org.uk/media-centre/press-releases/2013/09/8-out-of-10-firms-say-uk-must-stay-in-eu-cbi-yougov-survey/

'in 2011, The Migration Observatory calculated just over one million': 'Definitive data shows more than 1m UK-born migrants in other EU countries, but 2.6m EU migrants in the UK', The Migration Observatory website, 1 May 2014. http://www.migrationobservatory.ox.ac.uk/press-releases/definitive-data-shows-more-1m-uk-born-migrants-other-eu-countries-26m-eu-migrants-uk

[Monbiot] 'monstrous assault on democracy': George Monbiot, 'This transatlantic trade deal is a full-frontal assault on democracy, *Guardian*, 4 November 2013. http://www.theguardian.com/commentisfree/2013/nov/04/us-trade-deal-full-frontal-assault-on-democracy

[Cameron] 'Two million extra jobs, more choice and lower prices in our shops': Prime Minister's Speech, G8 Summit, HM Government website, 21 June 2013. https://www.gov.uk/government/speeches/g8-summit-us-eu-trade-statement

[Bennett] 'Chicken carcasses washed in bleach': 'Natalie Bennett: TTIP threatens both our sovereignty and democracy', Green Party website, 26 September 2014. http://greenparty.org.uk/news/ 2014/09/ 26/natalie-benett-ttip-threatens-both-our-sovereignty-and-democracy/

Miliband 'overwhelming economic case': 'EU referendum 'unlikely' under Labour, says Ed Miliband', BBC News website, 12 March 2014. http://www.bbc.co.uk/news/uk-politics-26538420

[Caroline Lucas] 'away from an obsessive focus on competition': 'Yes to an EU Referendum: Green MP calls for chance to build a better Europe', Green Party website. http://greenparty.org.uk/news/yes-to-an-eu-referendum-green-mp-calls-for-chance-to-build-a-better-europe.html

20. Inequality

'the 100 wealthiest people have as much money': 'The Equality Trust Wealth Tracker 2014', Equality Trust. http://www.equalitytrust. org.uk/sites/default/files/TET%20Wealth%20Report%202014.pdf

'the richest 10 per cent controlled 52 per cent of the nation's wealth': Jill Treanor and Sean Farrell, 'UK only G7 country with wider inequality since turn of century', Guardian, 14 October 2014. http://www.the guardian.com/society/2014/oct/14/uk-inequality-wealth-credit-suisse

[Emma Seery] 'economic recovery following the financial crisis has been skewed': 'Oxfam response to Credit Suisse global wealth report', Oxfam website, 14 October 2014. http://www.oxfam.org.uk/ blogs/2014/10/oxfam-response-to-credit-suisse-global-wealth-report-showing-rising-inequality

'for 20 per cent of voters "reducing inequality" is their top priority': ComRes/ITV poll, ITV website, 12 January 2015. http://www.itv.com/ news/2015-01-12/itv-news-index-poll-reveals-the-nhs-is-now-the-top-concern-for-voters/

[Boris Johnson] 'greed as a "valuable spur to economic activity"': Shruti Tripathi Chopra, 'Boris Johnson: economic inequality', London Loves Business website, 28 November 2013. http://www. londonlovesbusiness.com/business-news/politics/boris-johnson-economic-inequality-is-a-valuable-spur/6901.article

'56 per cent of the British public would prefer to see more equality': 'When it comes to the distribution of wealth in the UK, which would you prefer to see?', YouGov poll, 30 April 2014. https://yougov.co.uk/ news/2014/04/30/equality-more-important-wealth/

'In 1990, 36 per cent of the world's population were living in extreme poverty': Douglas A. Irwin, 'The Ultimate Global Antipoverty Program', *Wall Street Journal*, 2 November 2014. http://www.wsj. com/articles/douglas-irwin-the-ultimate-global-antipoverty-program-1414972491

[Cameron] 'inequality [in the UK] is at its lowest since 1986': Patrick Worrall, 'FactCheck: are child poverty and inequality falling?' Channel 4 website, 11 June 2014. http://blogs.channel4.com/factcheck/factcheck-child-poverty-inequality-falling/18387

'However, it had risen again in 2012/13': 'The Effects of Taxes and Benefits on Household Income, 2012/13', Office for National Statistics, 26 June 2014. http://www.ons.gov.uk/ons/dcp171778_367431.pdf

'the Institute for Fiscal Studies expects it to keep rising into 2015/16': Paul Johnson, 'Better-off hit hardest by recession initially', Institute for Fiscal Studies, 4 June 2013. http://www.ifs.org.uk/pr/inequality_recession_june2013.pdf

'poverty rate among pensioners is at an all-time low': 'Monitoring poverty and social exclusion 2014', Joseph Rowntree Foundation, 24 November 2014. http://www.jrf.org.uk/publications/monitoring-poverty-and-social-exclusion-2014

'only 13 per cent inherited their money, and 21 per cent are adding to existing fortunes': 'Inside the 2014 Forbes Billionaires List', Forbes website, 3 March 2014. http://www.forbes.com/sites/luisakroll/2014/03/03/inside-the-2014-forbes-billionaires-list-facts-and-figures/

[Duncan Exley] 'they are entry-level jobs that aren't going to go anywhere': Tracy McVeigh, 'Inequality "costs Britain £39bn a year"', *Guardian*, 16 March 2014. http://www.theguardian.com/society/2014/mar/16/inequality-costs-uk-billions

'child from a poor family in Denmark is three times more likely to do better than her parents': 'A Family Affair: Intergenerational Social Mobility across OECD Countries', OECD, 10 March 2010. http://www.oecd.org/tax/public-finance/chapter%205%20gfg%202010.pdf

'a child of a professional or managerial dad is twenty times more likely': Faiza Shaheen, 'Inequality in the UK', New Economics Foundation website, 10 November 2014. http://www.neweconomics. org/blog/entry/inequality-in-the-uk-whatever-happened-to-social-mobility

'a two-caste system is forming in the US': Robert Rector, 'Marriage', The Heritage Foundation, 5 September 2012. http://www. heritage. org/research/reports/2012/09/marriage-americas-greatest-weapon-against-child-poverty

'the rich and poor is costing the UK economy £39 billion': 'Inequality Costs UK £39 billion per year', Equality Trust, 14 March 2014. http://www.equalitytrust.org.uk/news/inequality-costs-uk-£39-billion-year

'top three thousand pay more income tax than the nine million lowest-paid': Jack Doyle, 'Britain's 3,000 top earners', Daily Mail, 16 November 2014. http://www.dailymail.co.uk/news/article-2836556/Britain-s-3-000-earners-pay-tax-9m-lowest-paid-workers-combined.html

'poorest 10 per cent of households pay 43 per cent of their income in taxes': Katie Allen, 'British public wrongly think rich pay most in tax', Guardian, 16 June 2014. http://www.theguardian.com/money/2014/jun/16/british-public-wrong-rich-poor-tax-research

'a report which details several ways to bring down inequality': Helen Kersley and Faiza Shaheen, 'Addressing economic inequality at root', New Economics Foundation website, 10 July 2014. http://www.neweconomics.org/publications/entry/addressing-economic-inequality-at-root

'there was a small increase in income inequality': Mike Brewer et al., 'Have the poor got poorer under Labour?' Institute for Fiscal Studies, 13 October 2009. http://www.ifs.org.uk/publications/4637

[Miliband] 'never accept an economy where the gap between rich and poor just grows wider': Ed Miliband's annual speech to Labour party conference 2012, Labour website, 2 October 2012. http://archive.labour.org.uk/ed-miliband-speech-conf-2012

21. Celebrity Involvement in Politics

'allegedly called him a "sanctimonious twat"': Richard Spilett, 'Russell Brand is a "sanctimonious t***"' says BBC's Nick Robinson', Daily Mail, 14 January 2015. http://www.dailymail.co.uk/news/article-2909519/Russell-Brand-sanctimonious-t-says-BBC-s-Nick-Robinson-comedian-refused-interviewed.html

'Jennifer Aniston's support of the Democrats': Anthony J Nownes, 'Information about celebrities' political activities can influence how

people think about political parties', LSE website. http://blogs.lse.ac.
uk/usappblog/2014/08/12/information-about-celebrities-political-
activities-can-influence-how-people-think-about-political-parties/

'Geri Halliwell described Margaret Thatcher as "the first Spice Girl":
Simon Sebag Montefiore, 'Time to add a bit of spice to politics',
Telegraph, 14 December 1996. http://www.telegraph.co.uk/
culture/4706704/Time-to-add-a-bit-of-spice-to-politics.html

'46 per cent thought that he was making a "negative contribution to
politics"': 'British public revolt against Brand', YouGov poll, 12
November 2014. https://yougov.co.uk/news/2014/11/12/public-
revolt-russell-brand/

'And rather than taking over, he gave us a much bigger audience to
speak to': Anthony Loewenstein, 'After New Era it's harder than ever to
mock Russell Brand', *Guardian*, 23 December 2013. http://www.
theguardian.com/commentisfree/ 2014/dec/23/after-new-era-its-harder-
than-ever-to-mock-russell-brand-as-a-hypocrite

'the first ever legal contract': Edmund Conway, 'Why a debt jubilee is
not the answer to Britain's prayers', *Telegraph*, 14 January 2010.
http://www.telegraph.co.uk/finance/comment/edmundconway/6986
140/Why-a-debt-jubilee-is-not-the-answer-to-Britains-prayers.html

'I will never vote and I don't think you should, either': Russell Brand,
'Russell Brand on revolution', *New Statesman* 24 October 2013.
http:// www.newstatesman.com/politics/2013/10/russell-brand-on-
revolution

'regardless of how many people agree with you on YouTube': Rod
Liddle, 'Russell Brand is duller than even the grimmest political
interview', *Spectator*, 13 September 2014. http://www.spectator.co.uk/
columnists/rod-liddle/9309752/russell-brand-is-duller-than-even-the-
grimmest-political-interview/

22. Alternatives to Our Democracy

'Lib Dems won 23 per cent of the overall votes, but only 8.8 per cent
of seats': 'general election 2010', Research Paper 10/36, House of
Commons Library, 2 February 2011.

'2010 election, more than half of all votes (52.8 per cent)': 'Wasted
Votes', Electoral Reform Society website. http://www.electoral-
reform.org.uk/ wasted-votes/

'Tony Blair and Labour won a very comfortable majority of seats':

'2001 General election results summary', UK Political Info website. http://www.ukpolitical.info/2001.htm

'Since 2011, there has been a government website': 'How e-petitions work', HM Government website. http://epetitions.direct.gov.uk/how-it-works#commons

'A party actually exists already called the UK's People's Administration Direct Democracy party': People's Administration Direct Democracy party website. http://www.paparty.co.uk

[Brennan] 'Technologically it is now possible. We could function as a direct democracy': Kevin Brennan quoted in Brian Wheeler, 'Why not let social media run the country?' BBC News website, 13 September 2013. http://www.bbc.co.uk/news/uk-politics-19555756

[Kellner] 'It is like a court case in which the jury and the defendants are the same people': Peter Kellner, 'Down With People Power', *Prospect Magazine*, 4 July 2009. http://www.prospectmagazine.co.uk/features/downwithpeoplepower

'Environmentalists believe that these campaigns are "subverting democracy"': Cahal Milmo, 'London airports' PR blitz is "subverting democracy"', *Independent*, 12 December 2014. http://www.independent.co.uk/travel/news-and-advice/london-airports-pr-blitz-is-subverting-democracy-9922081.html

'opposition parties already get state funding': Richard Kelly, 'Short Money', paper SN/PC/01663, House of Commons Library, 8 July 2014. http://www.parliament.uk/briefing-papers/SN01663.pdf

Thanks

First and foremost Emer, who suggested this book and was promptly rewarded by having to endure me at my worst; angry one moment, then excited, then depressed, then angry again. She's stayed in good humour whilst listening to me bang on about politics every day for six weeks. She's a keeper.

My boss Brendan, a man who knows everything about everything, and yet somehow manages not to be annoying. He is also the only person to have compared their loft to Holmand Province.

Adam, whose research and motivational comments ('Remember, caffeine goes in and then words come out – Ancient Essex proverb') made this book possible.

Abbie, my commissioning editor, who has shown remarkable stoicism in the face of midnight emails from me that sign off with 'I f***ing hate writing, it turns out'.

Jo, whose job as copy-editor was made infinitely harder by my repeated and stubborn inability to correctly format my words.

Caroline, my agent, who doesn't say 'No' when her

client, a TV presenter, says he's going to write a book about politics in less than two months.

Peter, a politics professor who pointed me in the direction of some interesting things, and didn't laugh at me.

The entire *Free Speech* team: Tina, Charlie, Lee, my 'excitable Chinese friend' Anthony, Rubina, Emily, Julie, Owen, Caroline, Jaz, Leanne and Hayley.

And The Doctors. They know who they are.

Outro

That's it! I hope this has helped.

If you have any questions that I haven't answered: sorry. Send me a message on Twitter, and I'll try and point you in the direction of an answer.

Just in case I haven't mentioned it – GO AND VOTE ON 7 MAY.

Thanks.